GRAVEYARD OF EMPIRES

created by
MARK SABLE & PAUL AZACETA

Dedicated to
Tim Hetherington

www.imagecomics.com

International Rights and Foreign Licensing:
foreignlicensing@imagecomics.com

GRAVEYARD OF EMPIRES

ISBN: 978-1-60706-739-9

First Printing.

GRAVEYARD OF EMPIRES

writer
MARK SABLE

artist
PAUL AZACETA

colorist
MATTHEW WILSON

letterer/designer
THOMAS MAUER

"CIRCLE"

writer/artist
PAUL AZACETA

letterer
THOMAS MAUER

CHAPTER 1

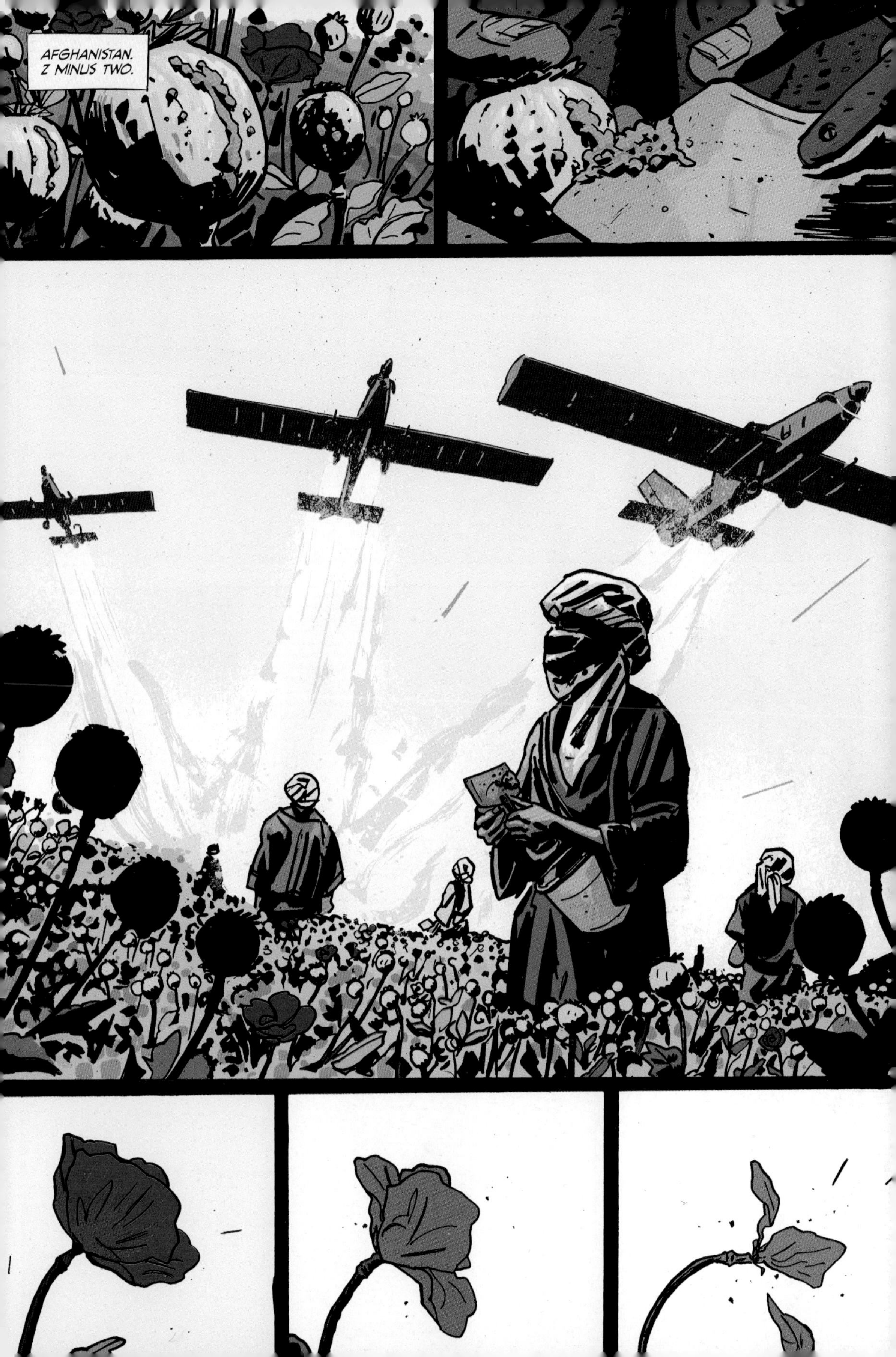
AFGHANISTAN.
Z MINUS TWO.

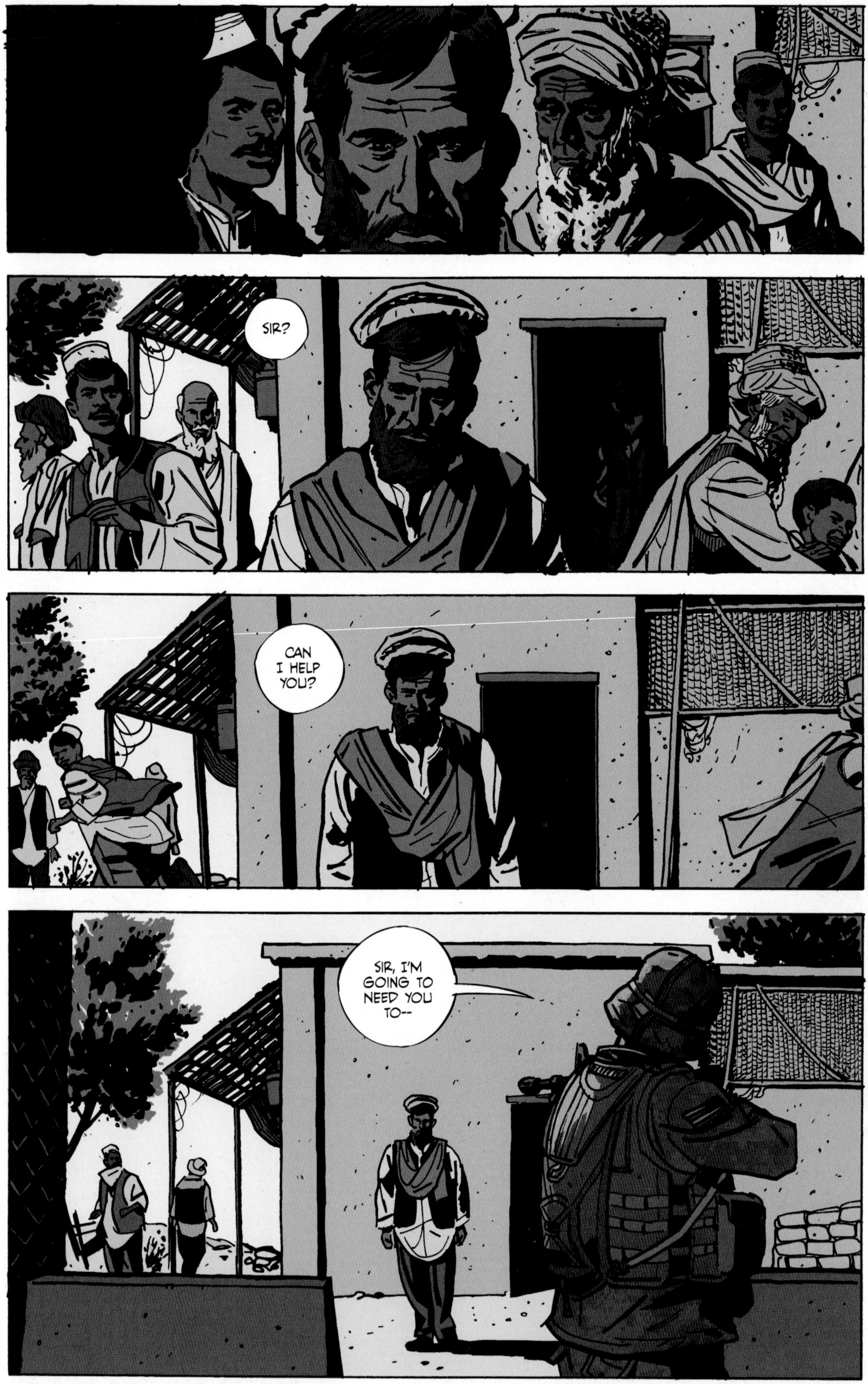
SIR?
CAN I HELP YOU?
SIR, I'M GOING TO NEED YOU TO--

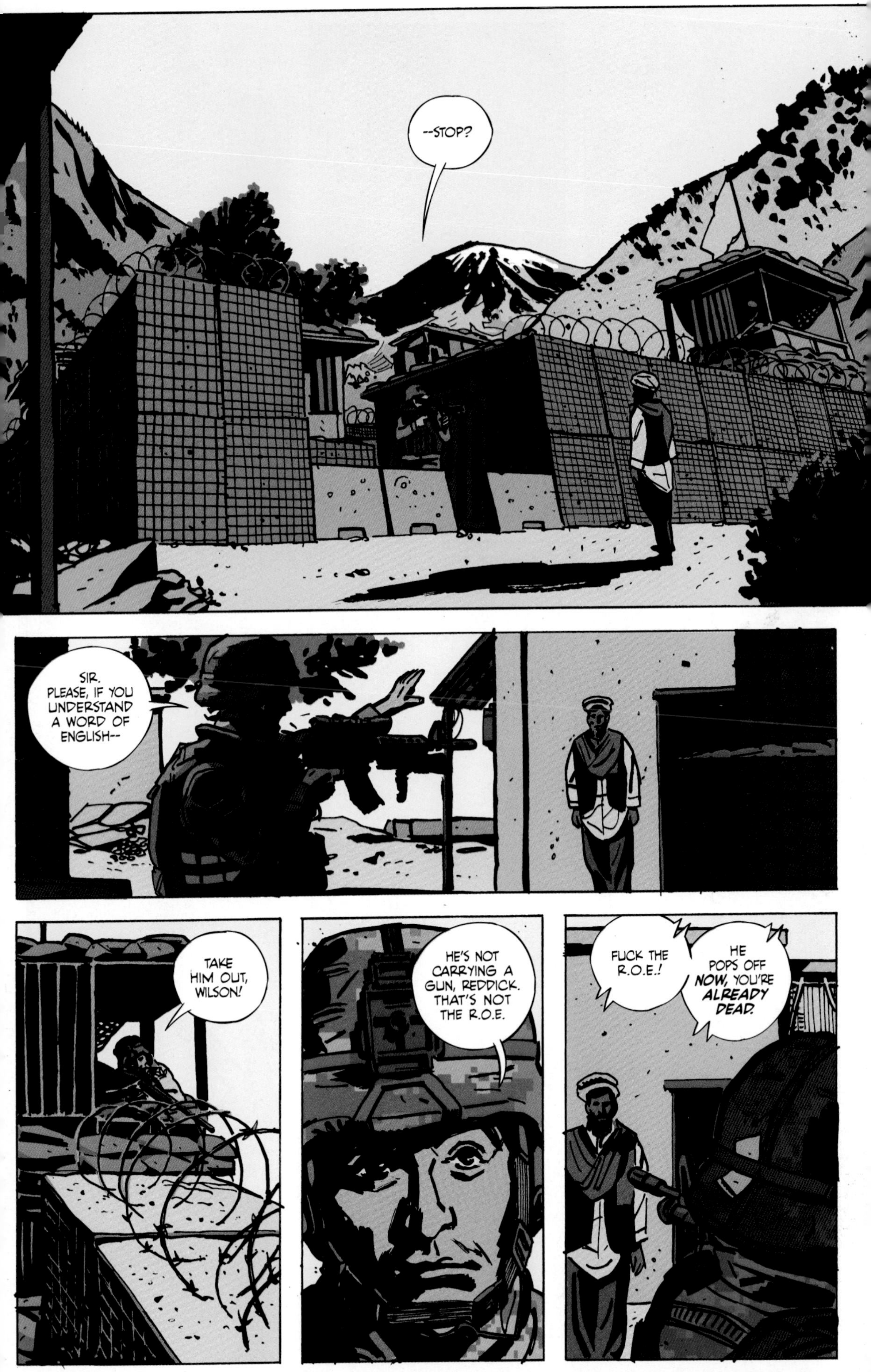
--STOP?
SIR. PLEASE, IF YOU UNDERSTAND A WORD OF ENGLISH--
TAKE HIM OUT, WILSON!
HE'S NOT CARRYING A GUN, REDDICK. THAT'S NOT THE R.O.E.
FUCK THE R.O.E.!
HE POPS OFF *NOW*, YOU'RE ***ALREADY DEAD.***

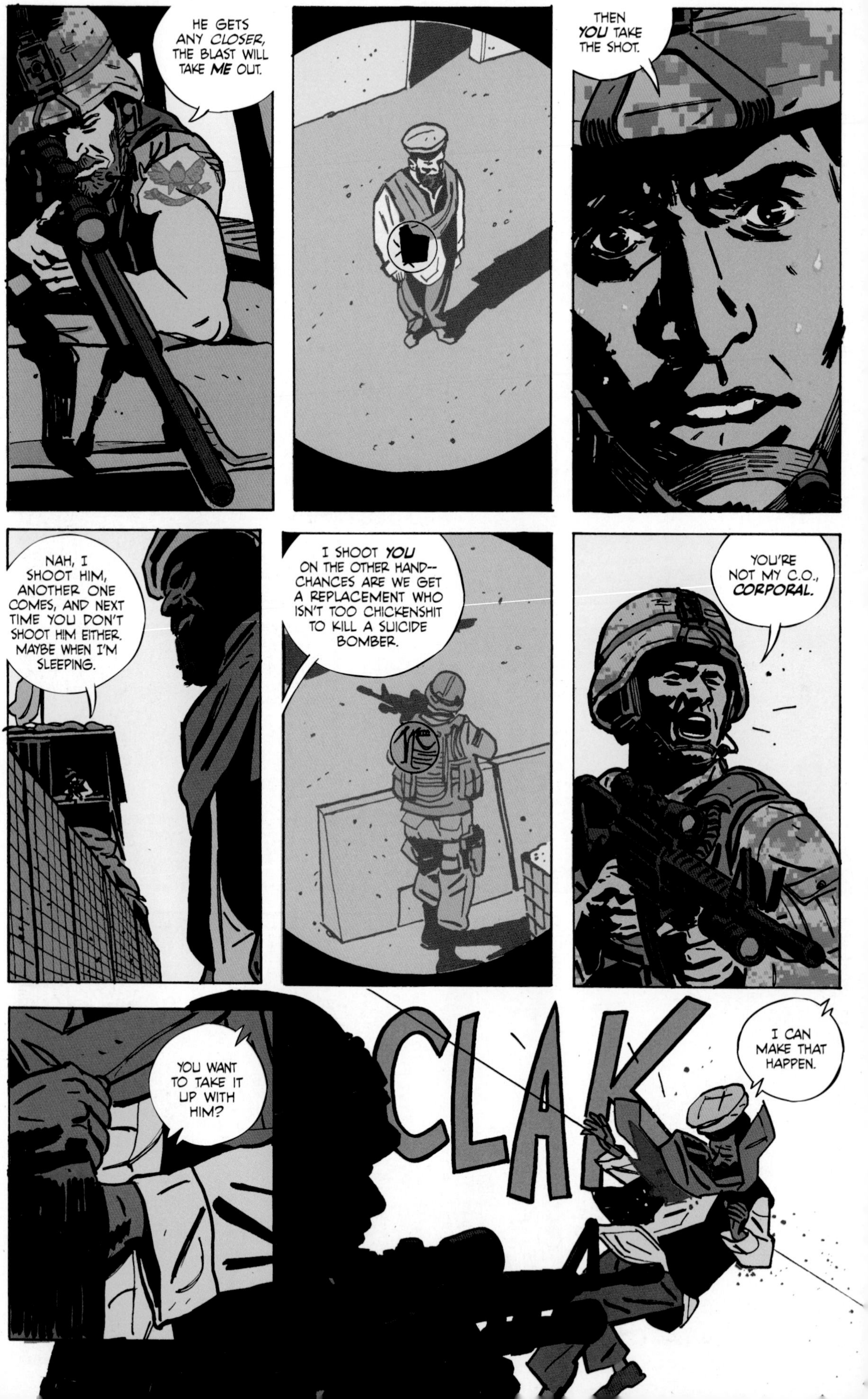
HE GETS ANY CLOSER, THE BLAST WILL TAKE ME OUT.
THEN YOU TAKE THE SHOT.
NAH, I SHOOT HIM, ANOTHER ONE COMES, AND NEXT TIME YOU DON'T SHOOT HIM EITHER. MAYBE WHEN I'M SLEEPING.
I SHOOT YOU ON THE OTHER HAND-- CHANCES ARE WE GET A REPLACEMENT WHO ISN'T TOO CHICKENSHIT TO KILL A SUICIDE BOMBER.
YOU'RE NOT MY C.O., CORPORAL.
YOU WANT TO TAKE IT UP WITH HIM?
CLAK
I CAN MAKE THAT HAPPEN.

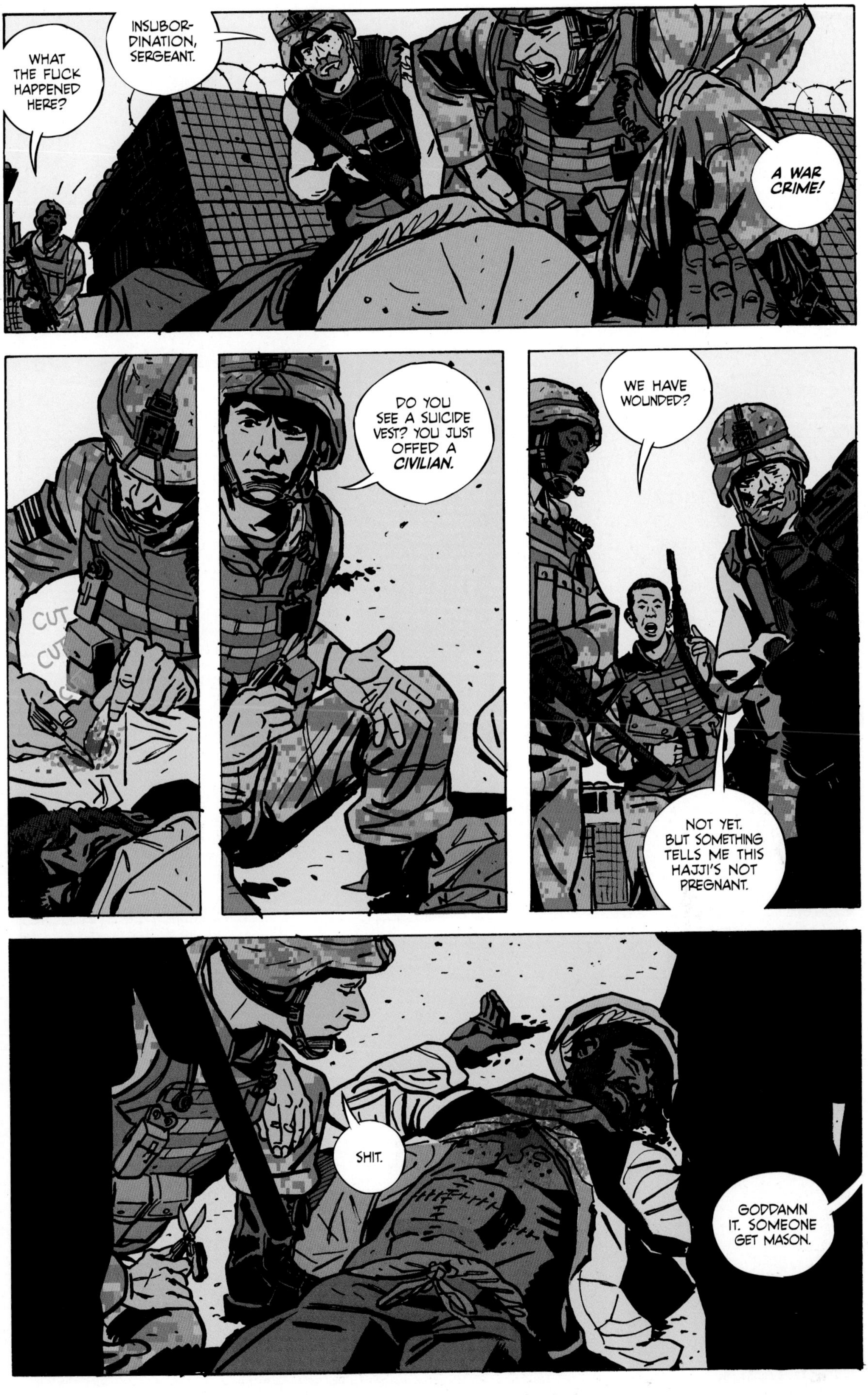
WHAT THE FUCK HAPPENED HERE?
INSUBOR-DINATION, SERGEANT.
A WAR CRIME!
CUT
CUT
DO YOU SEE A SUICIDE VEST? YOU JUST OFFED A *CIVILIAN.*
WE HAVE WOUNDED?
NOT YET. BUT SOMETHING TELLS ME THIS HAJJI'S NOT PREGNANT.
SHIT.
GODDAMN IT. SOMEONE GET MASON.

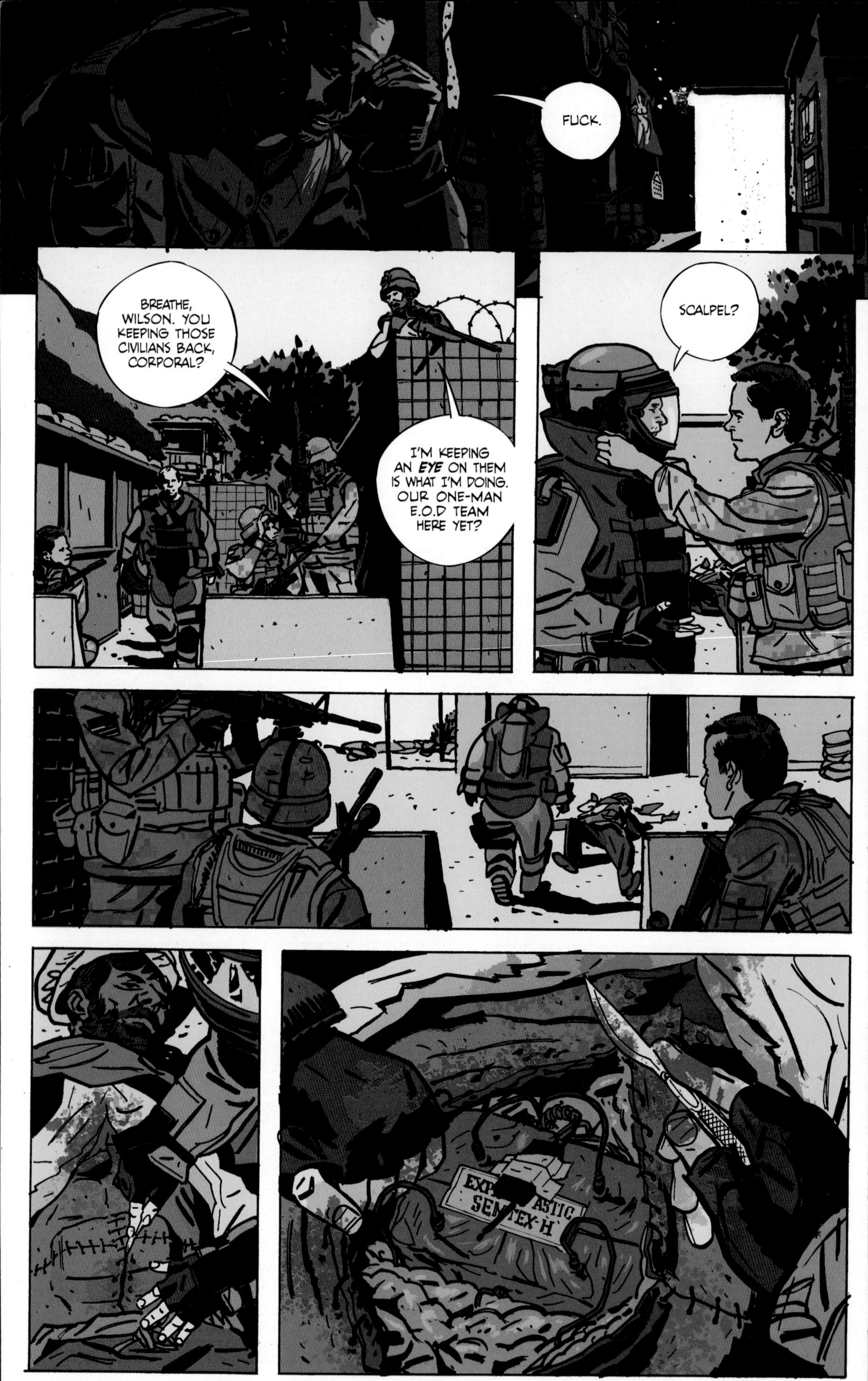
FUCK.
BREATHE, WILSON. YOU KEEPING THOSE CIVILIANS BACK, CORPORAL?
I'M KEEPING AN EYE ON THEM IS WHAT I'M DOING. OUR ONE-MAN E.O.D TEAM HERE YET?
SCALPEL?
SEMTEX-H

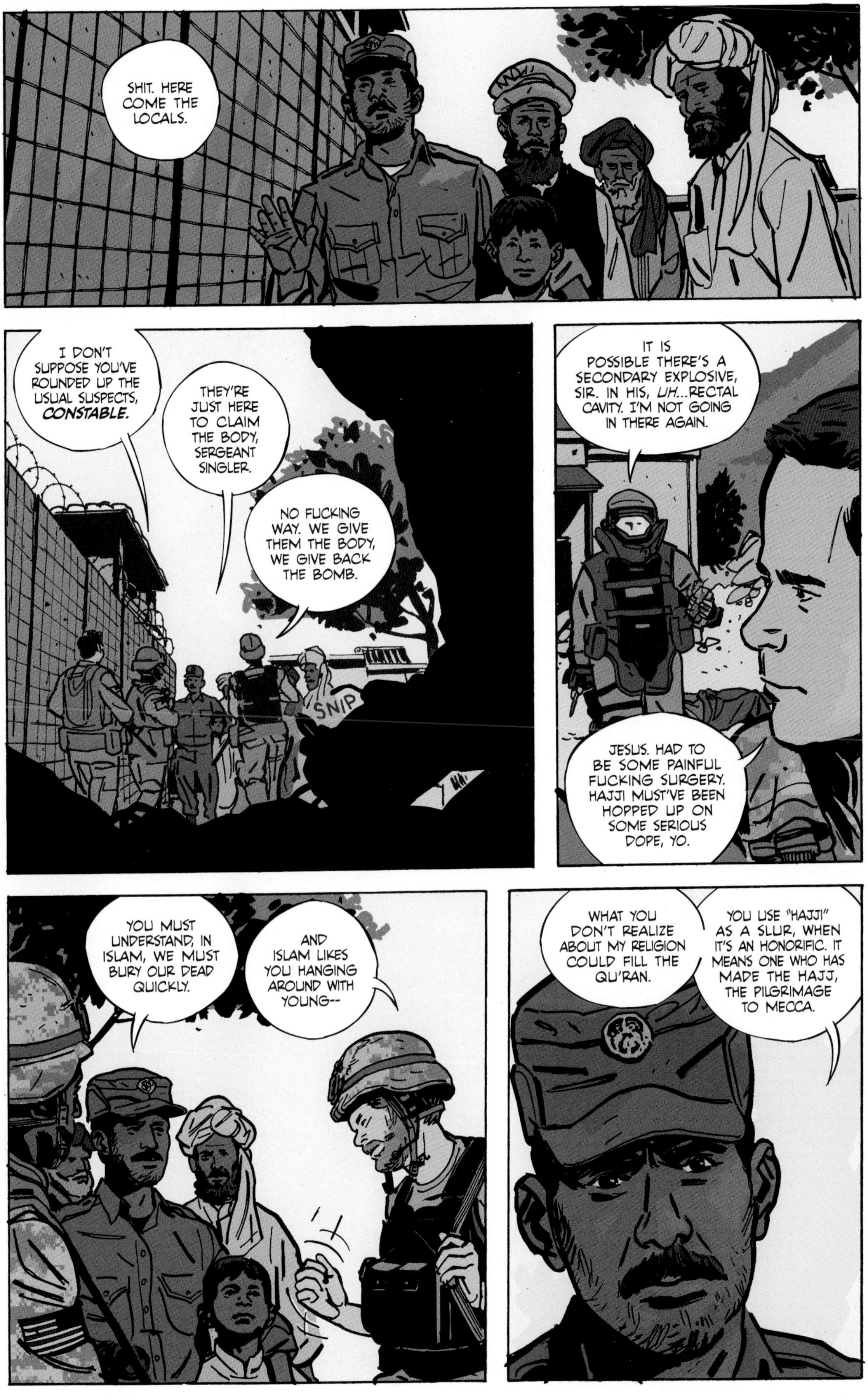
SHIT. HERE COME THE LOCALS.
I DON'T SUPPOSE YOU'VE ROUNDED UP THE USUAL SUSPECTS, CONSTABLE.
THEY'RE JUST HERE TO CLAIM THE BODY, SERGEANT SINGLER.
NO FUCKING WAY. WE GIVE THEM THE BODY, WE GIVE BACK THE BOMB.
SNIP
IT IS POSSIBLE THERE'S A SECONDARY EXPLOSIVE, SIR. IN HIS, UH...RECTAL CAVITY. I'M NOT GOING IN THERE AGAIN.
JESUS. HAD TO BE SOME PAINFUL FUCKING SURGERY. HAJJI MUST'VE BEEN HOPPED UP ON SOME SERIOUS DOPE, YO.
YOU MUST UNDERSTAND, IN ISLAM, WE MUST BURY OUR DEAD QUICKLY.
AND ISLAM LIKES YOU HANGING AROUND WITH YOUNG--
WHAT YOU DON'T REALIZE ABOUT MY RELIGION COULD FILL THE QU'RAN.
YOU USE "HAJJI" AS A SLUR, WHEN IT'S AN HONORIFIC. IT MEANS ONE WHO HAS MADE THE HAJJ, THE PILGRIMAGE TO MECCA.

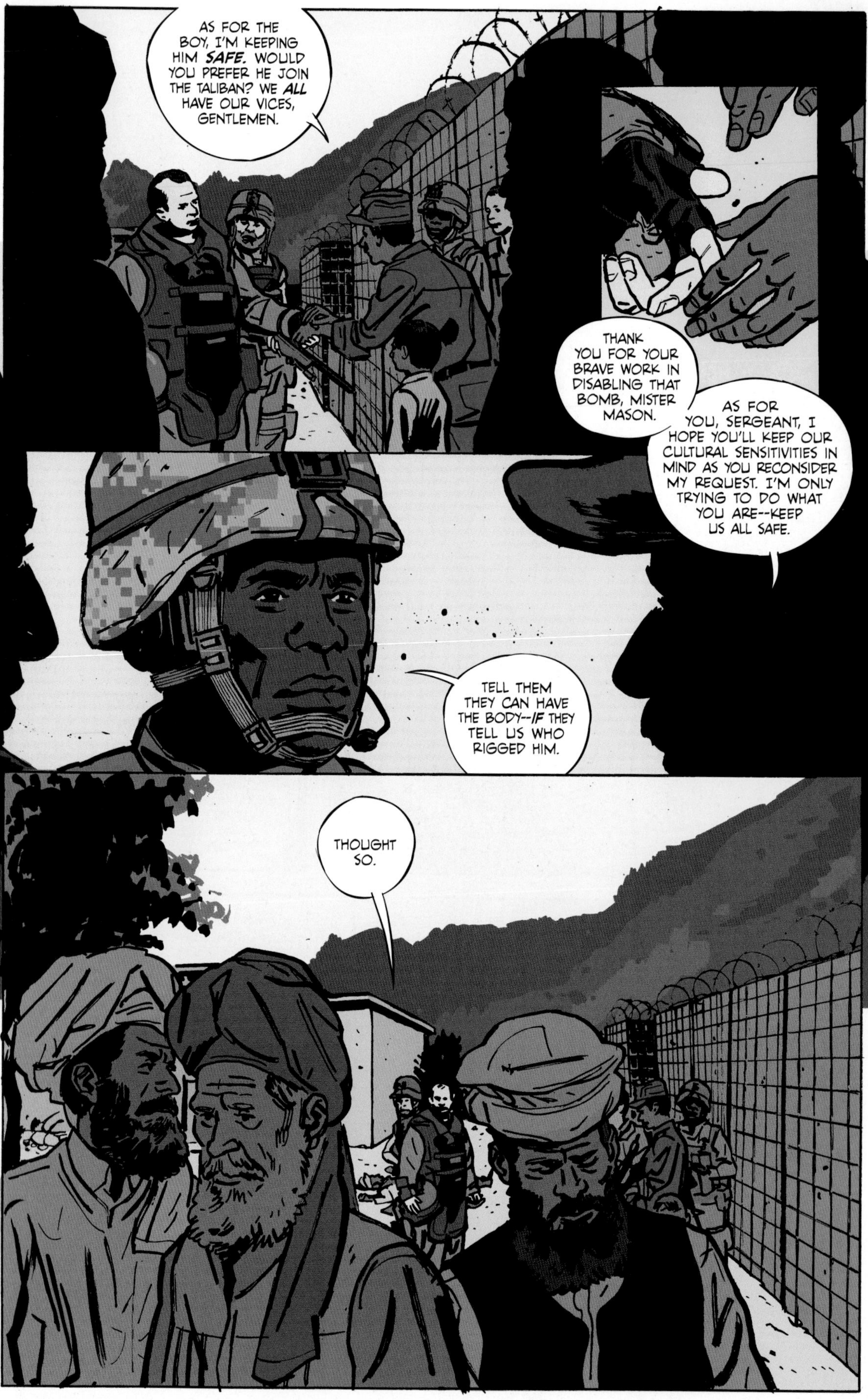
AS FOR THE BOY, I'M KEEPING HIM **SAFE.** WOULD YOU PREFER HE JOIN THE TALIBAN? WE **ALL** HAVE OUR VICES, GENTLEMEN.
THANK YOU FOR YOUR BRAVE WORK IN DISABLING THAT BOMB, MISTER MASON.
AS FOR YOU, SERGEANT, I HOPE YOU'LL KEEP OUR CULTURAL SENSITIVITIES IN MIND AS YOU RECONSIDER MY REQUEST. I'M ONLY TRYING TO DO WHAT YOU ARE--KEEP US ALL SAFE.
TELL THEM THEY CAN HAVE THE BODY--**IF** THEY TELL US WHO RIGGED HIM.
THOUGHT SO.

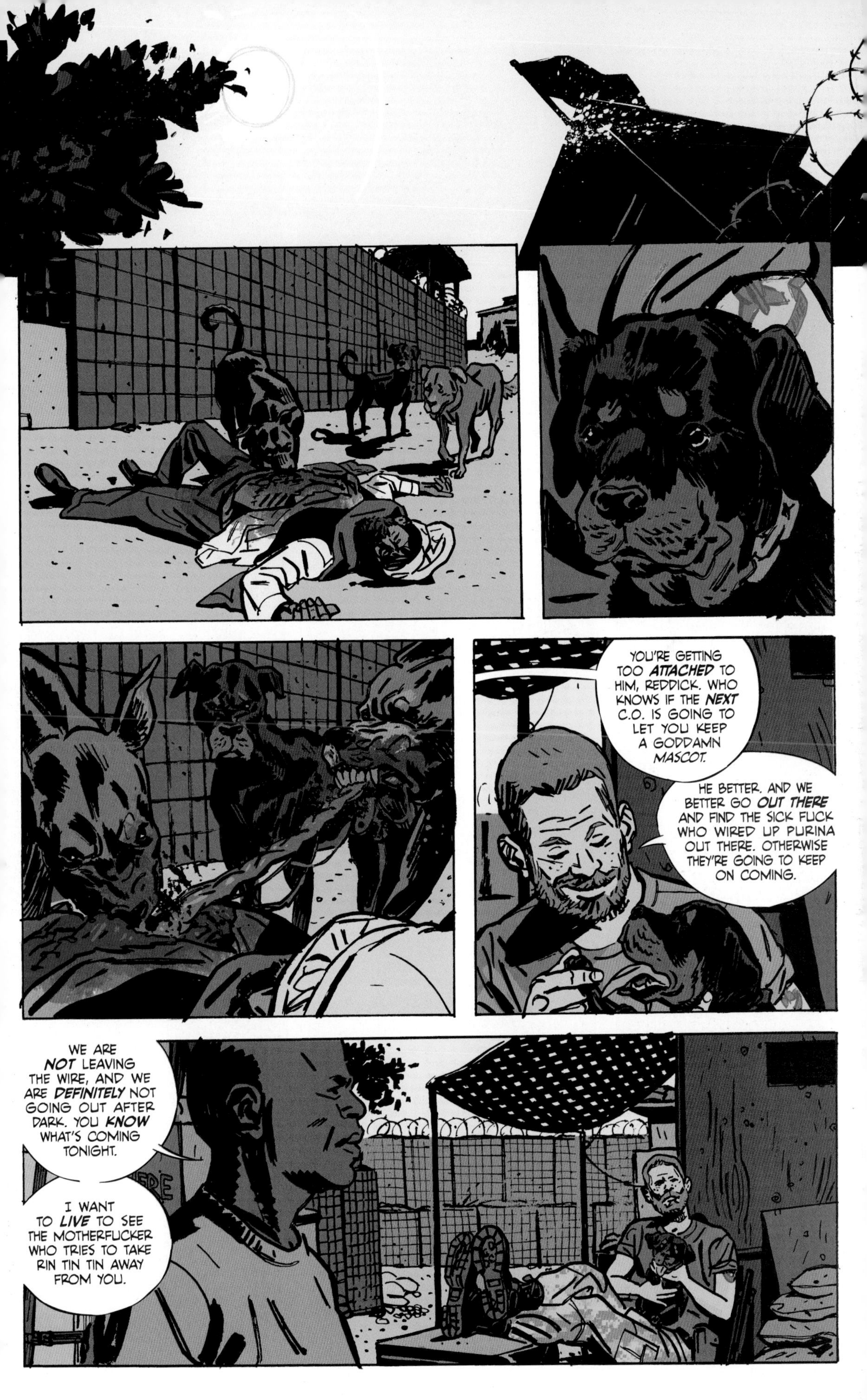
YOU'RE GETTING TOO ATTACHED TO HIM, REDDICK. WHO KNOWS IF THE NEXT C.O. IS GOING TO LET YOU KEEP A GODDAMN MASCOT.
HE BETTER. AND WE BETTER GO OUT THERE AND FIND THE SICK FUCK WHO WIRED UP PURINA OUT THERE. OTHERWISE THEY'RE GOING TO KEEP ON COMING.
WE ARE NOT LEAVING THE WIRE, AND WE ARE DEFINITELY NOT GOING OUT AFTER DARK. YOU KNOW WHAT'S COMING TONIGHT.
I WANT TO LIVE TO SEE THE MOTHERFUCKER WHO TRIES TO TAKE RIN TIN TIN AWAY FROM YOU.

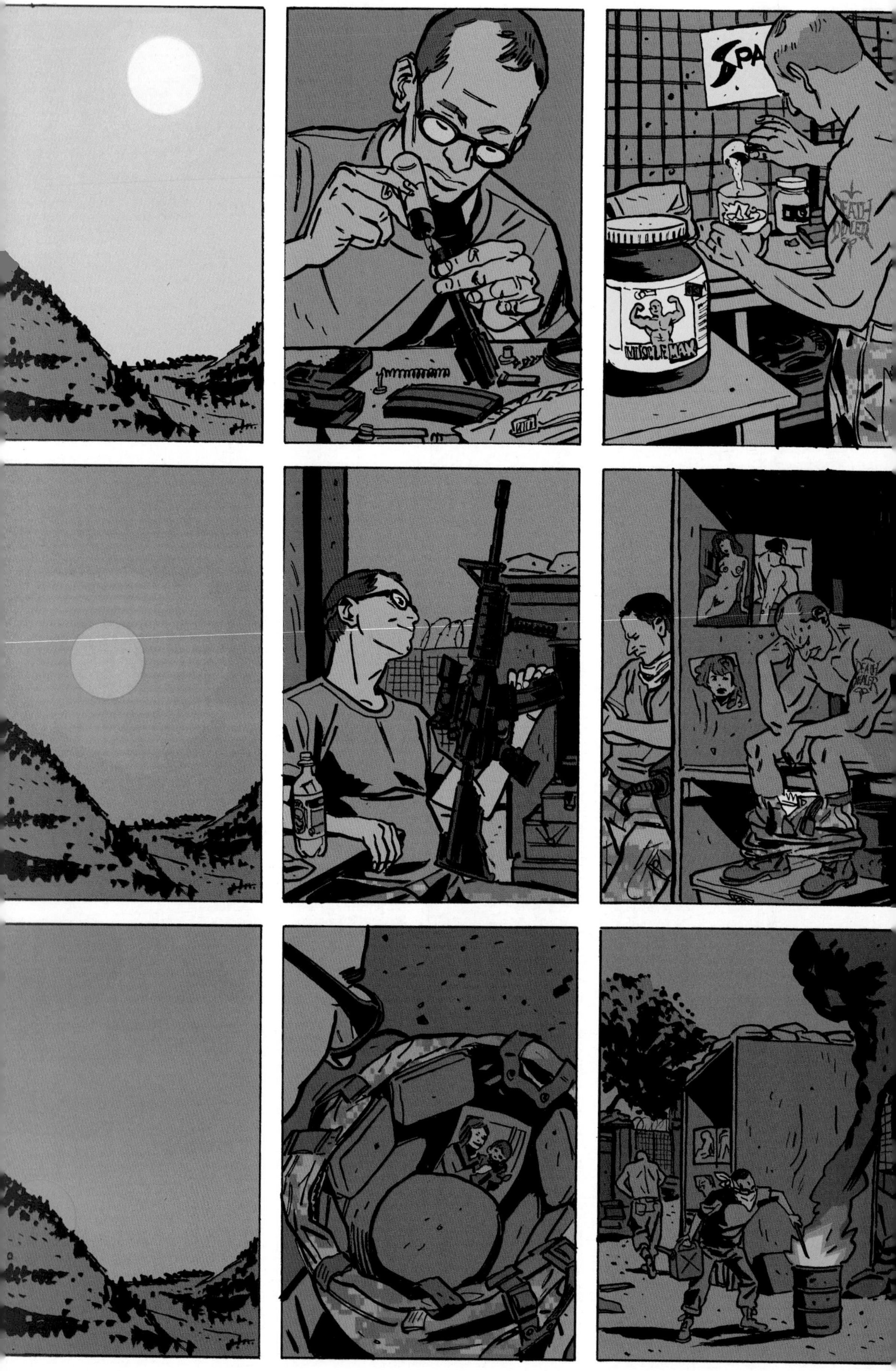
SPA
MUSCLE MAX
DEATH DEALER

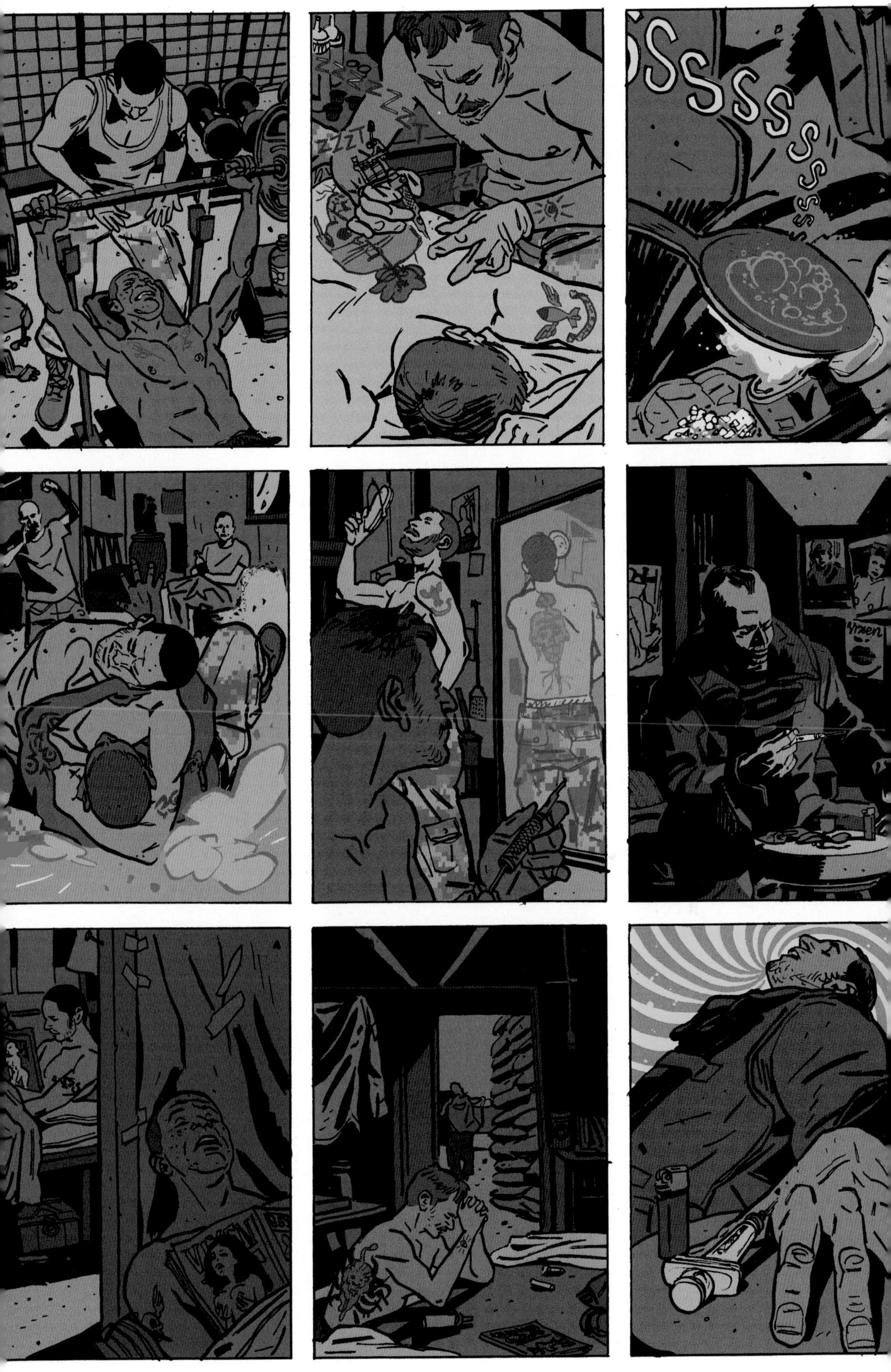
ZZZZT
SSSSSSSSS

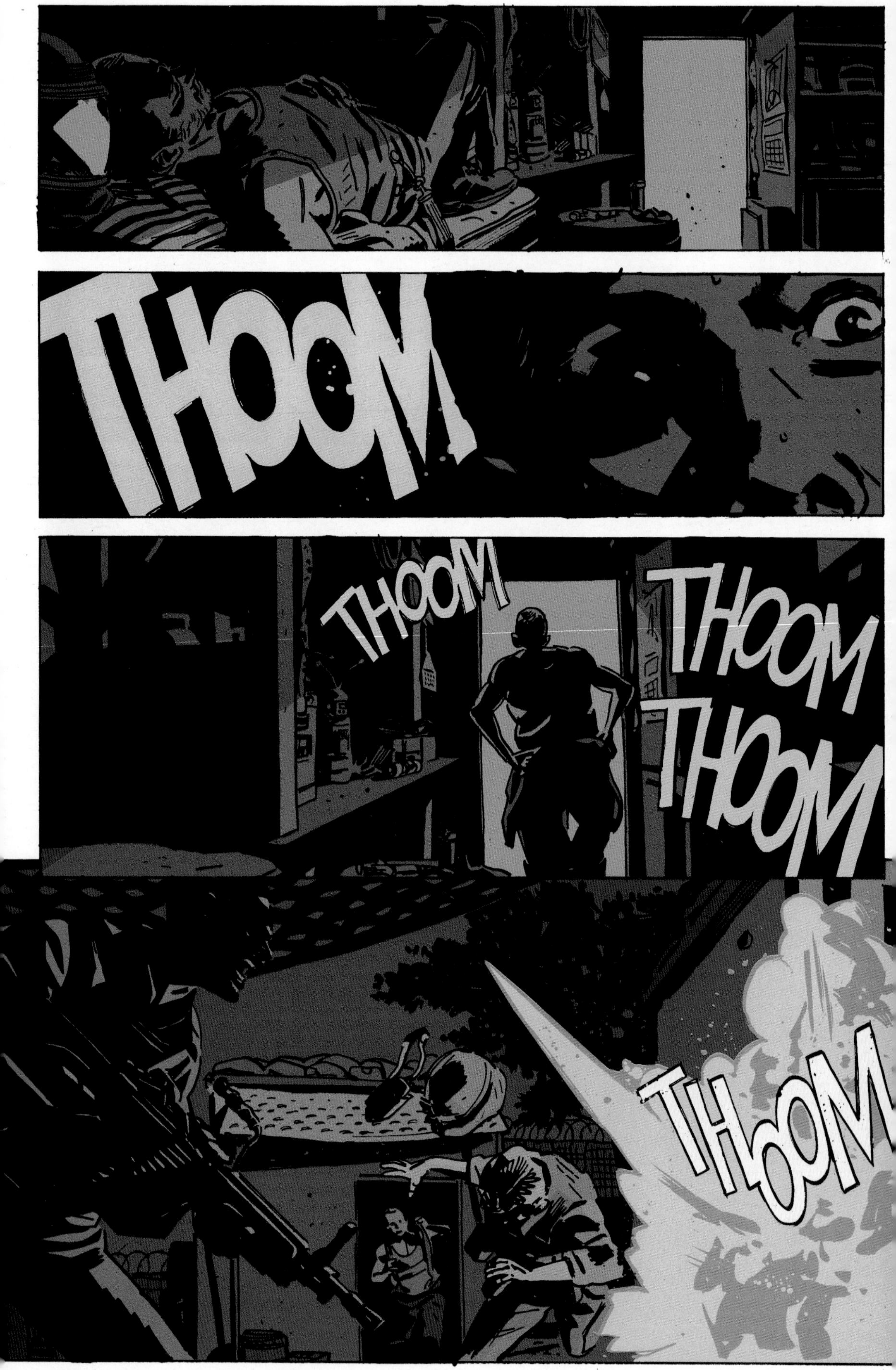
THOOM
THOOM
THOOM
THOOM
THOOM

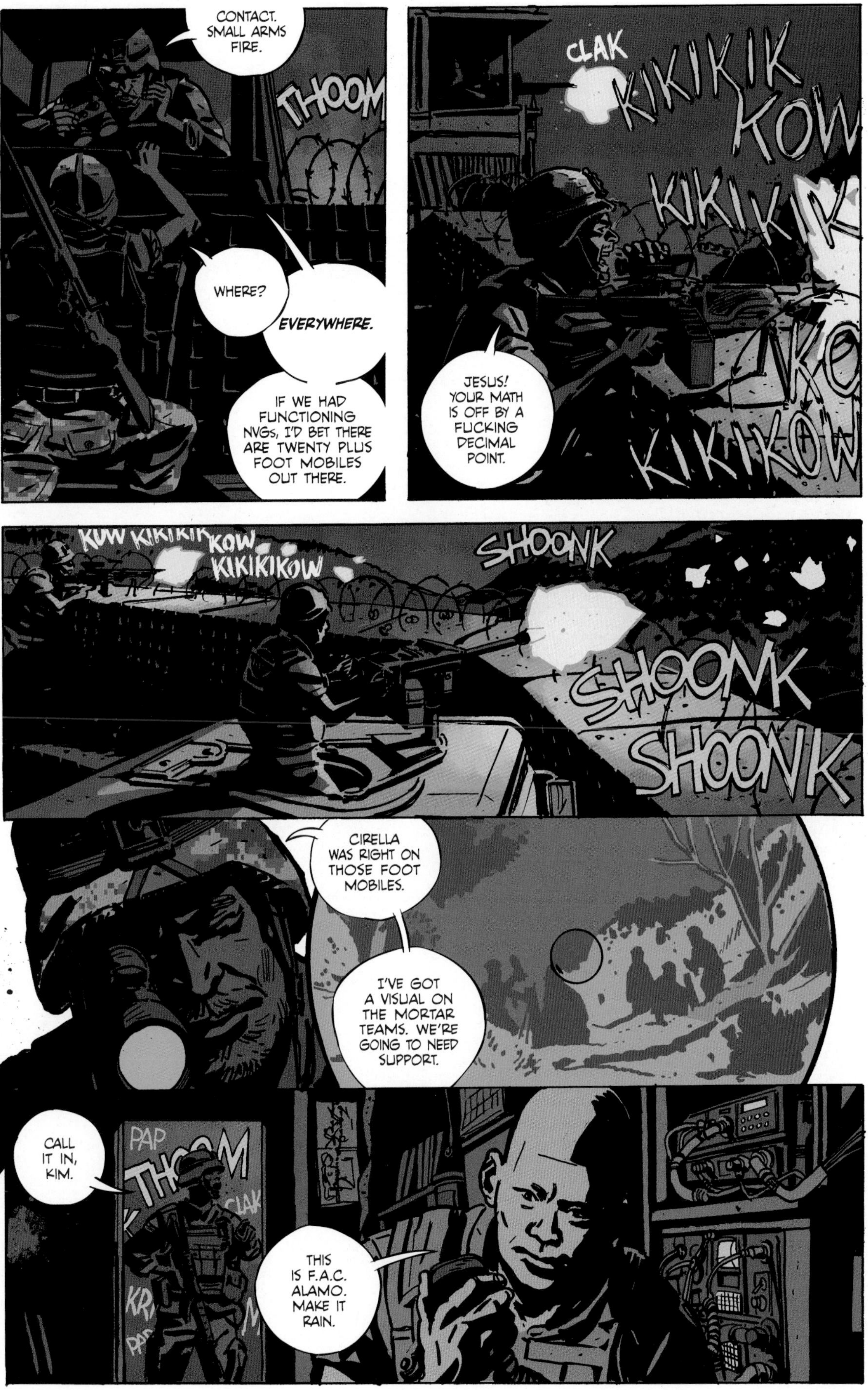
CONTACT. SMALL ARMS FIRE.
THOOM
WHERE?
EVERYWHERE.
IF WE HAD FUNCTIONING NVGs, I'D BET THERE ARE TWENTY PLUS FOOT MOBILES OUT THERE.
CLAK
KIKIKIK
KOW
KIKIKIK
JESUS! YOUR MATH IS OFF BY A FUCKING DECIMAL POINT.
KIKIKOW
KOW KIKIKIK KOW
KIKIKIKOW
SHOONK
SHOONK
SHOONK
CIRELLA WAS RIGHT ON THOSE FOOT MOBILES.
I'VE GOT A VISUAL ON THE MORTAR TEAMS. WE'RE GOING TO NEED SUPPORT.
CALL IT IN, KIM.
PAP
THOOM
CLAK
THIS IS F.A.C. ALAMO. MAKE IT RAIN.

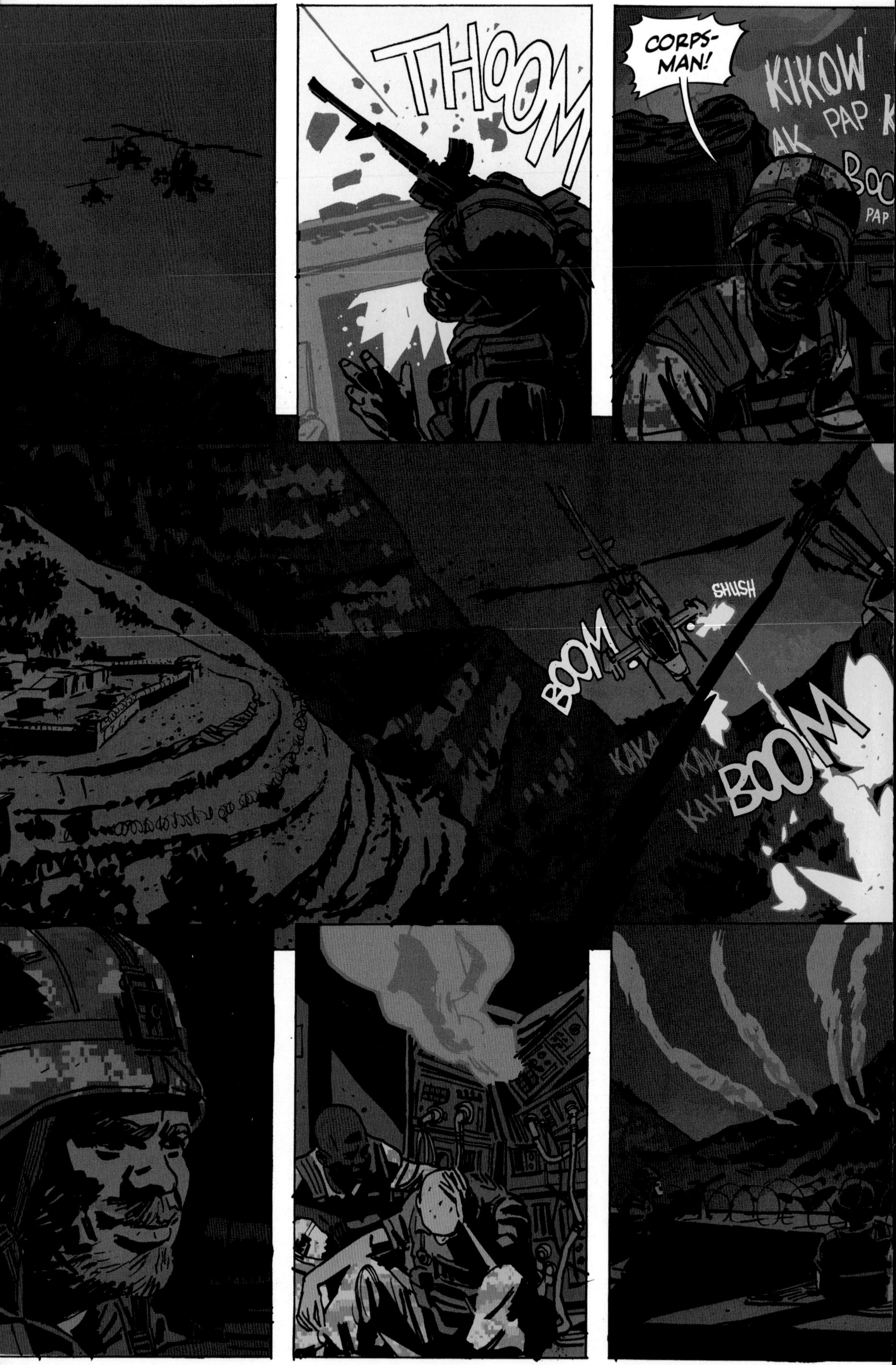
THOOM
CORPS-MAN!
KIKOW
AK
PAP
PAP
SHUSH
BOOM
KAKA
KAK
KAK
BOOM

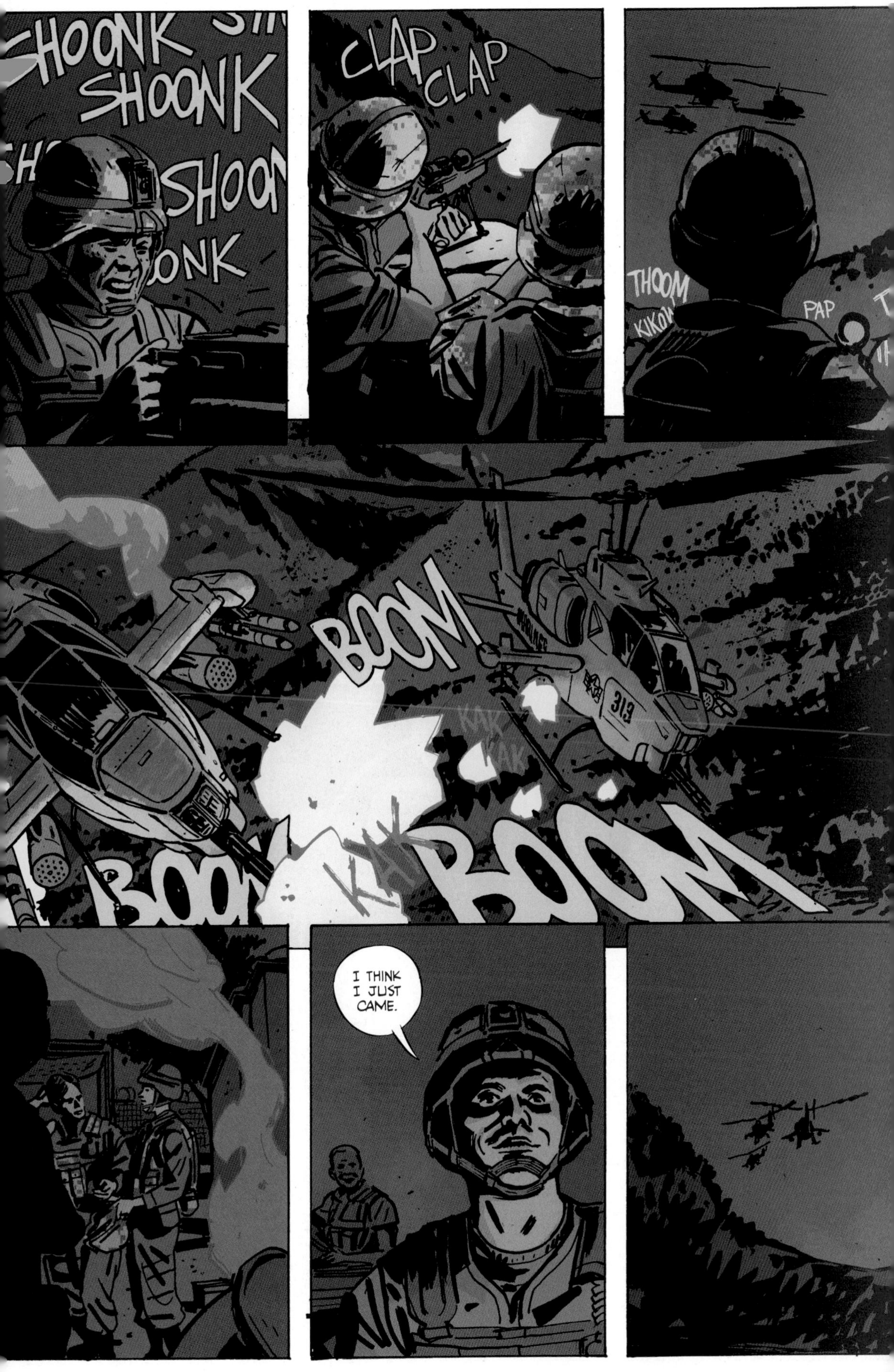
SHOONK
SHOONK
SHOON
ONK
CLAP
CLAP
THOOM
KIKOW
PAP
BOOM
KAK
KAK
BOOM
I THINK I JUST CAME.

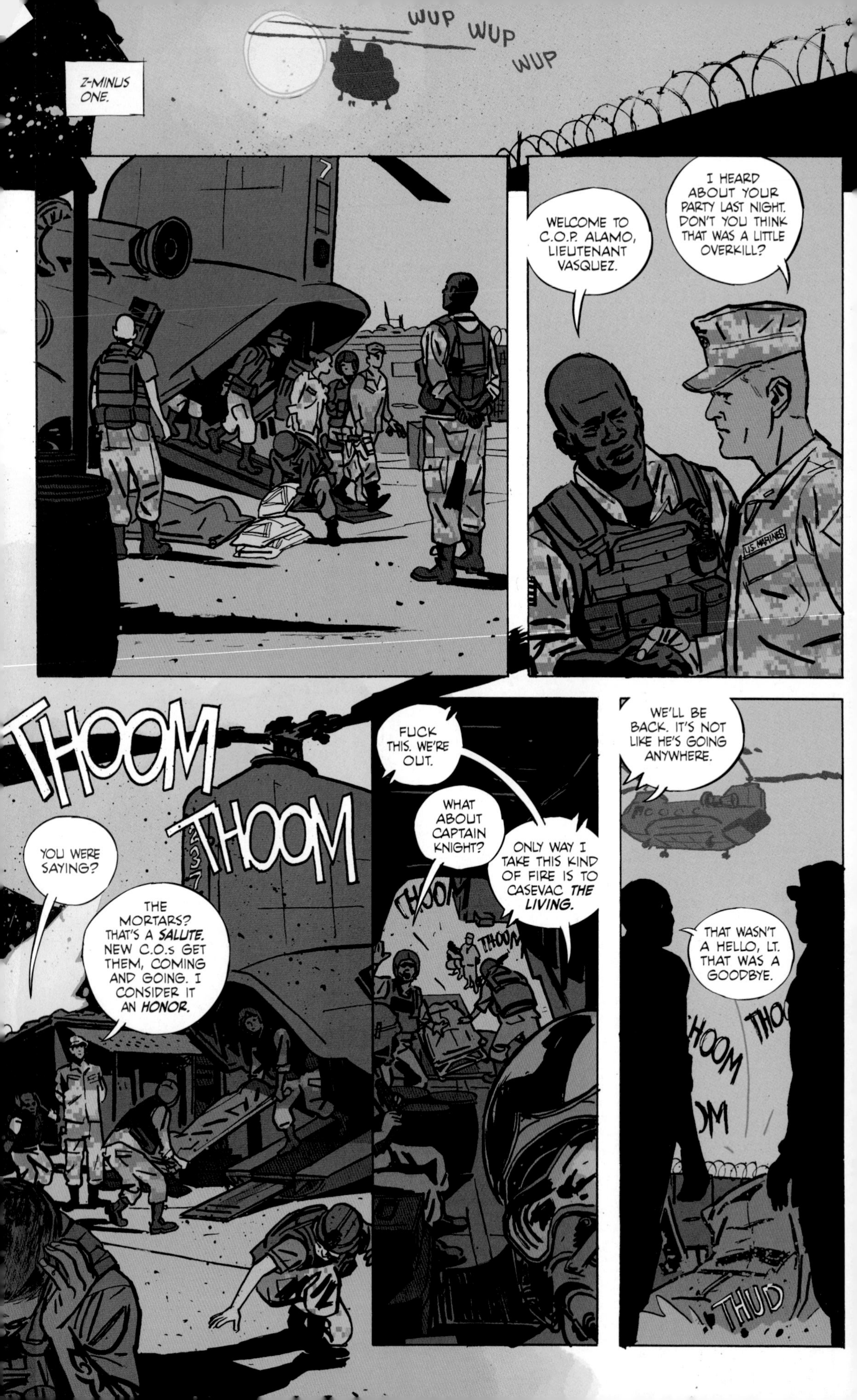

WUP WUP WUP
Z-MINUS ONE.
WELCOME TO C.O.P. ALAMO, LIEUTENANT VASQUEZ.
I HEARD ABOUT YOUR PARTY LAST NIGHT. DON'T YOU THINK THAT WAS A LITTLE OVERKILL?
U.S. MARINES
THOOM
THOOM
YOU WERE SAYING?
THE MORTARS? THAT'S A SALUTE. NEW C.O.s GET THEM, COMING AND GOING. I CONSIDER IT AN HONOR.
FUCK THIS. WE'RE OUT.
WHAT ABOUT CAPTAIN KNIGHT?
ONLY WAY I TAKE THIS KIND OF FIRE IS TO CASEVAC THE LIVING.
THOOM
THOOM
WE'LL BE BACK. IT'S NOT LIKE HE'S GOING ANYWHERE.
THAT WASN'T A HELLO, LT. THAT WAS A GOODBYE.
THOOM
THOOM
THUD

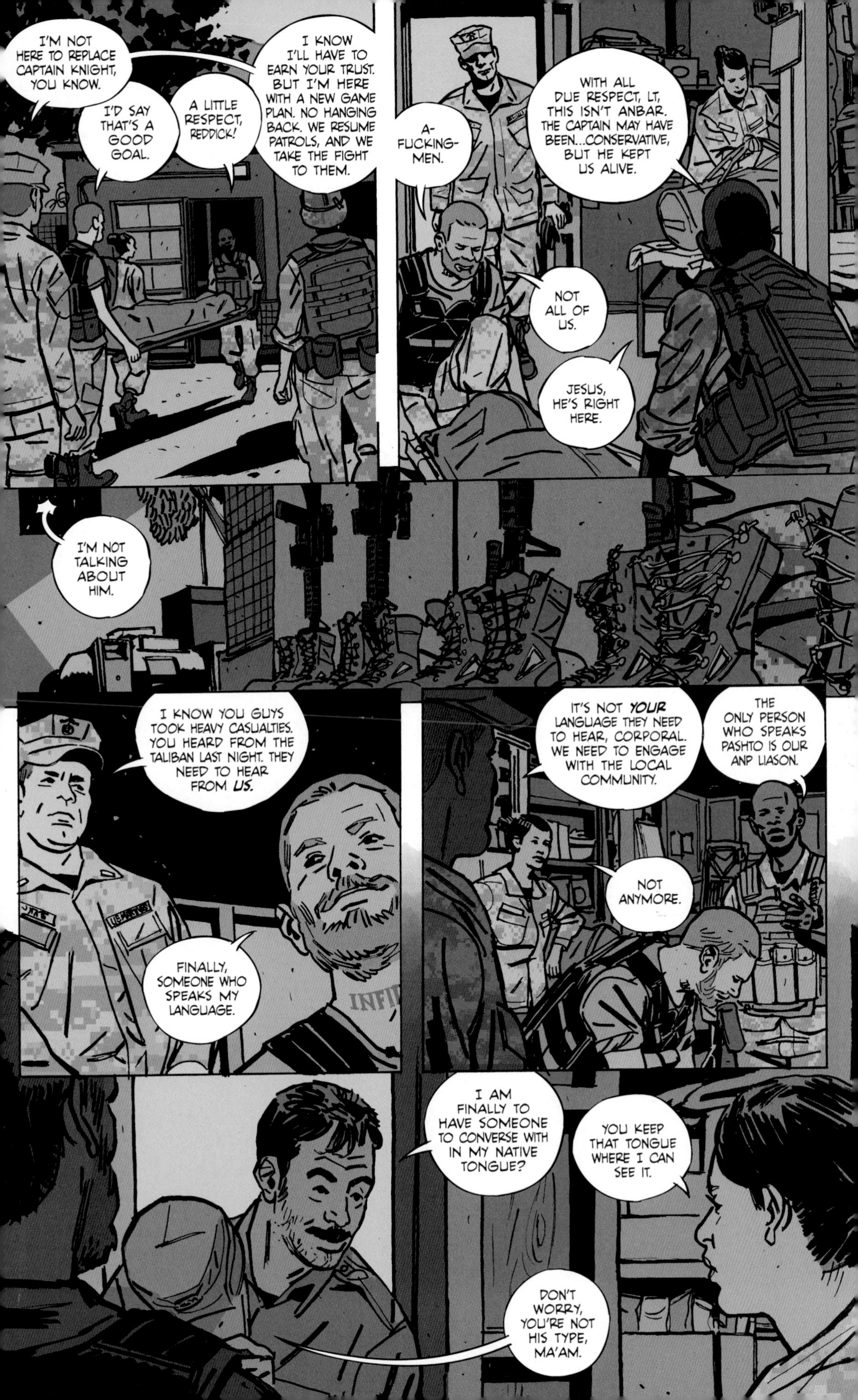
I'M NOT HERE TO REPLACE CAPTAIN KNIGHT, YOU KNOW.
I'D SAY THAT'S A GOOD GOAL.
A LITTLE RESPECT, REDDICK!
I KNOW I'LL HAVE TO EARN YOUR TRUST. BUT I'M HERE WITH A NEW GAME PLAN. NO HANGING BACK. WE RESUME PATROLS, AND WE TAKE THE FIGHT TO THEM.
A-FUCKING-MEN.
WITH ALL DUE RESPECT, LT, THIS ISN'T ANBAR. THE CAPTAIN MAY HAVE BEEN...CONSERVATIVE, BUT HE KEPT US ALIVE.
NOT ALL OF US.
JESUS, HE'S RIGHT HERE.
I'M NOT TALKING ABOUT HIM.
I KNOW YOU GUYS TOOK HEAVY CASUALTIES. YOU HEARD FROM THE TALIBAN LAST NIGHT. THEY NEED TO HEAR FROM *US.*
FINALLY, SOMEONE WHO SPEAKS MY LANGUAGE.
IT'S NOT *YOUR* LANGUAGE THEY NEED TO HEAR, CORPORAL. WE NEED TO ENGAGE WITH THE LOCAL COMMUNITY.
THE ONLY PERSON WHO SPEAKS PASHTO IS OUR ANP LIASON.
NOT ANYMORE.
I AM FINALLY TO HAVE SOMEONE TO CONVERSE WITH IN MY NATIVE TONGUE?
YOU KEEP THAT TONGUE WHERE I CAN SEE IT.
DON'T WORRY, YOU'RE NOT HIS TYPE, MA'AM.

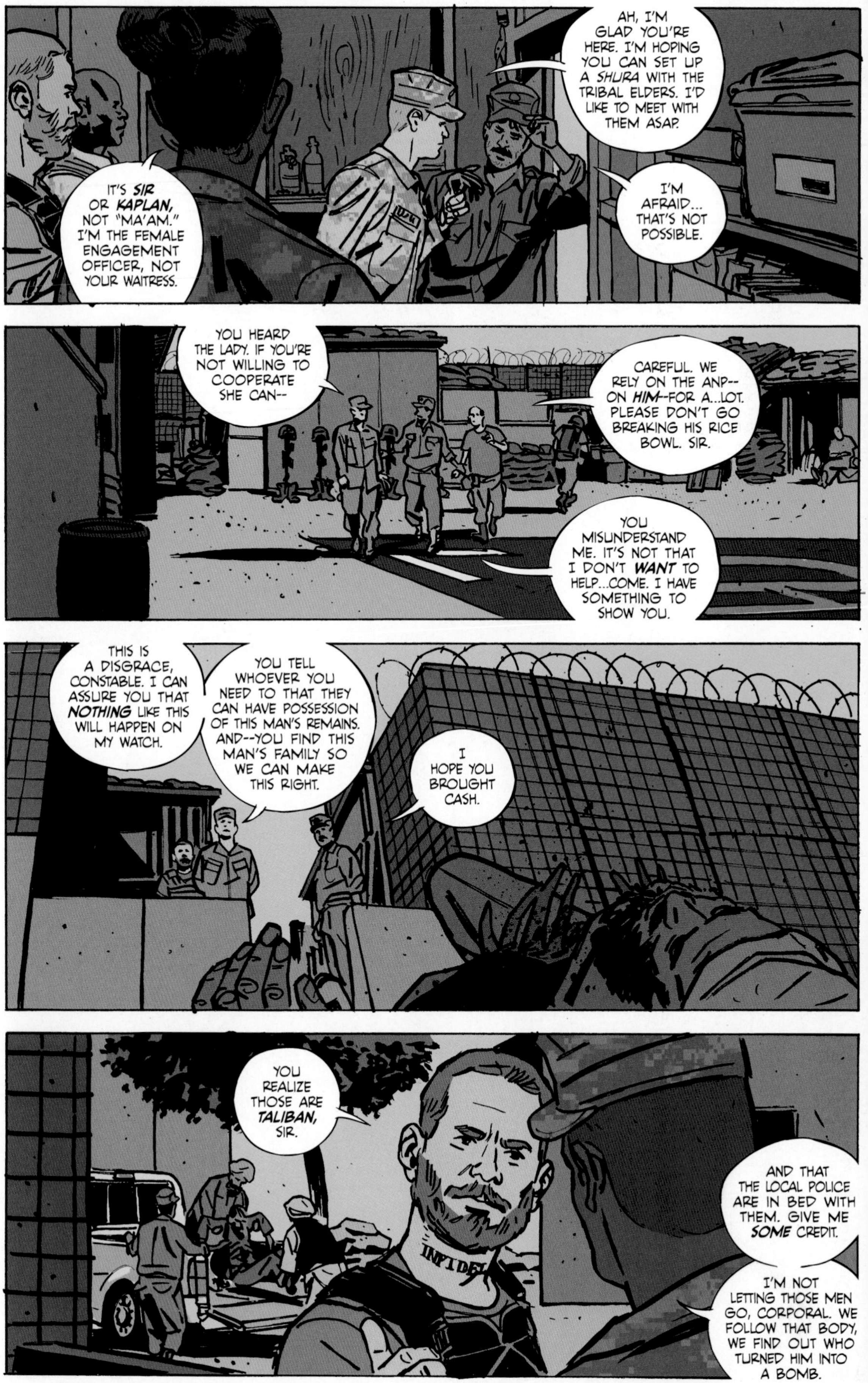
AH, I'M GLAD YOU'RE HERE. I'M HOPING YOU CAN SET UP A *SHURA* WITH THE TRIBAL ELDERS. I'D LIKE TO MEET WITH THEM ASAP.
IT'S ***SIR*** OR ***KAPLAN,*** NOT "MA'AM." I'M THE FEMALE ENGAGEMENT OFFICER, NOT YOUR WAITRESS.
I'M AFRAID... THAT'S NOT POSSIBLE.
YOU HEARD THE LADY. IF YOU'RE NOT WILLING TO COOPERATE SHE CAN--
CAREFUL. WE RELY ON THE ANP-- ON ***HIM***--FOR A...LOT. PLEASE DON'T GO BREAKING HIS RICE BOWL. SIR.
YOU MISUNDERSTAND ME. IT'S NOT THAT I DON'T ***WANT*** TO HELP...COME. I HAVE SOMETHING TO SHOW YOU.
THIS IS A DISGRACE, CONSTABLE. I CAN ASSURE YOU THAT ***NOTHING*** LIKE THIS WILL HAPPEN ON MY WATCH.
YOU TELL WHOEVER YOU NEED TO THAT THEY CAN HAVE POSSESSION OF THIS MAN'S REMAINS. AND--YOU FIND THIS MAN'S FAMILY SO WE CAN MAKE THIS RIGHT.
I HOPE YOU BROUGHT CASH.
YOU REALIZE THOSE ARE ***TALIBAN,*** SIR.
INFIDEL
AND THAT THE LOCAL POLICE ARE IN BED WITH THEM. GIVE ME ***SOME*** CREDIT.
I'M NOT LETTING THOSE MEN GO, CORPORAL. WE FOLLOW THAT BODY, WE FIND OUT WHO TURNED HIM INTO A BOMB.

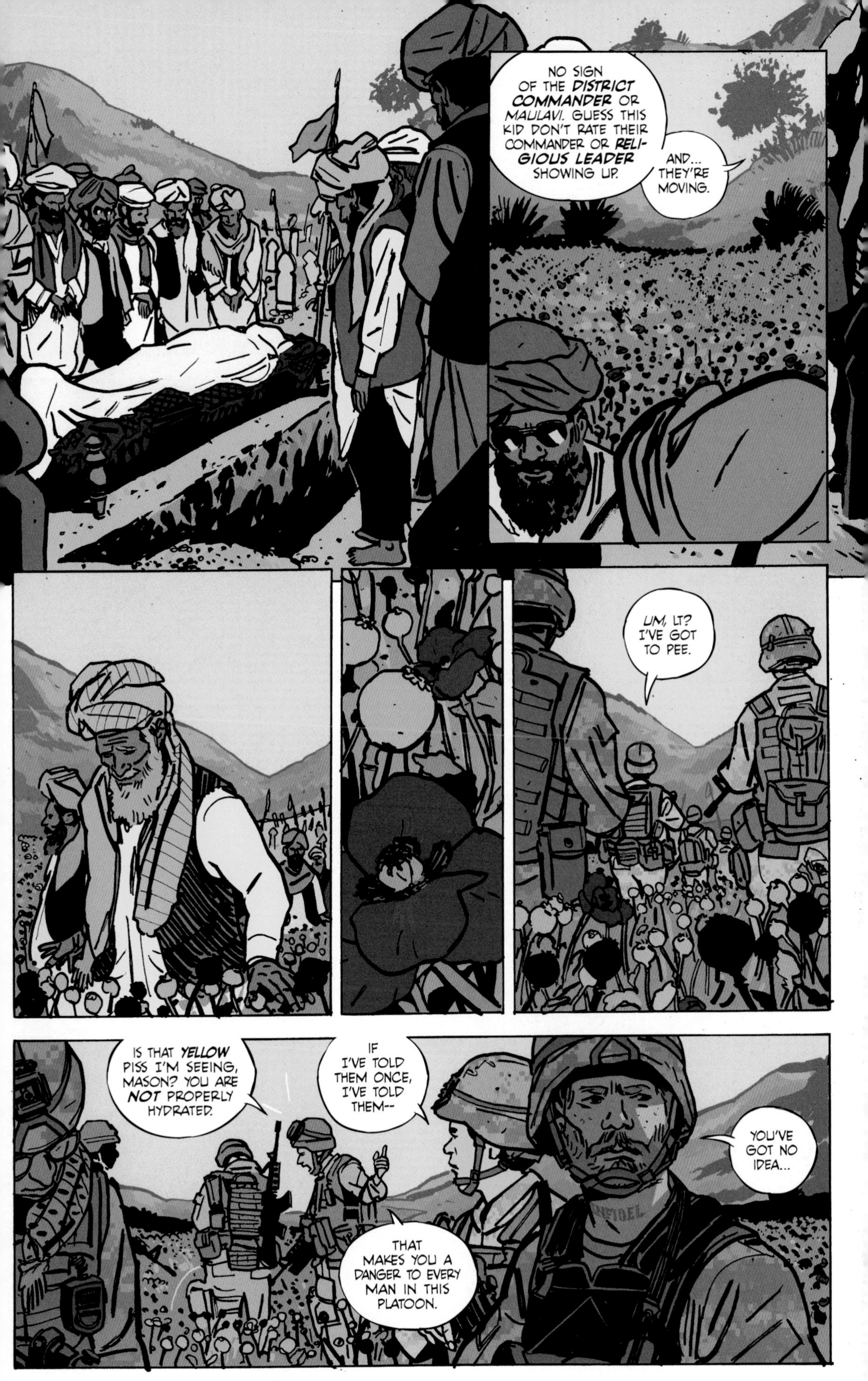
NO SIGN OF THE DISTRICT COMMANDER OR MAULAVI. GUESS THIS KID DON'T RATE THEIR COMMANDER OR RELIGIOUS LEADER SHOWING UP.
AND... THEY'RE MOVING.
UM, LT? I'VE GOT TO PEE.
IS THAT YELLOW PISS I'M SEEING, MASON? YOU ARE NOT PROPERLY HYDRATED.
IF I'VE TOLD THEM ONCE, I'VE TOLD THEM--
THAT MAKES YOU A DANGER TO EVERY MAN IN THIS PLATOON.
YOU'VE GOT NO IDEA...

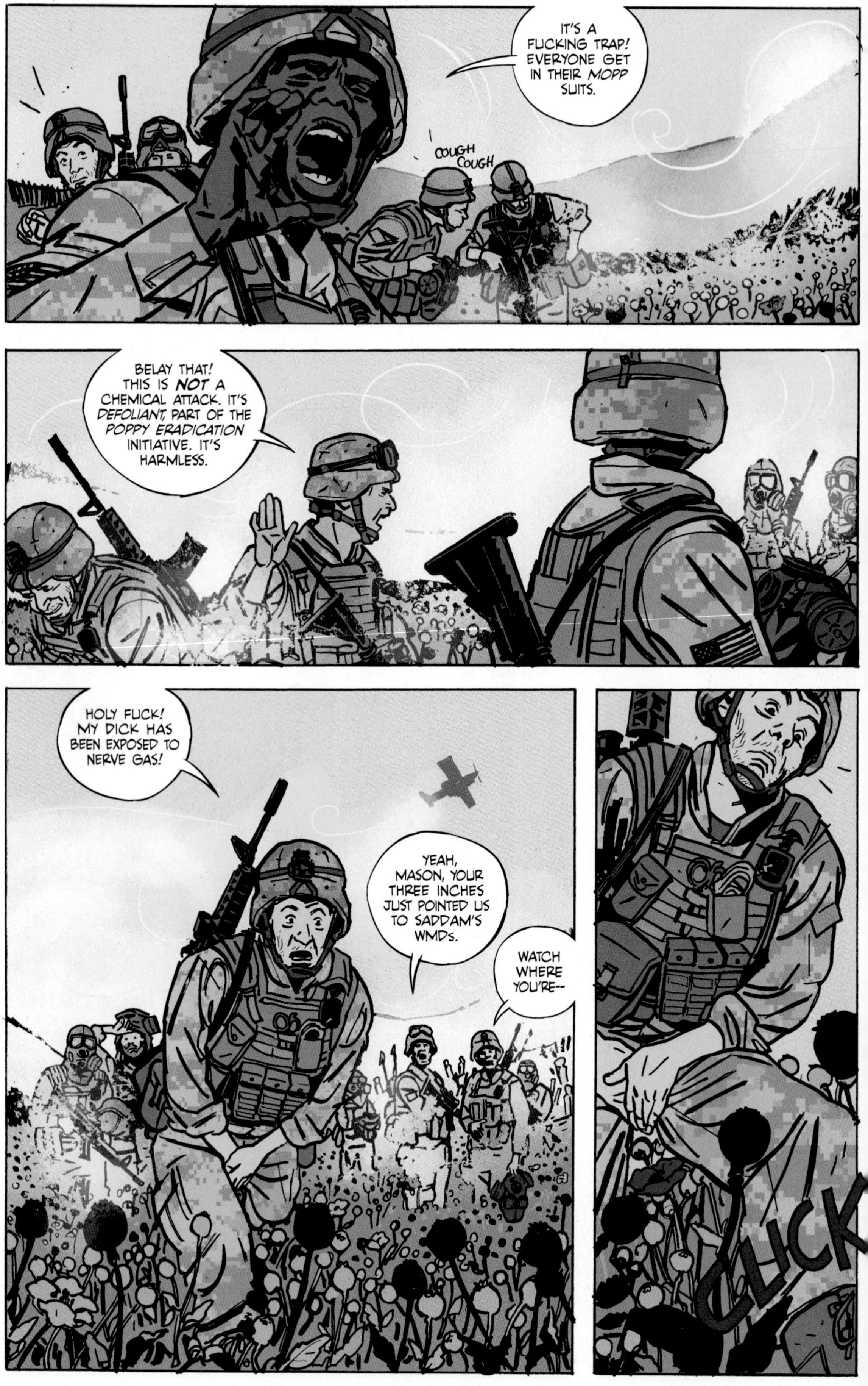
IT'S A FUCKING TRAP! EVERYONE GET IN THEIR MOPP SUITS.
COUGH COUGH
BELAY THAT! THIS IS NOT A CHEMICAL ATTACK. IT'S DEFOLIANT, PART OF THE POPPY ERADICATION INITIATIVE. IT'S HARMLESS.
HOLY FUCK! MY DICK HAS BEEN EXPOSED TO NERVE GAS!
YEAH, MASON, YOUR THREE INCHES JUST POINTED US TO SADDAM'S WMDs.
WATCH WHERE YOU'RE--
CLICK

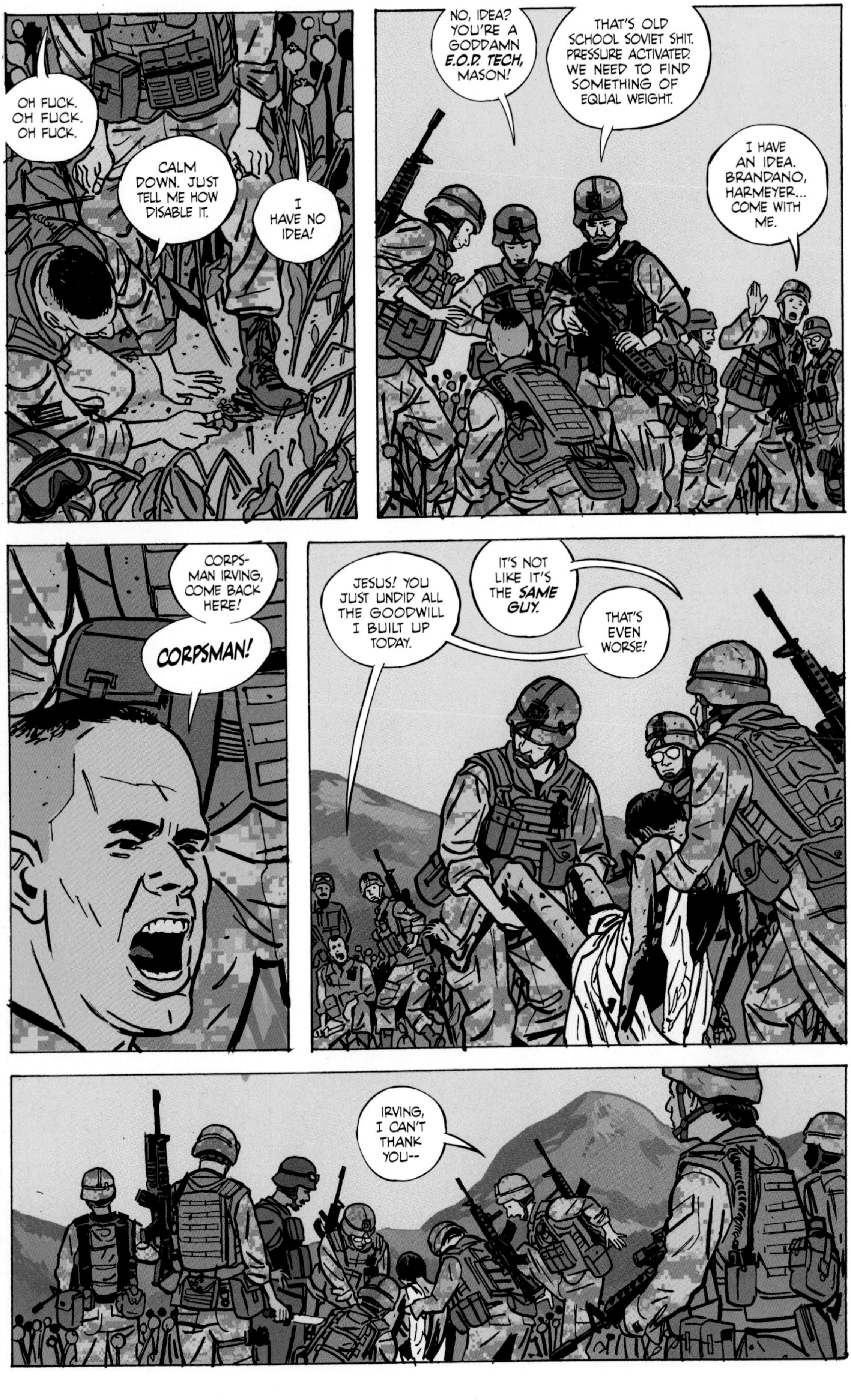
OH FUCK. OH FUCK. OH FUCK.
CALM DOWN. JUST TELL ME HOW DISABLE IT.
I HAVE NO IDEA!
NO, IDEA? YOU'RE A GODDAMN E.O.D. TECH, MASON!
THAT'S OLD SCHOOL SOVIET SHIT. PRESSURE ACTIVATED. WE NEED TO FIND SOMETHING OF EQUAL WEIGHT.
I HAVE AN IDEA. BRANDANO, HARMEYER... COME WITH ME.
CORPS-MAN IRVING, COME BACK HERE!
CORPSMAN!
JESUS! YOU JUST UNDID ALL THE GOODWILL I BUILT UP TODAY.
IT'S NOT LIKE IT'S THE SAME GUY.
THAT'S EVEN WORSE!
IRVING, I CAN'T THANK YOU--

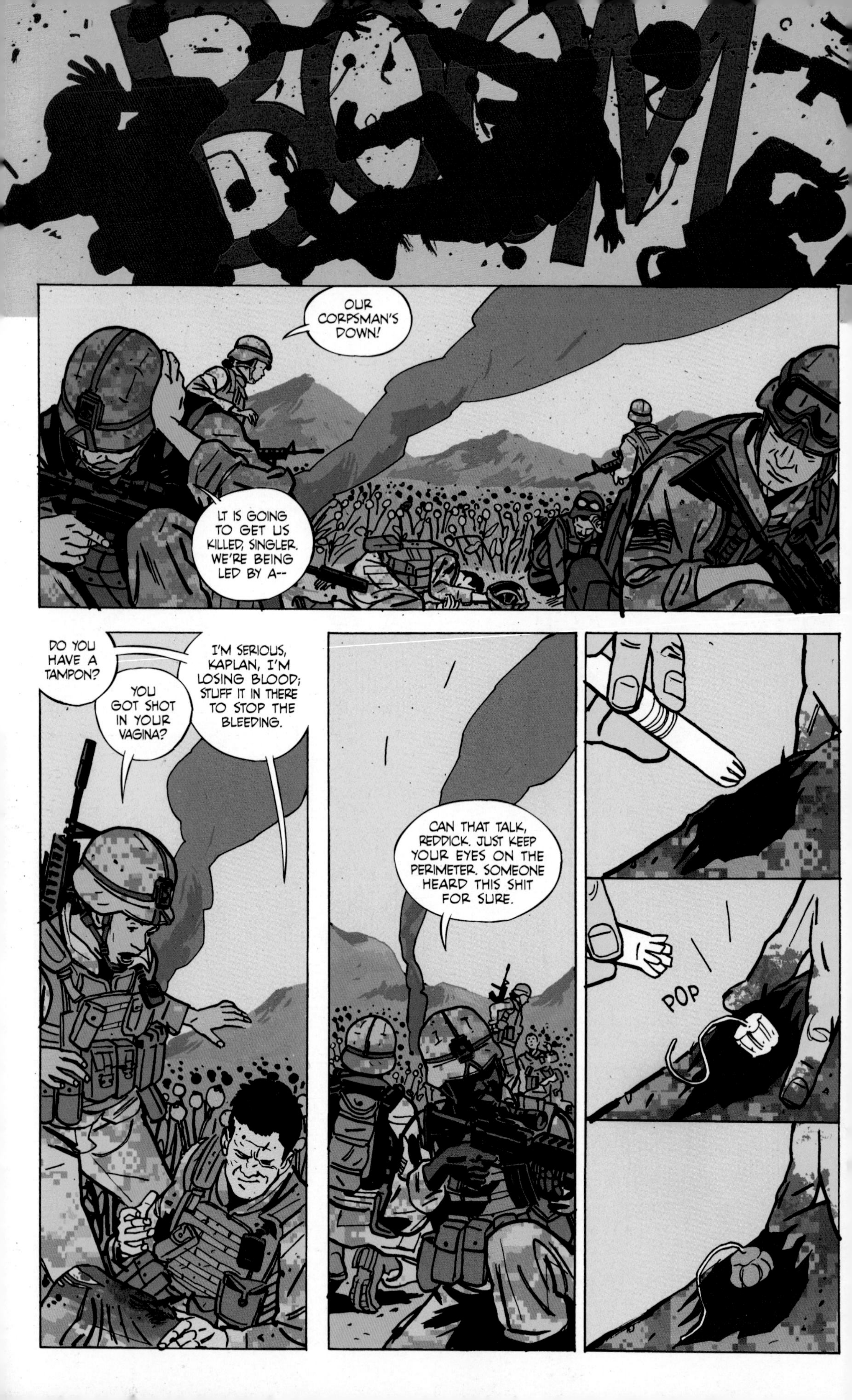
BOOM
OUR CORPSMAN'S DOWN!
LT IS GOING TO GET US KILLED, SINGLER. WE'RE BEING LED BY A--
DO YOU HAVE A TAMPON?
YOU GOT SHOT IN YOUR VAGINA?
I'M SERIOUS, KAPLAN, I'M LOSING BLOOD; STUFF IT IN THERE TO STOP THE BLEEDING.
CAN THAT TALK, REDDICK. JUST KEEP YOUR EYES ON THE PERIMETER. SOMEONE HEARD THIS SHIT FOR SURE.
POP

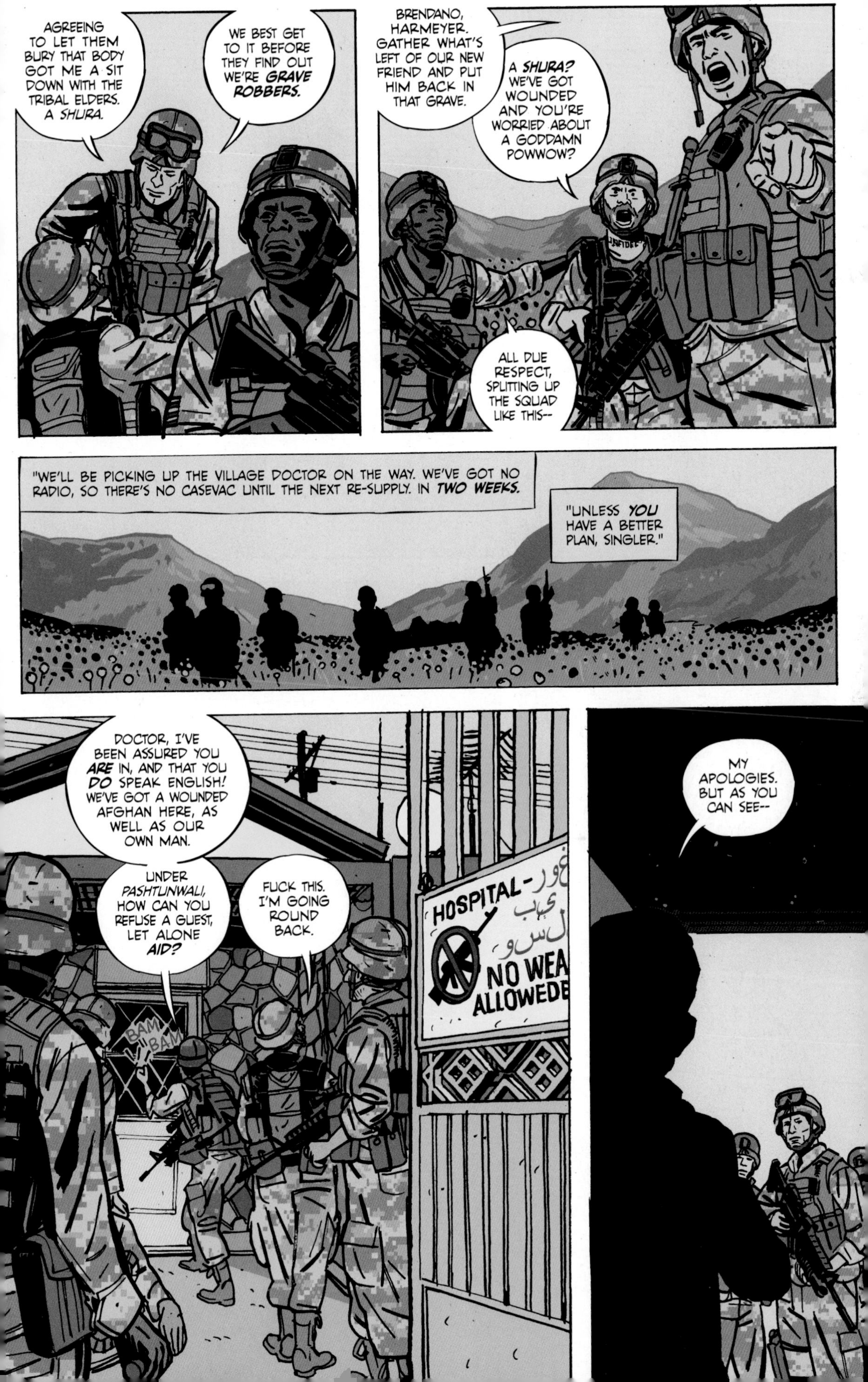
AGREEING TO LET THEM BURY THAT BODY GOT ME A SIT DOWN WITH THE TRIBAL ELDERS. A *SHURA*.
WE BEST GET TO IT BEFORE THEY FIND OUT WE'RE ***GRAVE ROBBERS.***
BRENDANO, HARMEYER. GATHER WHAT'S LEFT OF OUR NEW FRIEND AND PUT HIM BACK IN THAT GRAVE.
A ***SHURA?*** WE'VE GOT WOUNDED AND YOU'RE WORRIED ABOUT A GODDAMN POWWOW?
ALL DUE RESPECT, SPLITTING UP THE SQUAD LIKE THIS--
"WE'LL BE PICKING UP THE VILLAGE DOCTOR ON THE WAY. WE'VE GOT NO RADIO, SO THERE'S NO CASEVAC UNTIL THE NEXT RE-SUPPLY. IN ***TWO WEEKS.***
"UNLESS ***YOU*** HAVE A BETTER PLAN, SINGLER."
DOCTOR, I'VE BEEN ASSURED YOU ***ARE*** IN, AND THAT YOU ***DO*** SPEAK ENGLISH! WE'VE GOT A WOUNDED AFGHAN HERE, AS WELL AS OUR OWN MAN.
UNDER *PASHTUNWALI*, HOW CAN YOU REFUSE A GUEST, LET ALONE ***AID?***
BAM BAM
FUCK THIS. I'M GOING ROUND BACK.
HOSPITAL
MY APOLOGIES. BUT AS YOU CAN SEE--

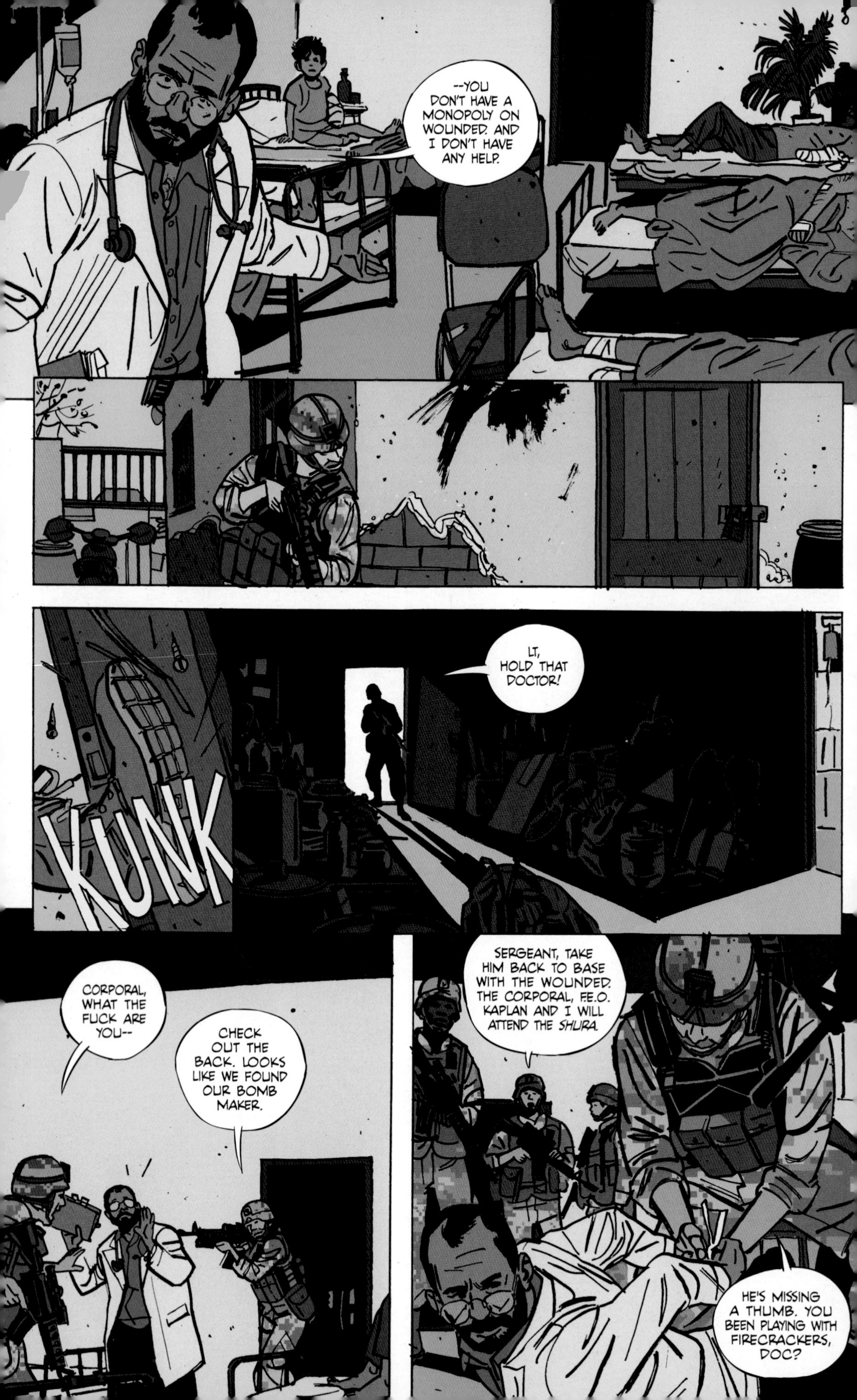
--YOU DON'T HAVE A MONOPOLY ON WOUNDED. AND I DON'T HAVE ANY HELP.
LT, HOLD THAT DOCTOR!
KUNK
CORPORAL, WHAT THE FUCK ARE YOU--
CHECK OUT THE BACK. LOOKS LIKE WE FOUND OUR BOMB MAKER.
SERGEANT, TAKE HIM BACK TO BASE WITH THE WOUNDED. THE CORPORAL, F.E.O. KAPLAN AND I WILL ATTEND THE SHURA.
HE'S MISSING A THUMB. YOU BEEN PLAYING WITH FIRECRACKERS, DOC?

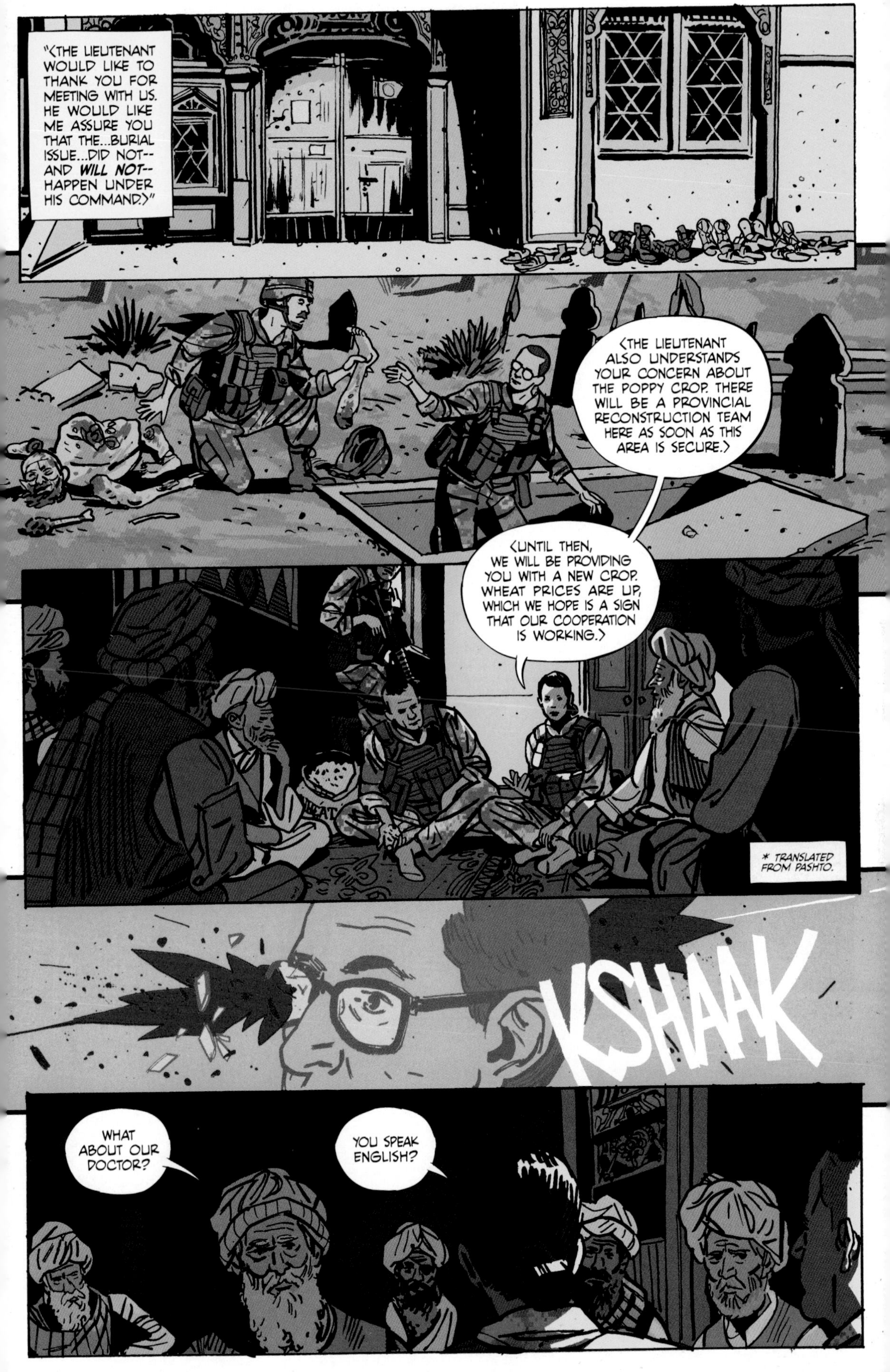
"<THE LIEUTENANT WOULD LIKE TO THANK YOU FOR MEETING WITH US. HE WOULD LIKE ME ASSURE YOU THAT THE...BURIAL ISSUE...DID NOT-- AND WILL NOT-- HAPPEN UNDER HIS COMMAND.>"
<THE LIEUTENANT ALSO UNDERSTANDS YOUR CONCERN ABOUT THE POPPY CROP. THERE WILL BE A PROVINCIAL RECONSTRUCTION TEAM HERE AS SOON AS THIS AREA IS SECURE.>
<UNTIL THEN, WE WILL BE PROVIDING YOU WITH A NEW CROP. WHEAT PRICES ARE UP, WHICH WE HOPE IS A SIGN THAT OUR COOPERATION IS WORKING.>
* TRANSLATED FROM PASHTO.
KSHAAK
WHAT ABOUT OUR DOCTOR?
YOU SPEAK ENGLISH?

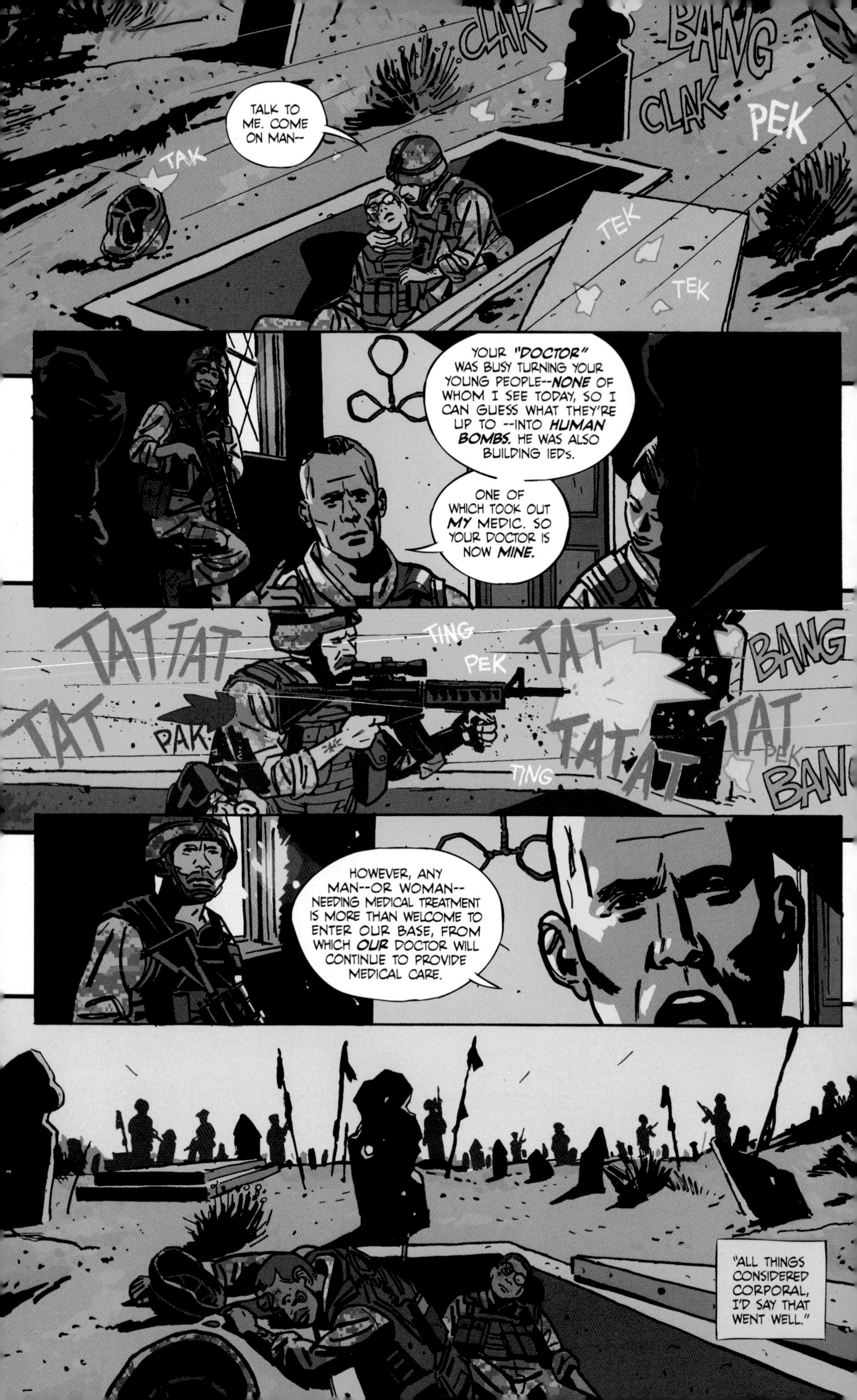
CLAK
BANG
CLAK
PEK
TALK TO ME. COME ON MAN--
TAK
TEK
TEK
YOUR "DOCTOR" WAS BUSY TURNING YOUR YOUNG PEOPLE--NONE OF WHOM I SEE TODAY, SO I CAN GUESS WHAT THEY'RE UP TO --INTO HUMAN BOMBS. HE WAS ALSO BUILDING IEDs.
ONE OF WHICH TOOK OUT MY MEDIC. SO YOUR DOCTOR IS NOW MINE.
TAT TAT TAT
TING
PEK
TAT
BANG
TAT
PAK
TATAT
TAT
TING
PEK
BAN
HOWEVER, ANY MAN--OR WOMAN--NEEDING MEDICAL TREATMENT IS MORE THAN WELCOME TO ENTER OUR BASE, FROM WHICH OUR DOCTOR WILL CONTINUE TO PROVIDE MEDICAL CARE.
"ALL THINGS CONSIDERED CORPORAL, I'D SAY THAT WENT WELL."

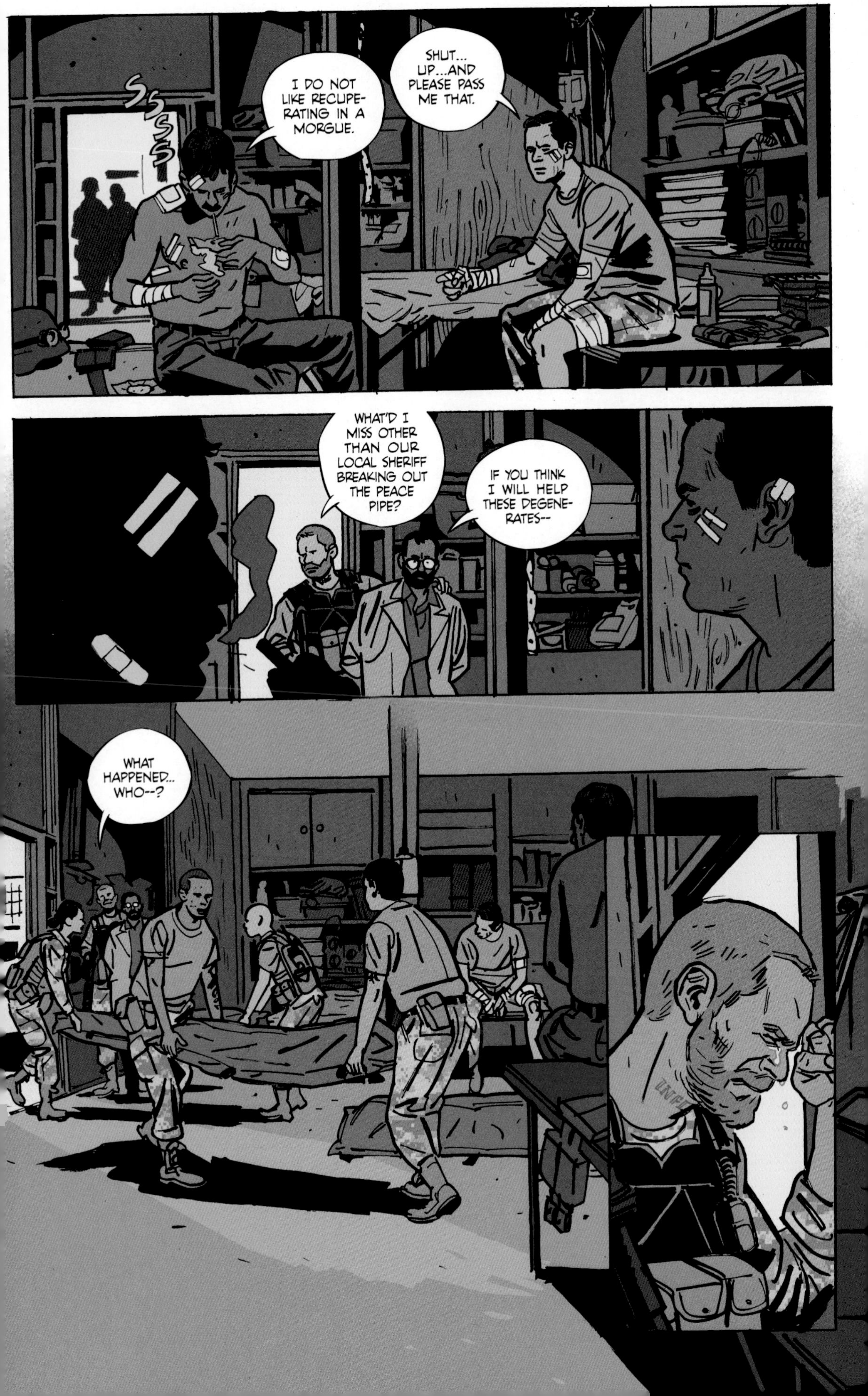
SSSS
I DO NOT LIKE RECUPE-RATING IN A MORGUE.
SHUT... UP...AND PLEASE PASS ME THAT.
WHAT'D I MISS OTHER THAN OUR LOCAL SHERIFF BREAKING OUT THE PEACE PIPE?
IF YOU THINK I WILL HELP THESE DEGENE-RATES--
WHAT HAPPENED... WHO--?

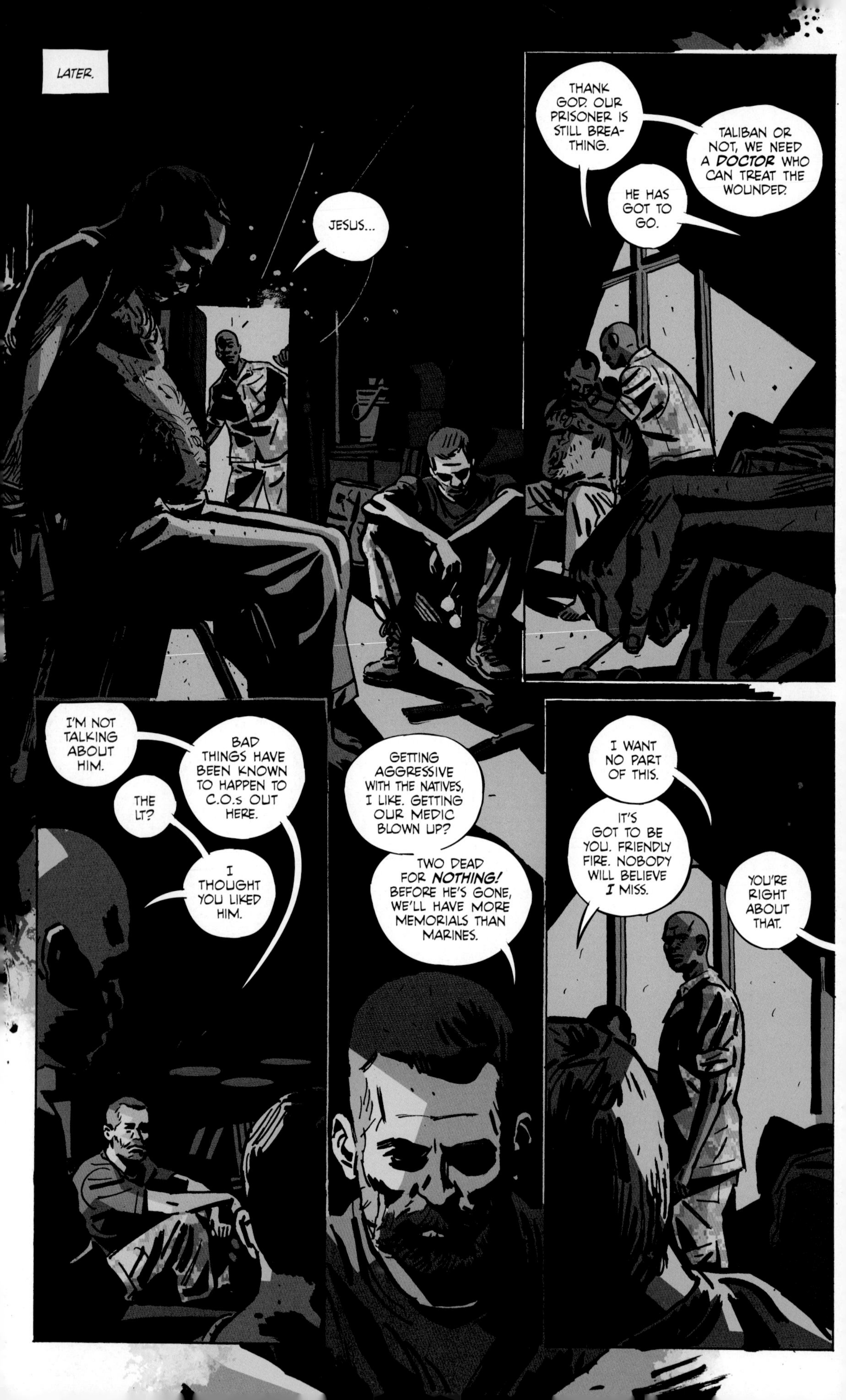
LATER.
JESUS...
THANK GOD. OUR PRISONER IS STILL BREA-THING.
TALIBAN OR NOT, WE NEED A DOCTOR WHO CAN TREAT THE WOUNDED.
HE HAS GOT TO GO.
I'M NOT TALKING ABOUT HIM.
BAD THINGS HAVE BEEN KNOWN TO HAPPEN TO C.O.s OUT HERE.
THE LT?
I THOUGHT YOU LIKED HIM.
GETTING AGGRESSIVE WITH THE NATIVES, I LIKE. GETTING OUR MEDIC BLOWN UP?
TWO DEAD FOR NOTHING! BEFORE HE'S GONE, WE'LL HAVE MORE MEMORIALS THAN MARINES.
I WANT NO PART OF THIS.
IT'S GOT TO BE YOU. FRIENDLY FIRE. NOBODY WILL BELIEVE I MISS.
YOU'RE RIGHT ABOUT THAT.

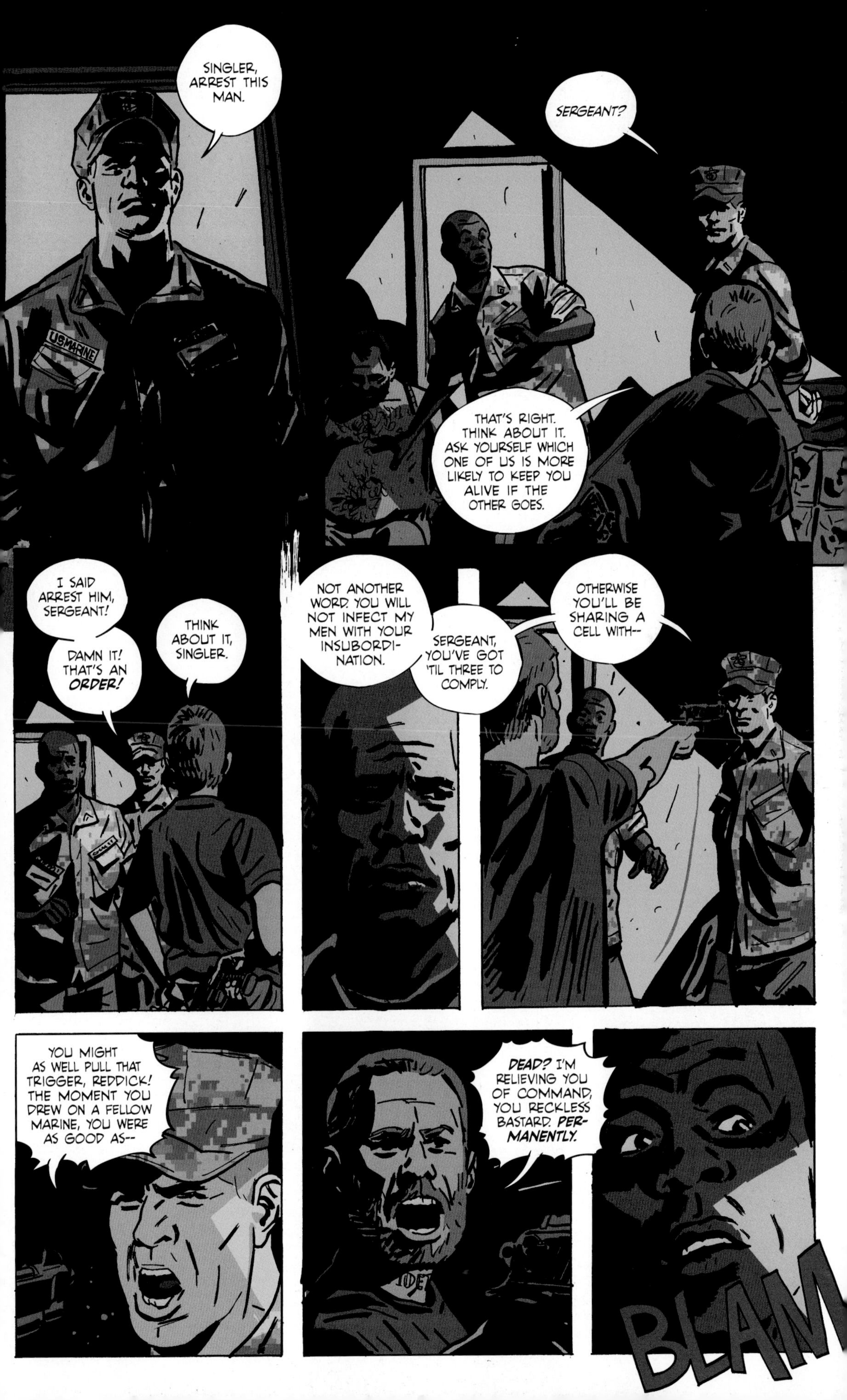
SINGLER, ARREST THIS MAN.
SERGEANT?
THAT'S RIGHT. THINK ABOUT IT. ASK YOURSELF WHICH ONE OF US IS MORE LIKELY TO KEEP YOU ALIVE IF THE OTHER GOES.
I SAID ARREST HIM, SERGEANT!
DAMN IT! THAT'S AN ORDER!
THINK ABOUT IT, SINGLER.
NOT ANOTHER WORD. YOU WILL NOT INFECT MY MEN WITH YOUR INSUBORDI-NATION.
SERGEANT, YOU'VE GOT 'TIL THREE TO COMPLY.
OTHERWISE YOU'LL BE SHARING A CELL WITH--
YOU MIGHT AS WELL PULL THAT TRIGGER, REDDICK! THE MOMENT YOU DREW ON A FELLOW MARINE, YOU WERE AS GOOD AS--
DEAD? I'M RELIEVING YOU OF COMMAND, YOU RECKLESS BASTARD. PER-MANENTLY.
BLAM

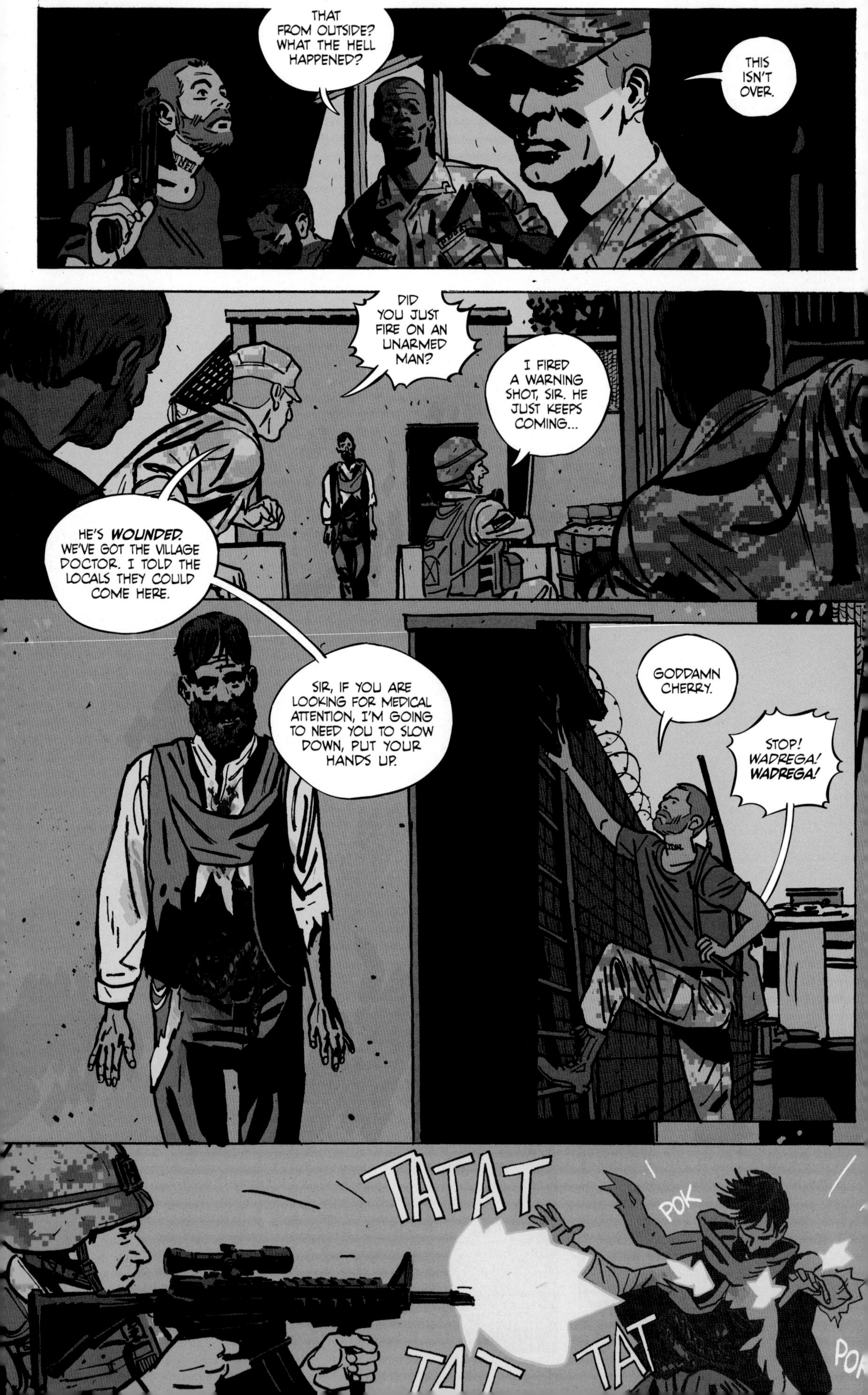
THAT FROM OUTSIDE? WHAT THE HELL HAPPENED?
THIS ISN'T OVER.
DID YOU JUST FIRE ON AN UNARMED MAN?
I FIRED A WARNING SHOT, SIR. HE JUST KEEPS COMING...
HE'S *WOUNDED.* WE'VE GOT THE VILLAGE DOCTOR. I TOLD THE LOCALS THEY COULD COME HERE.
SIR, IF YOU ARE LOOKING FOR MEDICAL ATTENTION, I'M GOING TO NEED YOU TO SLOW DOWN, PUT YOUR HANDS UP.
GODDAMN CHERRY.
STOP! *WADREGA!* ***WADREGA!***
TATAT
POK
TAT TAT

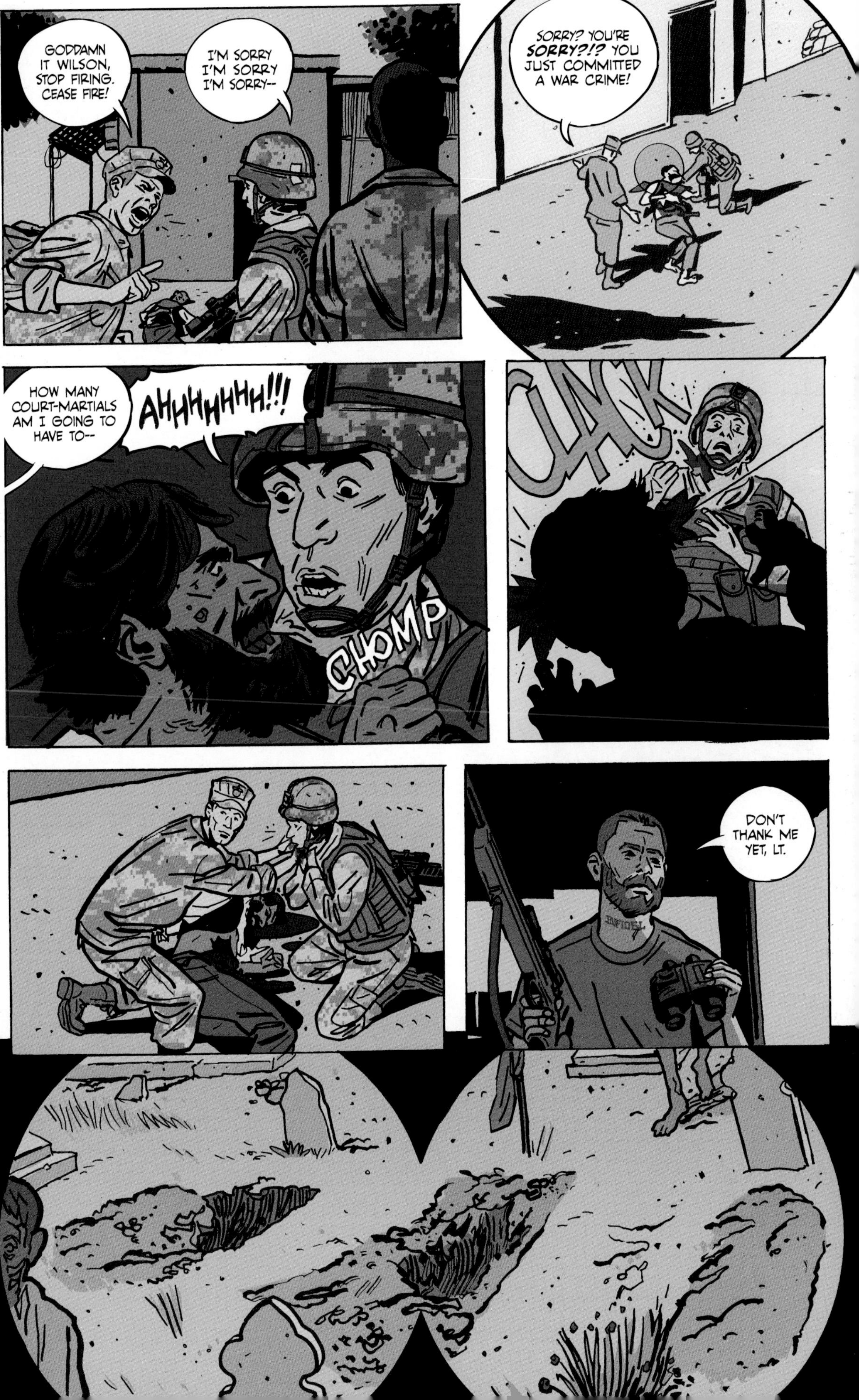
GODDAMN IT WILSON, STOP FIRING. CEASE FIRE!
I'M SORRY I'M SORRY I'M SORRY--
SORRY? YOU'RE SORRY?!? YOU JUST COMMITTED A WAR CRIME!
HOW MANY COURT-MARTIALS AM I GOING TO HAVE TO--
AHHHHHHH!!!
CHOMP
DON'T THANK ME YET, LT.

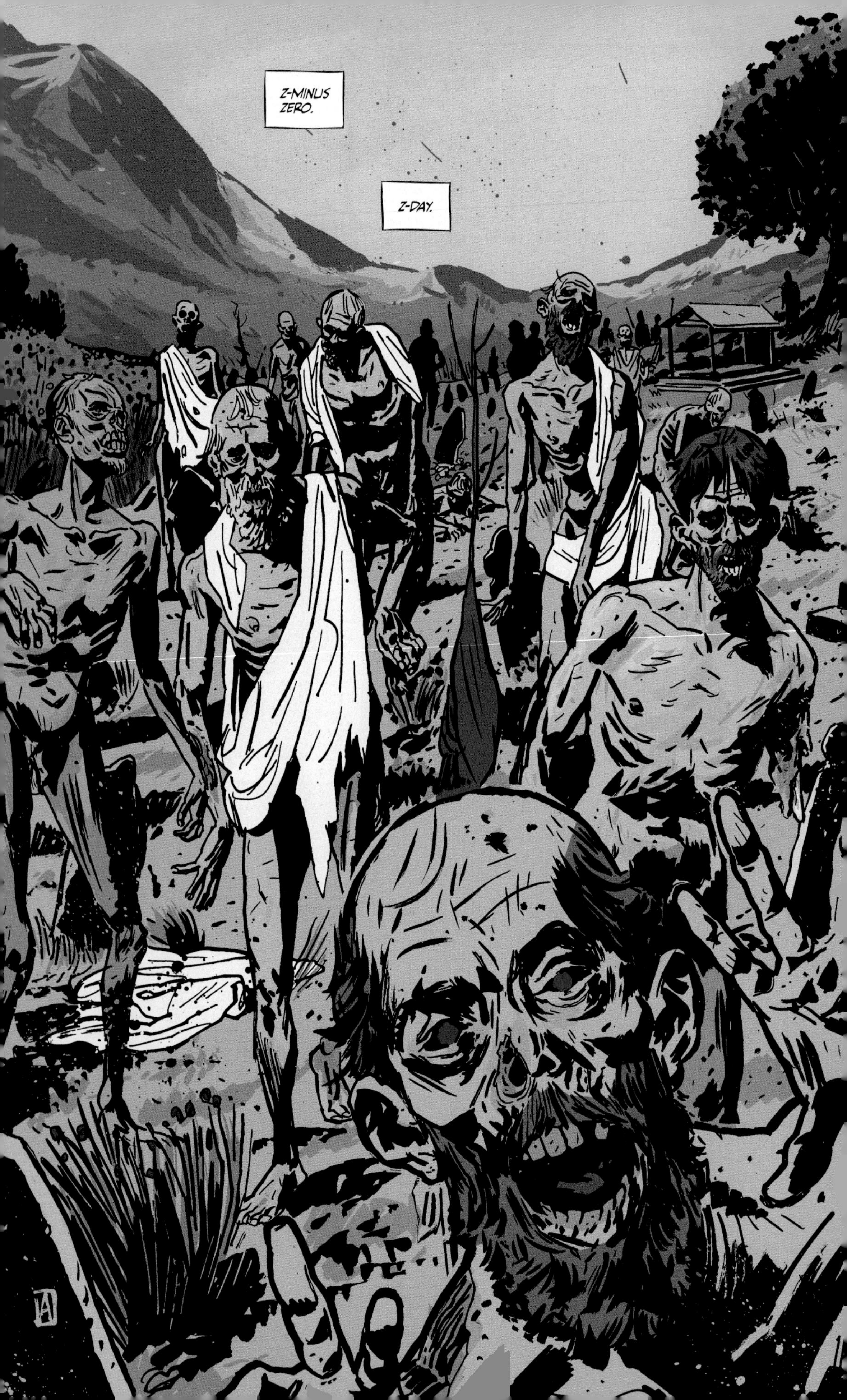
Z-MINUS ZERO.
Z-DAY.

CHAPTER 2

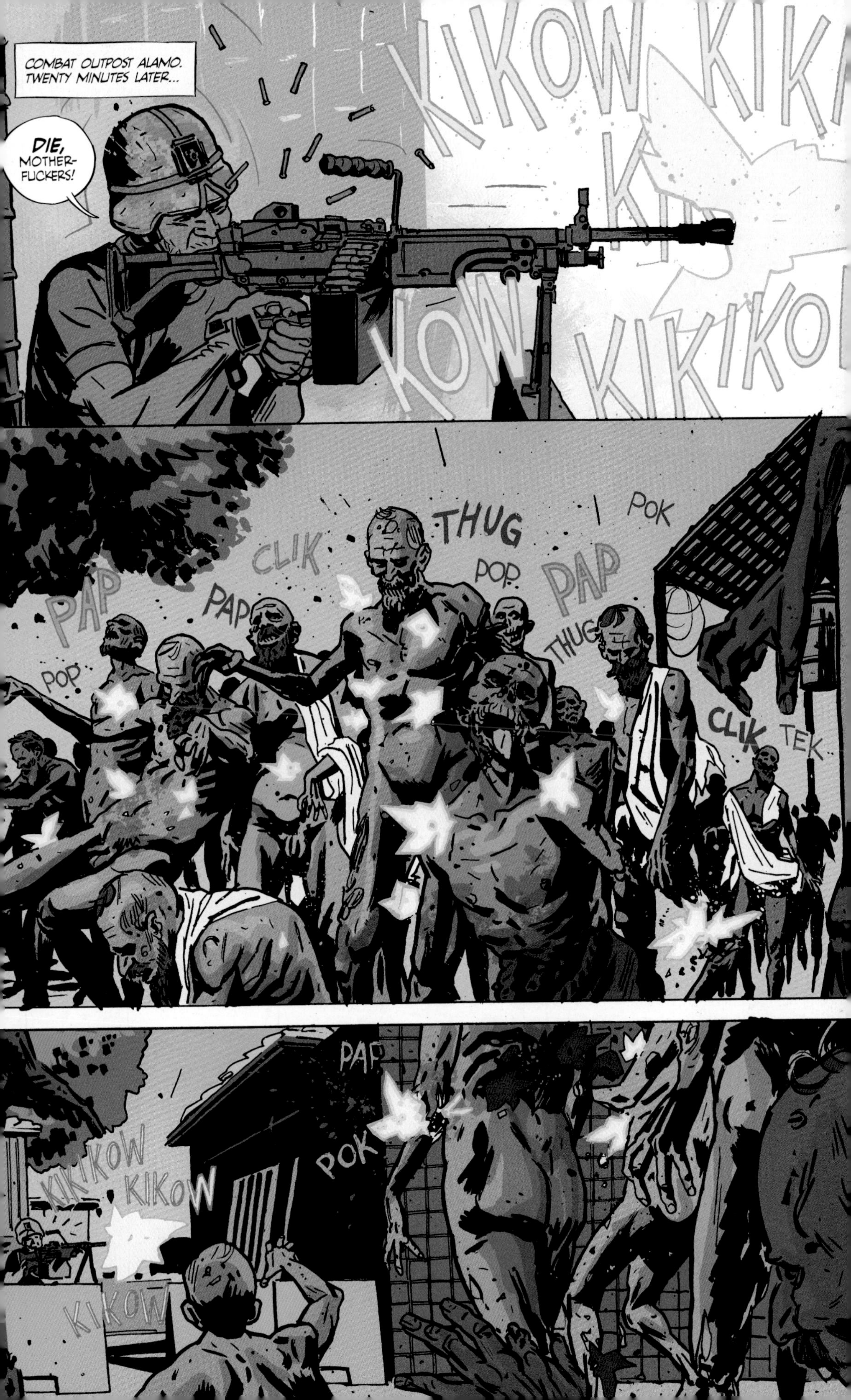
COMBAT OUTPOST ALAMO. TWENTY MINUTES LATER...
DIE, MOTHER-FUCKERS!
KIKOW KIKI
KI
KIKO
KOW
KIKIKOI
THUG
POK
CLIK
POP
PAP
PAP
PAP
THUG
POP
CLIK TEK...
PAP
POK
KIKOW
KIKOW
KIKOW

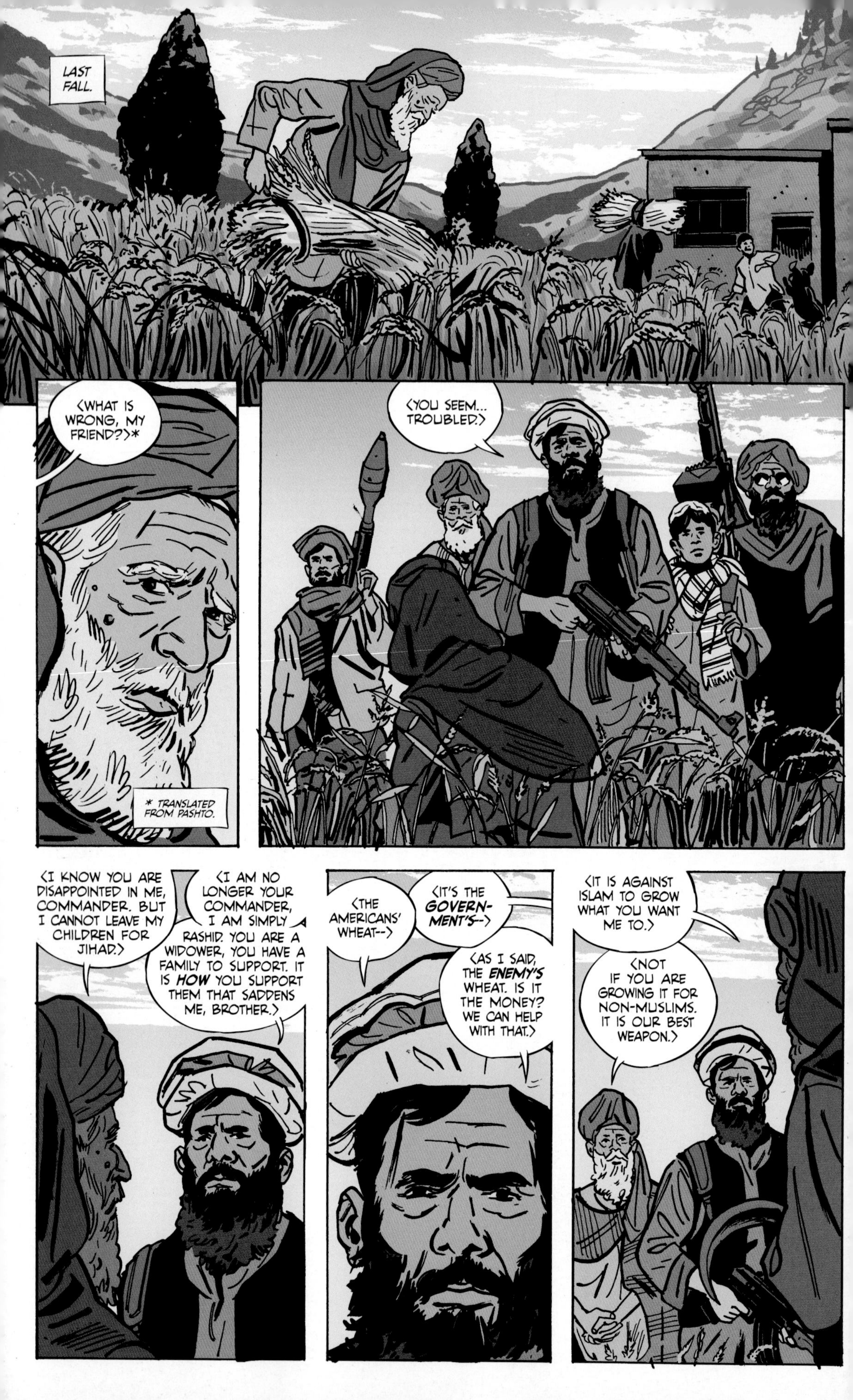
LAST FALL.
<WHAT IS WRONG, MY FRIEND?>*
* TRANSLATED FROM PASHTO.
<YOU SEEM... TROUBLED.>
<I KNOW YOU ARE DISAPPOINTED IN ME, COMMANDER. BUT I CANNOT LEAVE MY CHILDREN FOR JIHAD.>
<I AM NO LONGER YOUR COMMANDER, I AM SIMPLY RASHID. YOU ARE A WIDOWER, YOU HAVE A FAMILY TO SUPPORT. IT IS **HOW** YOU SUPPORT THEM THAT SADDENS ME, BROTHER.>
<THE AMERICANS' WHEAT-->
<IT'S THE ***GOVERNMENT'S***-->
<AS I SAID, THE ***ENEMY'S*** WHEAT. IS IT THE MONEY? WE CAN HELP WITH THAT.>
<IT IS AGAINST ISLAM TO GROW WHAT YOU WANT ME TO.>
<NOT IF YOU ARE GROWING IT FOR NON-MUSLIMS. IT IS OUR BEST WEAPON.>

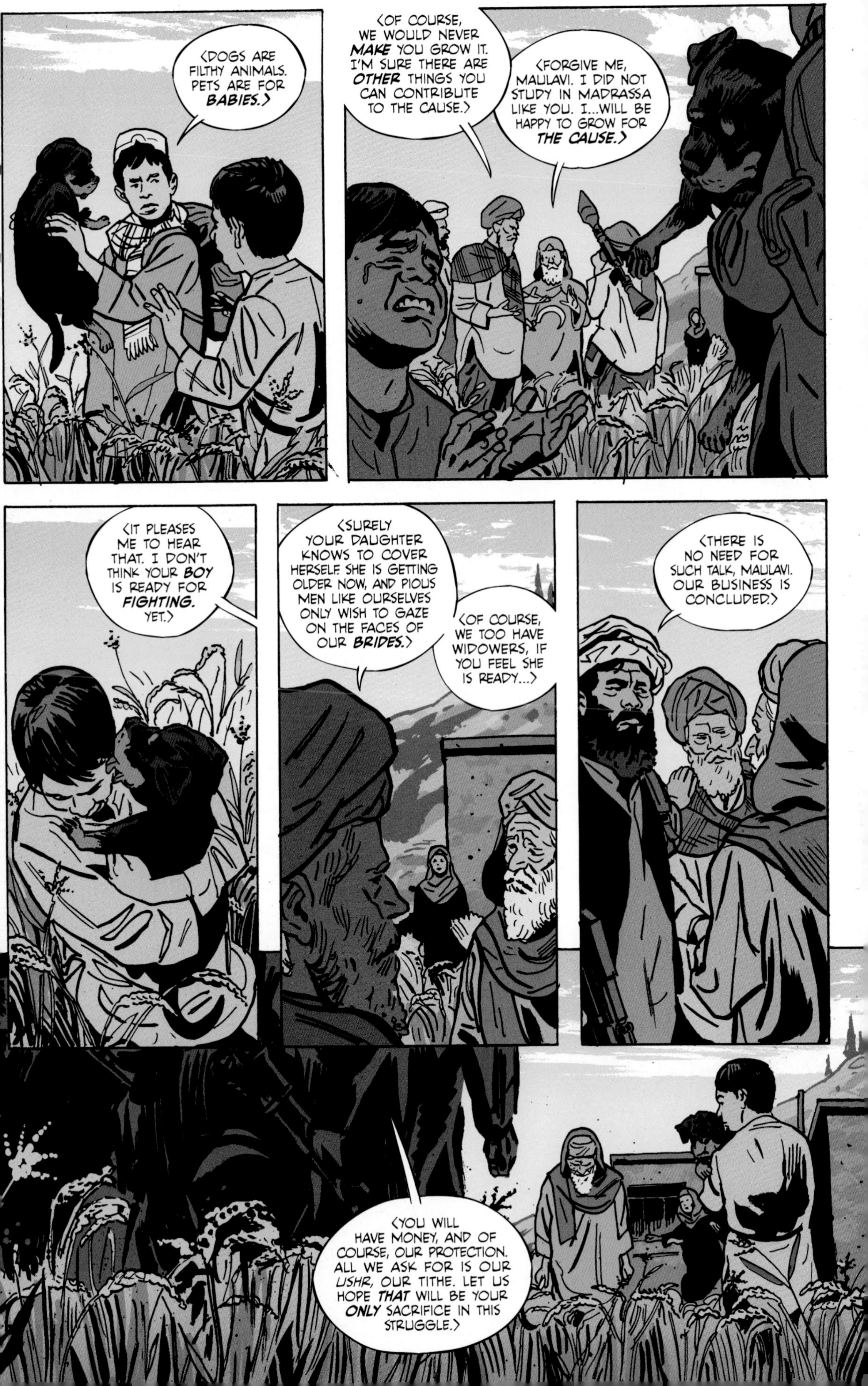

<DOGS ARE FILTHY ANIMALS. PETS ARE FOR BABIES.>
<OF COURSE, WE WOULD NEVER MAKE YOU GROW IT. I'M SURE THERE ARE OTHER THINGS YOU CAN CONTRIBUTE TO THE CAUSE.>
<FORGIVE ME, MAULAVI. I DID NOT STUDY IN MADRASSA LIKE YOU. I...WILL BE HAPPY TO GROW FOR THE CAUSE.>
<IT PLEASES ME TO HEAR THAT. I DON'T THINK YOUR BOY IS READY FOR FIGHTING. YET.>
<SURELY YOUR DAUGHTER KNOWS TO COVER HERSELF. SHE IS GETTING OLDER NOW, AND PIOUS MEN LIKE OURSELVES ONLY WISH TO GAZE ON THE FACES OF OUR BRIDES.>
<OF COURSE, WE TOO HAVE WIDOWERS, IF YOU FEEL SHE IS READY...>
<THERE IS NO NEED FOR SUCH TALK, MAULAVI. OUR BUSINESS IS CONCLUDED.>
<YOU WILL HAVE MONEY, AND OF COURSE, OUR PROTECTION. ALL WE ASK FOR IS OUR USHR, OUR TITHE. LET US HOPE THAT WILL BE YOUR ONLY SACRIFICE IN THIS STRUGGLE.>

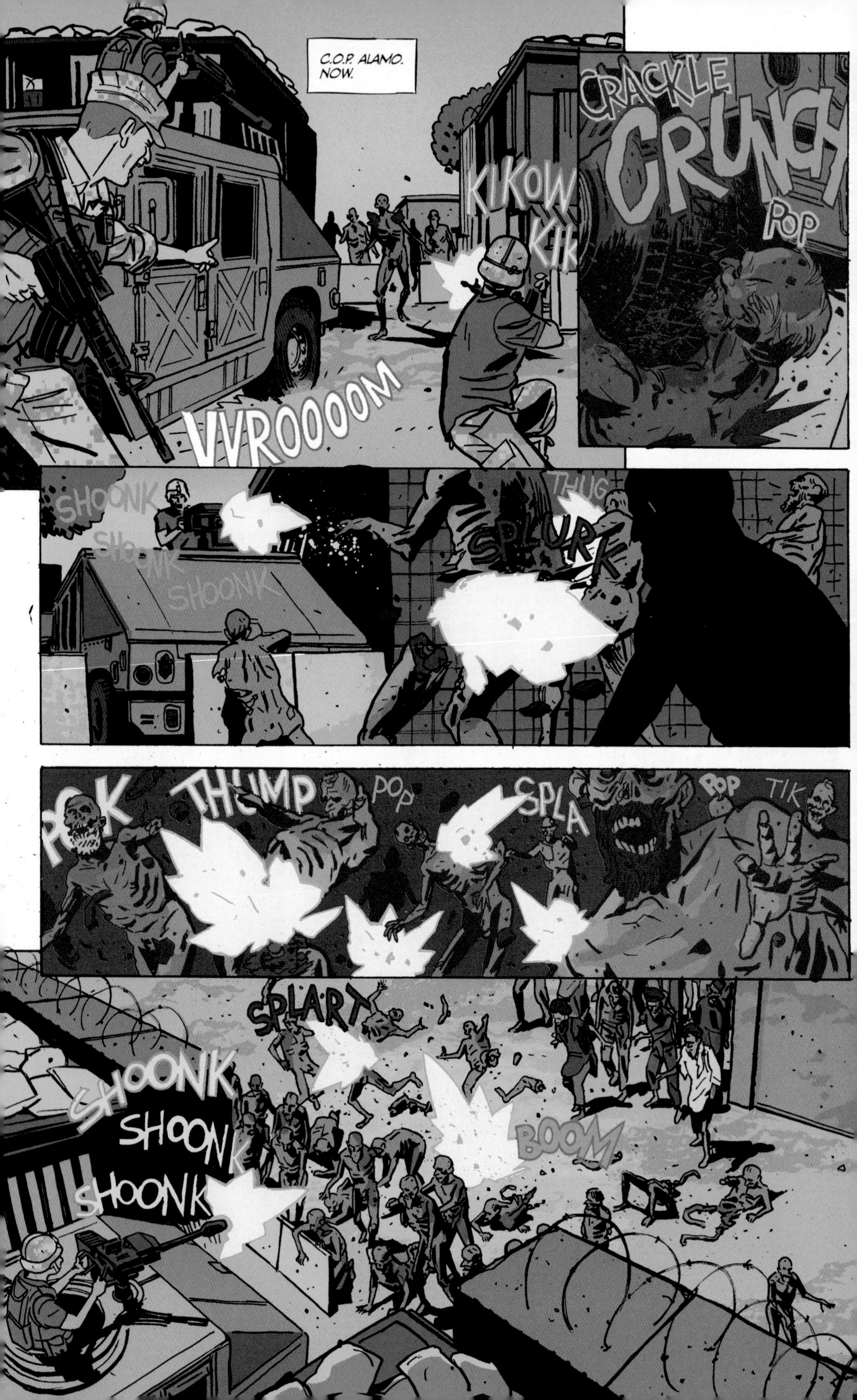
C.O.P. ALAMO. NOW.
KIKOW
KIK
VVROOOOM
CRACKLE
CRUNCH
POP
SHOONK
SHOONK
SHOONK
THUG
SPLURK
POK
THUMP
POP
SPLA
POP
TIK
SPLART
SHOONK
SHOONK
SHOONK
BOOM

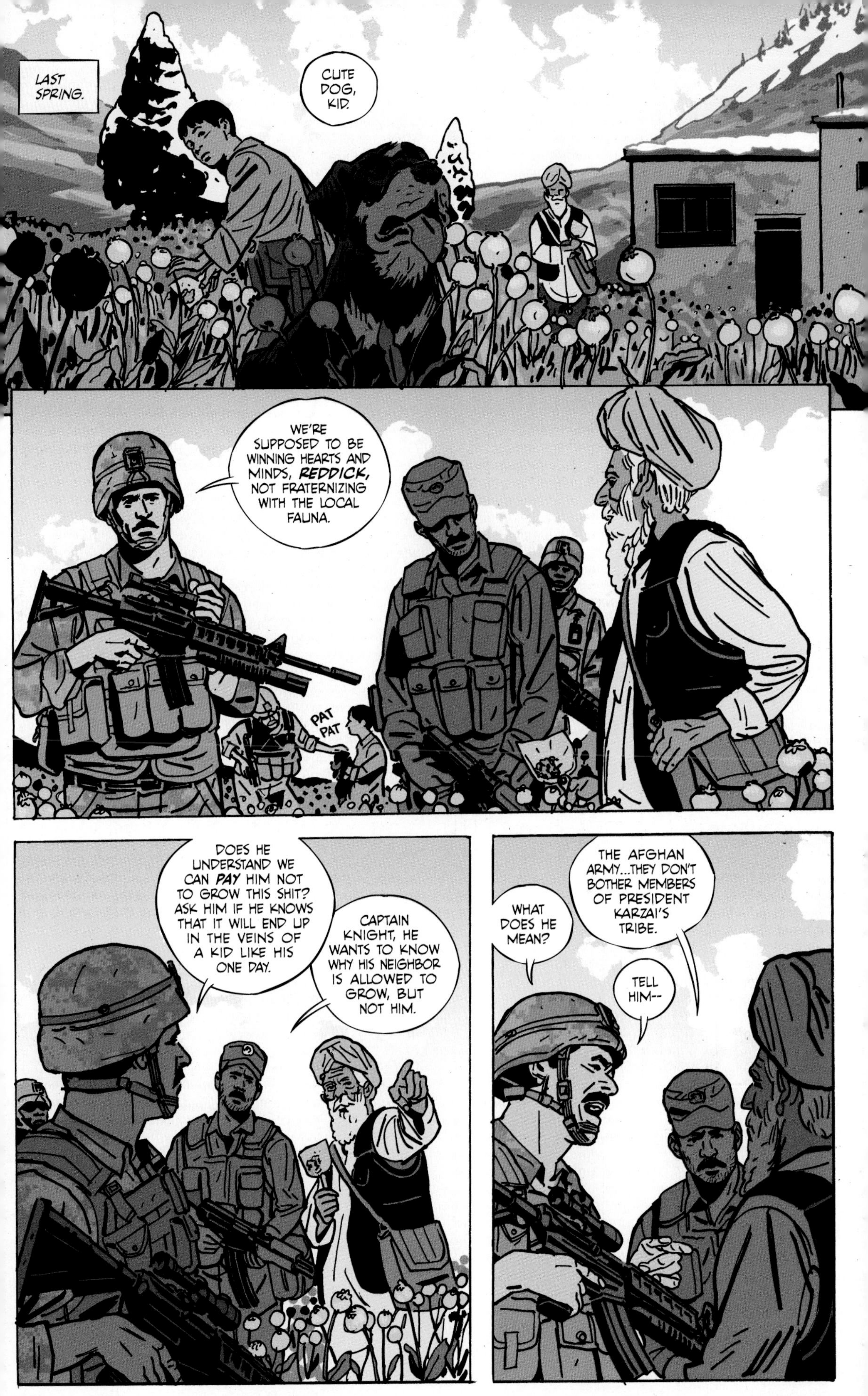
LAST SPRING.
CUTE DOG, KID.
WE'RE SUPPOSED TO BE WINNING HEARTS AND MINDS, REDDICK, NOT FRATERNIZING WITH THE LOCAL FAUNA.
PAT PAT
DOES HE UNDERSTAND WE CAN PAY HIM NOT TO GROW THIS SHIT? ASK HIM IF HE KNOWS THAT IT WILL END UP IN THE VEINS OF A KID LIKE HIS ONE DAY.
CAPTAIN KNIGHT, HE WANTS TO KNOW WHY HIS NEIGHBOR IS ALLOWED TO GROW, BUT NOT HIM.
WHAT DOES HE MEAN?
THE AFGHAN ARMY...THEY DON'T BOTHER MEMBERS OF PRESIDENT KARZAI'S TRIBE.
TELL HIM--

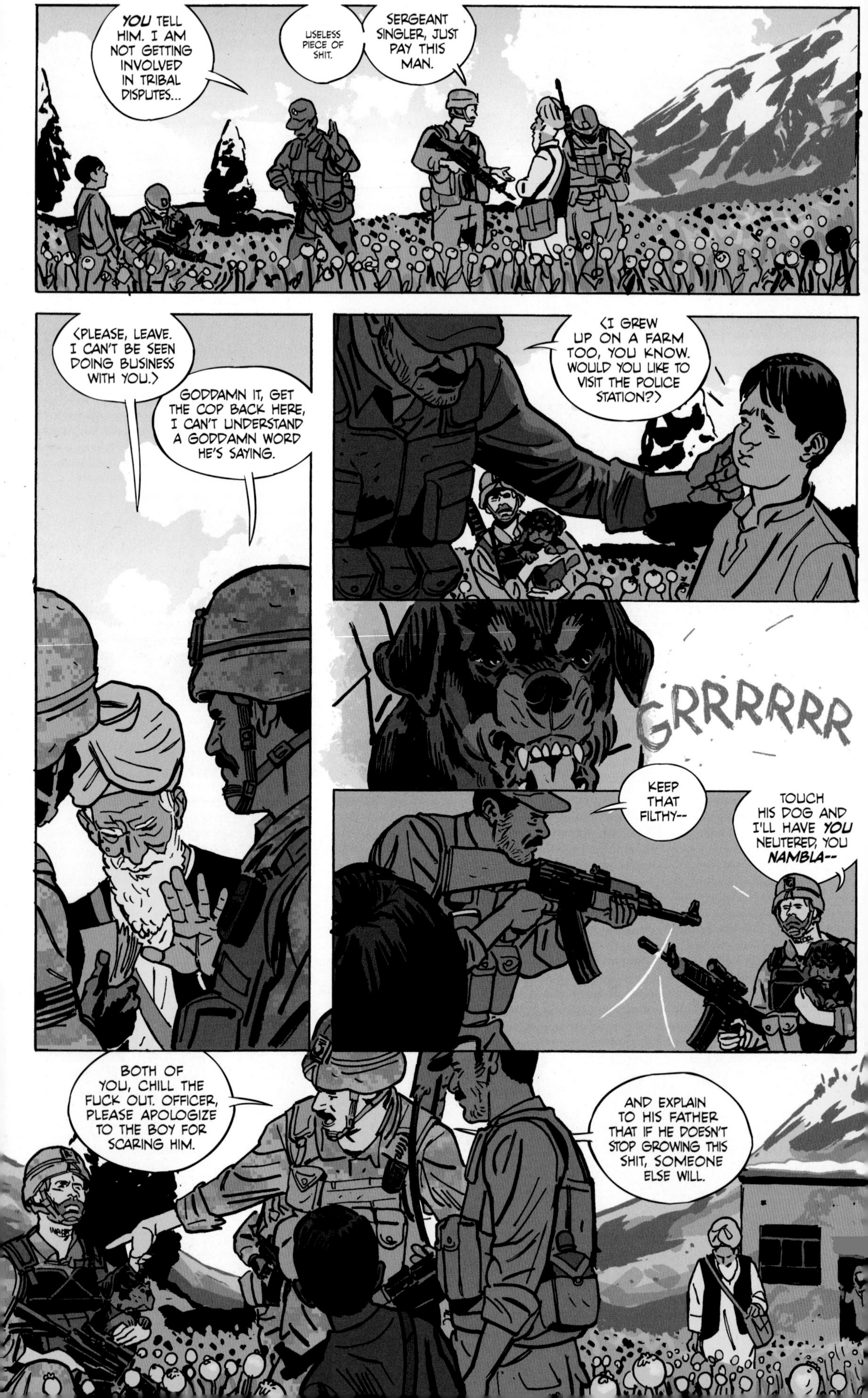
YOU TELL HIM. I AM NOT GETTING INVOLVED IN TRIBAL DISPUTES...
USELESS PIECE OF SHIT.
SERGEANT SINGLER, JUST PAY THIS MAN.
<PLEASE, LEAVE. I CAN'T BE SEEN DOING BUSINESS WITH YOU.>
GODDAMN IT, GET THE COP BACK HERE, I CAN'T UNDERSTAND A GODDAMN WORD HE'S SAYING.
<I GREW UP ON A FARM TOO, YOU KNOW. WOULD YOU LIKE TO VISIT THE POLICE STATION?>
GRRRRRR
KEEP THAT FILTHY--
TOUCH HIS DOG AND I'LL HAVE YOU NEUTERED, YOU NAMBLA--
BOTH OF YOU, CHILL THE FUCK OUT. OFFICER, PLEASE APOLOGIZE TO THE BOY FOR SCARING HIM.
AND EXPLAIN TO HIS FATHER THAT IF HE DOESN'T STOP GROWING THIS SHIT, SOMEONE ELSE WILL.

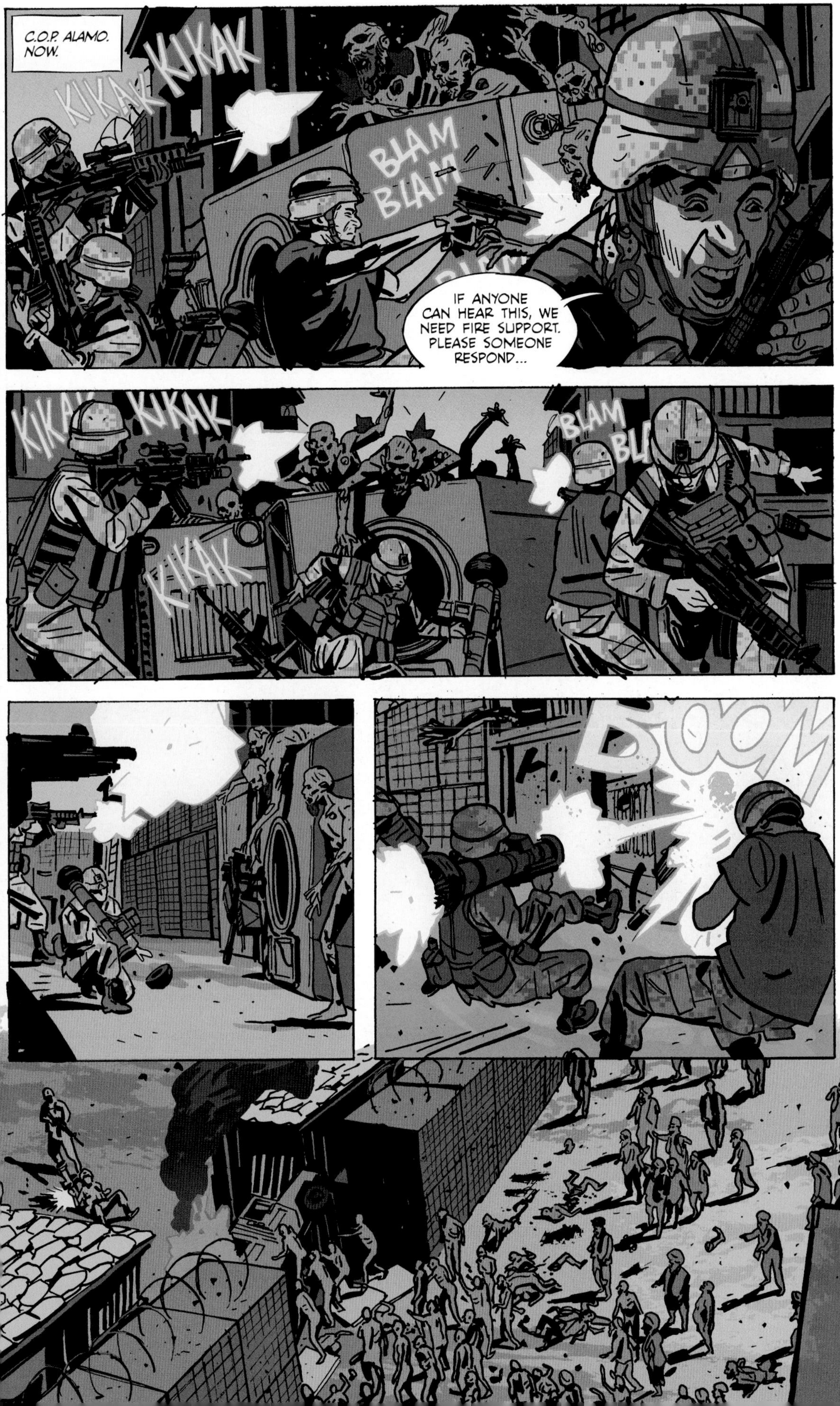
C.O.P. ALAMO. NOW.
KIKAK KIKAK
BLAM BLAM
IF ANYONE CAN HEAR THIS, WE NEED FIRE SUPPORT. PLEASE SOMEONE RESPOND...
KIKAK KIKAK
BLAM
KIKAK
BOOM

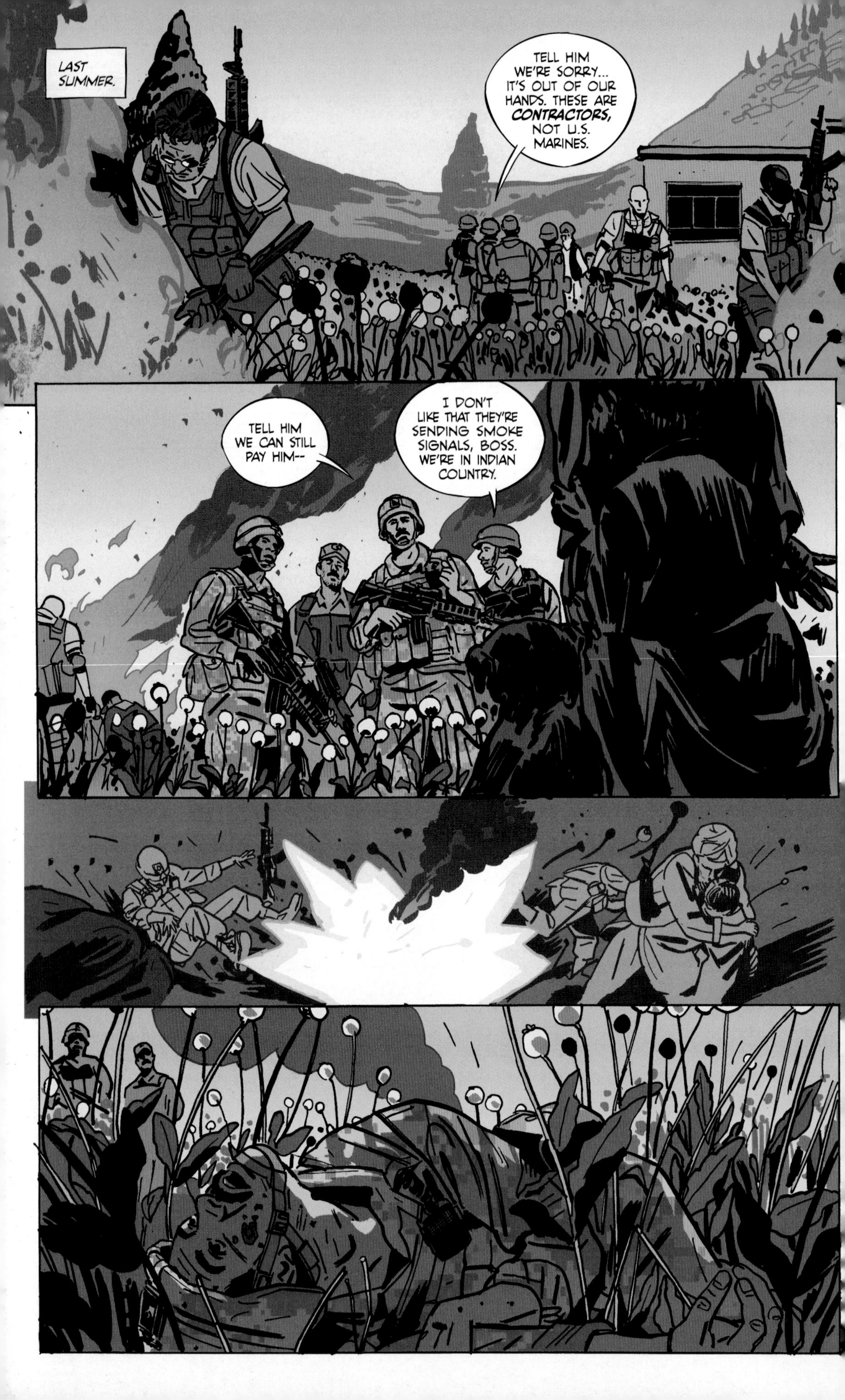
LAST SUMMER.
TELL HIM WE'RE SORRY... IT'S OUT OF OUR HANDS. THESE ARE CONTRACTORS, NOT U.S. MARINES.
TELL HIM WE CAN STILL PAY HIM--
I DON'T LIKE THAT THEY'RE SENDING SMOKE SIGNALS, BOSS. WE'RE IN INDIAN COUNTRY.

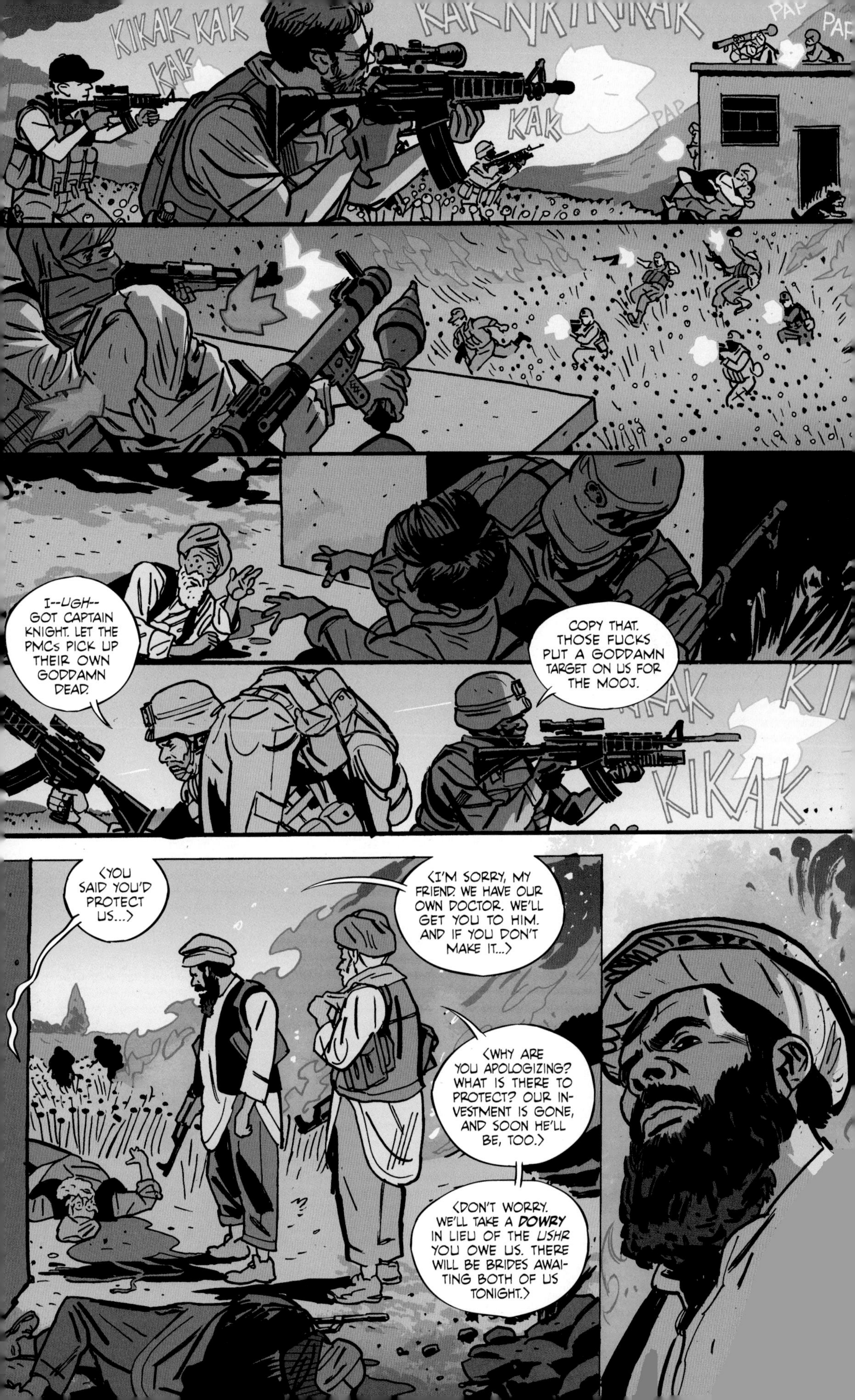
KIKAK KAK
KAK
KAKAKIKIKAK
PAP
PAP
KAK
PAP
I--UGH--
GOT CAPTAIN
KNIGHT. LET THE
PMCs PICK UP
THEIR OWN
GODDAMN
DEAD.
COPY THAT.
THOSE FUCKS
PUT A GODDAMN
TARGET ON US FOR
THE MOOJ.
KIKAK...
<YOU SAID YOU'D PROTECT US...>
<I'M SORRY, MY FRIEND. WE HAVE OUR OWN DOCTOR. WE'LL GET YOU TO HIM. AND IF YOU DON'T MAKE IT...>
<WHY ARE YOU APOLOGIZING? WHAT IS THERE TO PROTECT? OUR INVESTMENT IS GONE, AND SOON HE'LL BE, TOO.>
<DON'T WORRY. WE'LL TAKE A DOWRY IN LIEU OF THE USHR YOU OWE US. THERE WILL BE BRIDES AWAITING BOTH OF US TONIGHT.>

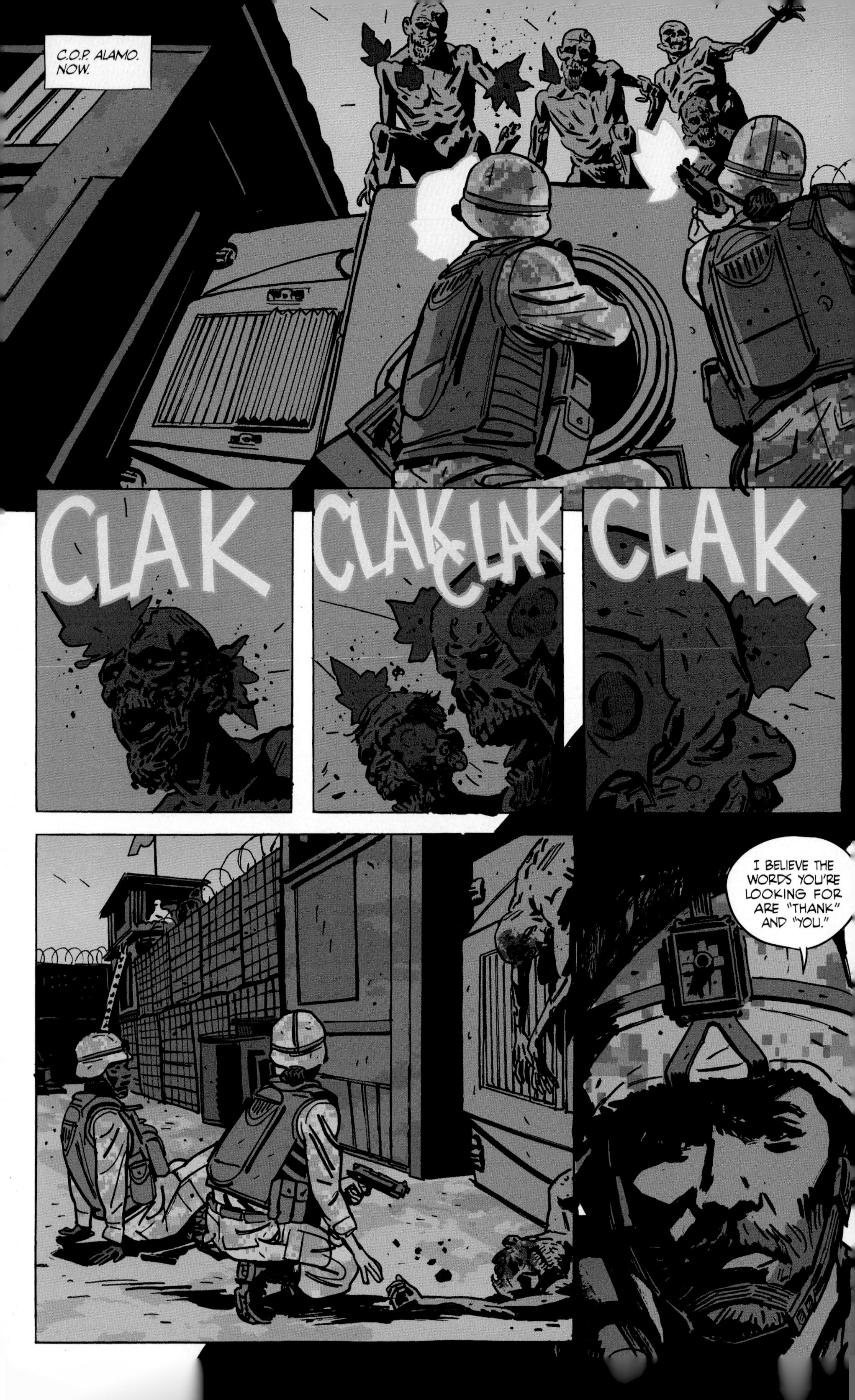
C.O.P. ALAMO. NOW.
CLAK
CLAK CLAK CLAK
CLAK
I BELIEVE THE WORDS YOU'RE LOOKING FOR ARE "THANK" AND "YOU."

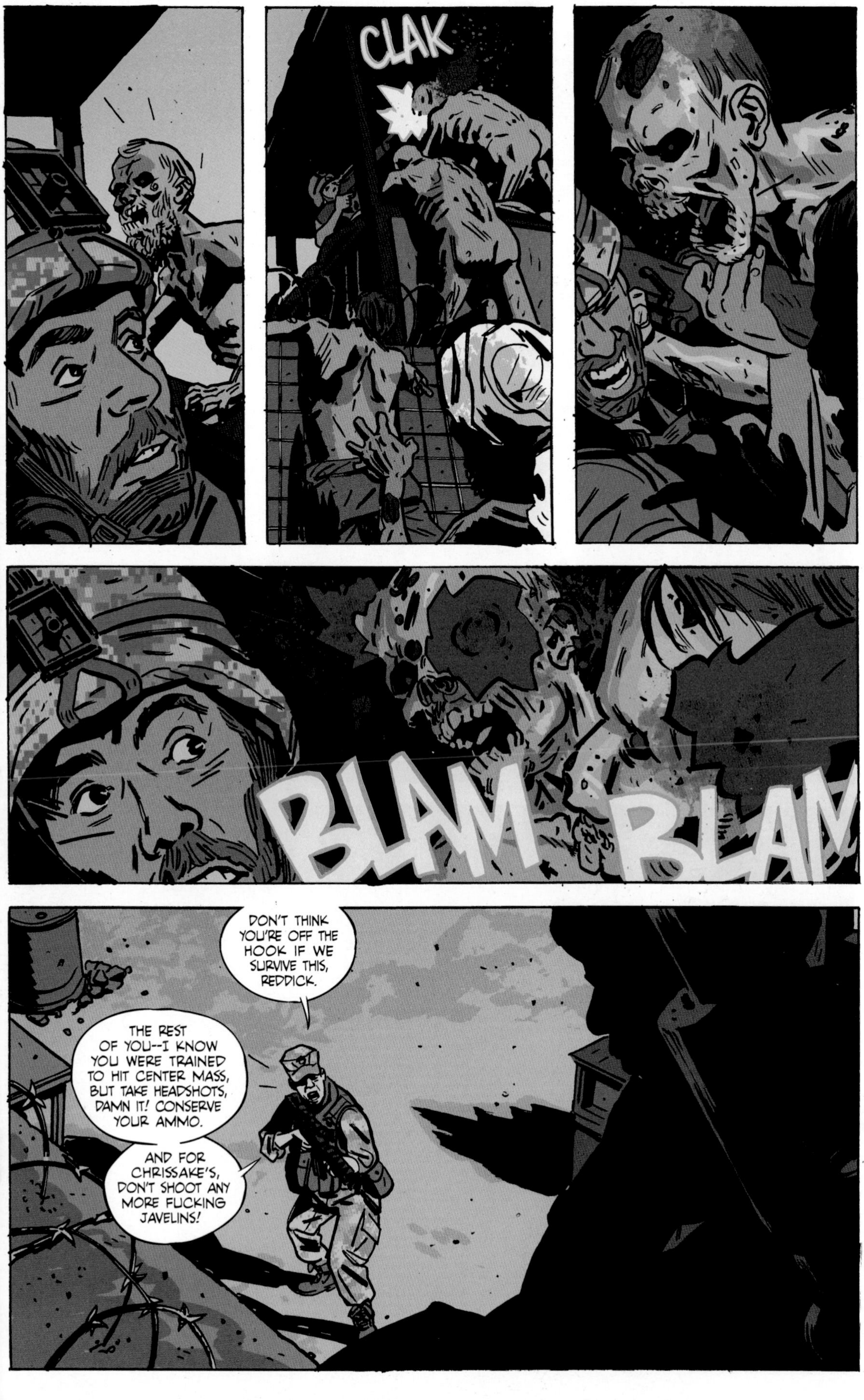
CLAK
BLAM BLAM
DON'T THINK YOU'RE OFF THE HOOK IF WE SURVIVE THIS, REDDICK.
THE REST OF YOU--I KNOW YOU WERE TRAINED TO HIT CENTER MASS, BUT TAKE HEADSHOTS, DAMN IT! CONSERVE YOUR AMMO.
AND FOR CHRISSAKE'S, DON'T SHOOT ANY MORE FUCKING JAVELINS!

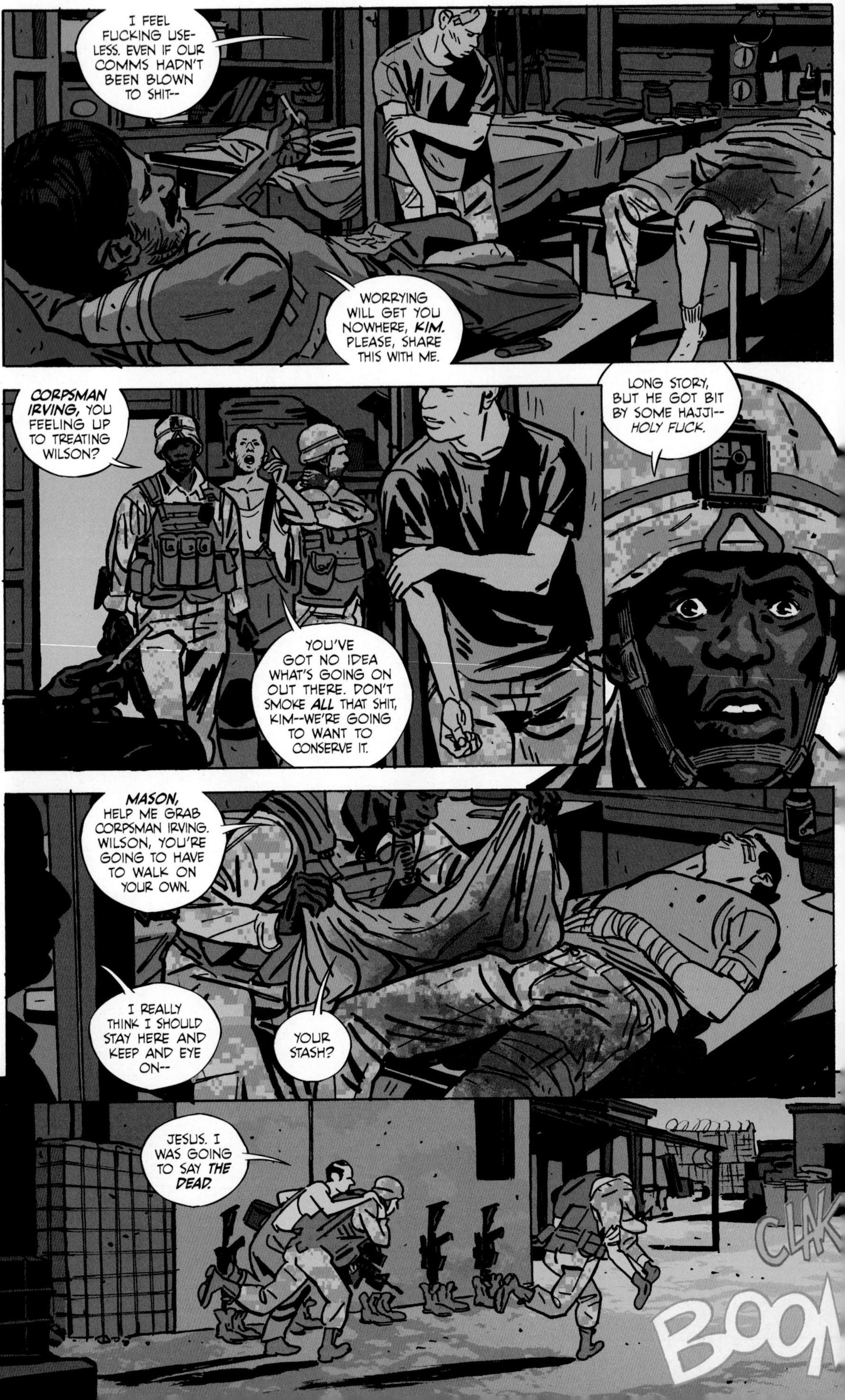
I FEEL FUCKING USELESS. EVEN IF OUR COMMS HADN'T BEEN BLOWN TO SHIT--
WORRYING WILL GET YOU NOWHERE, KIM. PLEASE, SHARE THIS WITH ME.
CORPSMAN IRVING, YOU FEELING UP TO TREATING WILSON?
YOU'VE GOT NO IDEA WHAT'S GOING ON OUT THERE. DON'T SMOKE ALL THAT SHIT, KIM--WE'RE GOING TO WANT TO CONSERVE IT.
LONG STORY, BUT HE GOT BIT BY SOME HAJJI-- HOLY FUCK.
MASON, HELP ME GRAB CORPSMAN IRVING. WILSON, YOU'RE GOING TO HAVE TO WALK ON YOUR OWN.
I REALLY THINK I SHOULD STAY HERE AND KEEP AND EYE ON--
YOUR STASH?
JESUS. I WAS GOING TO SAY THE DEAD.
CLAK
BOOM

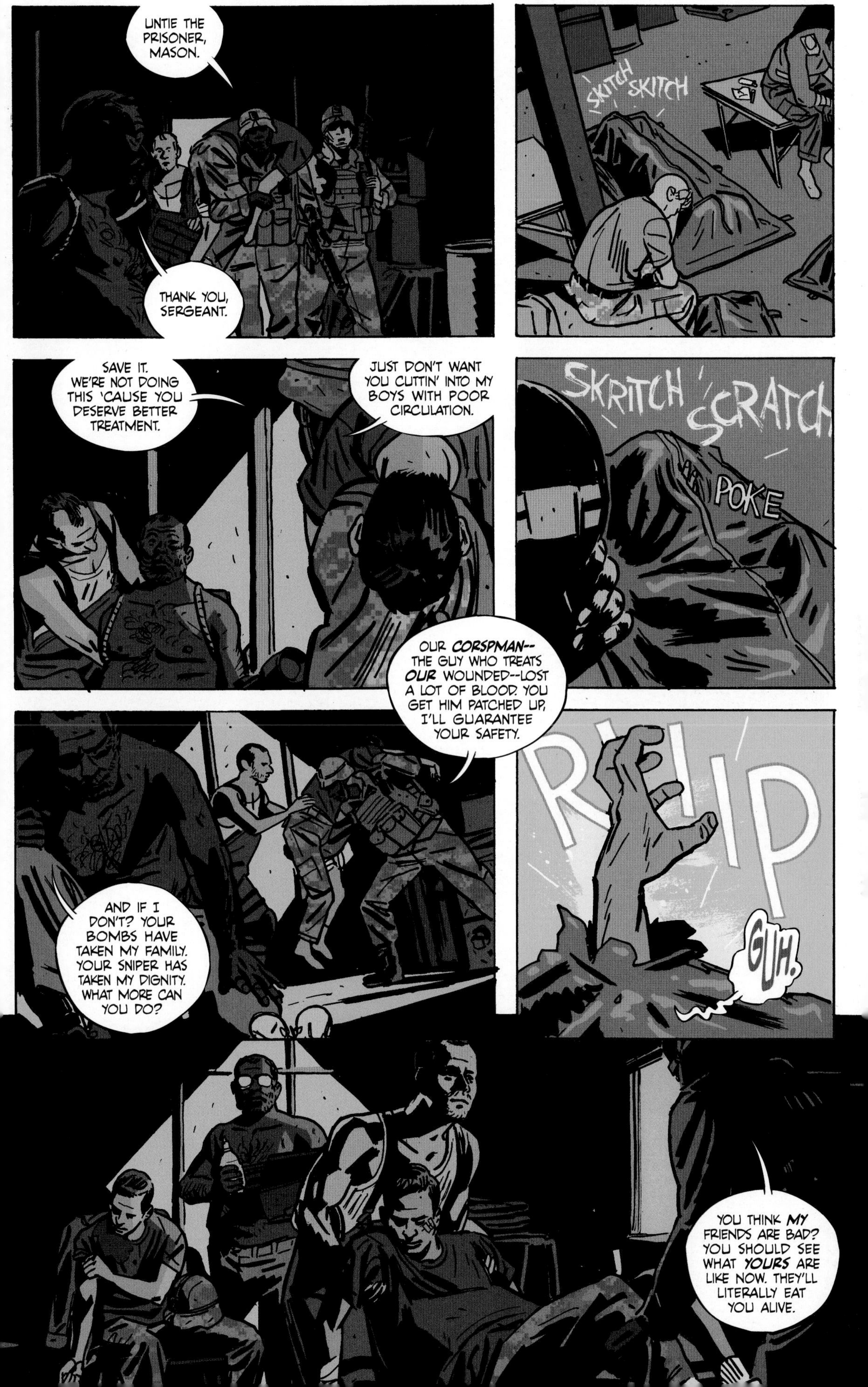
UNTIE THE PRISONER, MASON.
THANK YOU, SERGEANT.
SKITCH SKITCH
SAVE IT. WE'RE NOT DOING THIS 'CAUSE YOU DESERVE BETTER TREATMENT.
JUST DON'T WANT YOU CUTTIN' INTO MY BOYS WITH POOR CIRCULATION.
SKRITCH SCRATCH
POKE
OUR CORSPMAN-- THE GUY WHO TREATS OUR WOUNDED--LOST A LOT OF BLOOD. YOU GET HIM PATCHED UP, I'LL GUARANTEE YOUR SAFETY.
AND IF I DON'T? YOUR BOMBS HAVE TAKEN MY FAMILY. YOUR SNIPER HAS TAKEN MY DIGNITY. WHAT MORE CAN YOU DO?
RIIIP
GUH.
YOU THINK MY FRIENDS ARE BAD? YOU SHOULD SEE WHAT YOURS ARE LIKE NOW. THEY'LL LITERALLY EAT YOU ALIVE.

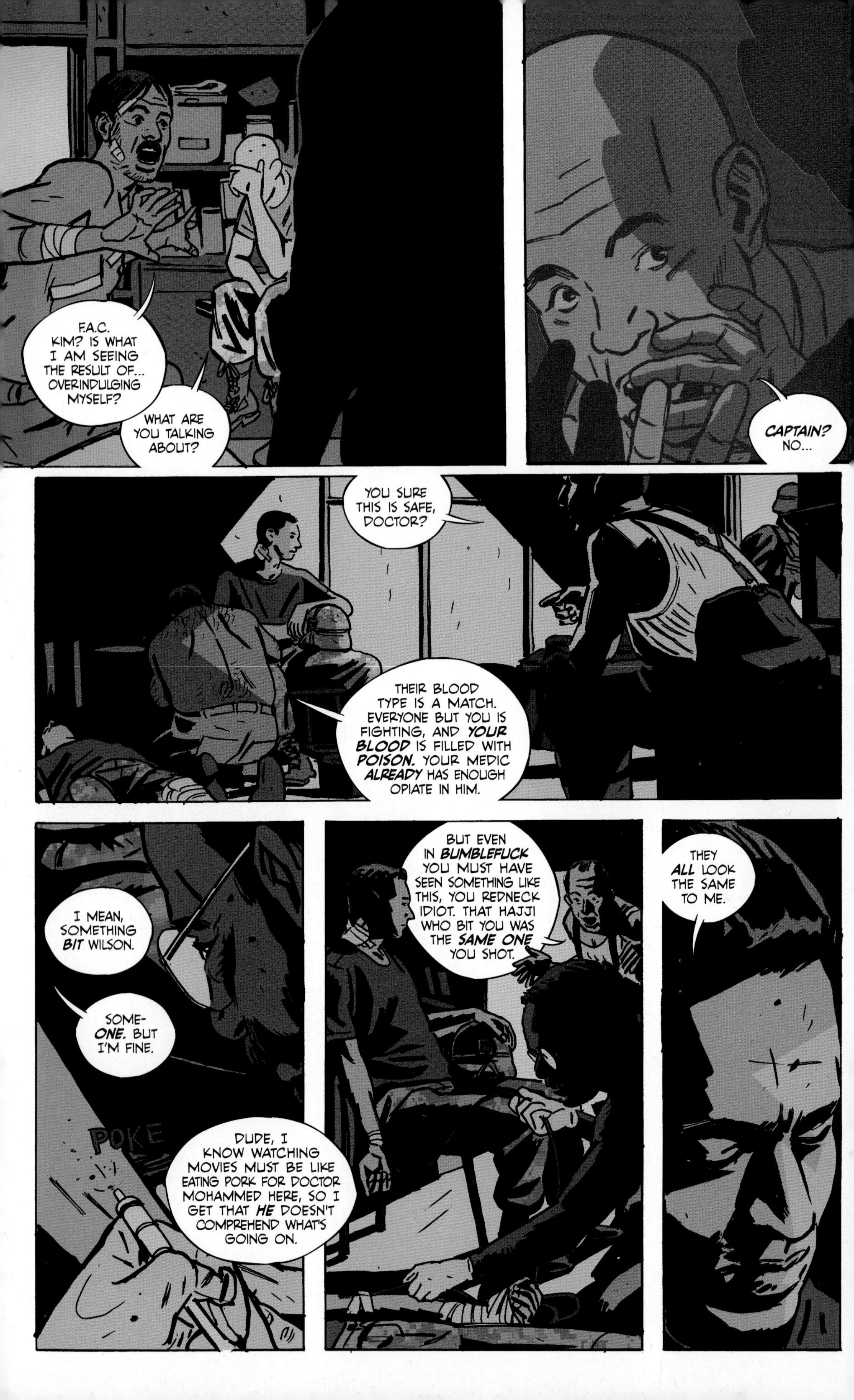
F.A.C. KIM? IS WHAT I AM SEEING THE RESULT OF... OVERINDULGING MYSELF?
WHAT ARE YOU TALKING ABOUT?
CAPTAIN? NO...
YOU SURE THIS IS SAFE, DOCTOR?
THEIR BLOOD TYPE IS A MATCH. EVERYONE BUT YOU IS FIGHTING, AND YOUR BLOOD IS FILLED WITH POISON. YOUR MEDIC ALREADY HAS ENOUGH OPIATE IN HIM.
I MEAN, SOMETHING BIT WILSON.
SOME-ONE. BUT I'M FINE.
POKE
DUDE, I KNOW WATCHING MOVIES MUST BE LIKE EATING PORK FOR DOCTOR MOHAMMED HERE, SO I GET THAT HE DOESN'T COMPREHEND WHAT'S GOING ON.
BUT EVEN IN BUMBLEFUCK YOU MUST HAVE SEEN SOMETHING LIKE THIS, YOU REDNECK IDIOT. THAT HAJJI WHO BIT YOU WAS THE SAME ONE YOU SHOT.
THEY ALL LOOK THE SAME TO ME.

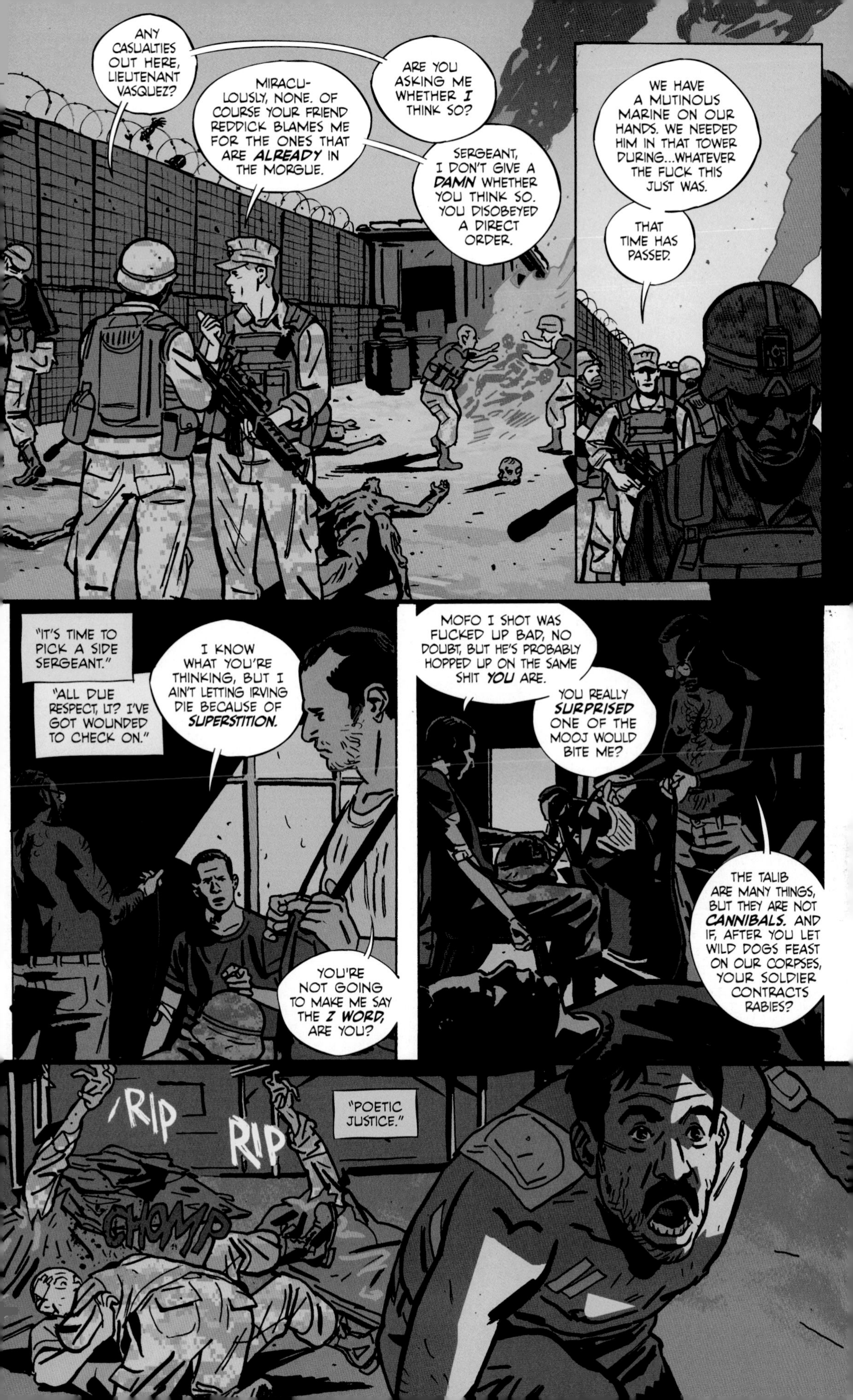

ANY CASUALTIES OUT HERE, LIEUTENANT VASQUEZ?
ARE YOU ASKING ME WHETHER I THINK SO?
MIRACU-LOUSLY, NONE. OF COURSE YOUR FRIEND REDDICK BLAMES ME FOR THE ONES THAT ARE ALREADY IN THE MORGUE.
SERGEANT, I DON'T GIVE A DAMN WHETHER YOU THINK SO. YOU DISOBEYED A DIRECT ORDER.
WE HAVE A MUTINOUS MARINE ON OUR HANDS. WE NEEDED HIM IN THAT TOWER DURING...WHATEVER THE FUCK THIS JUST WAS.
THAT TIME HAS PASSED.
"IT'S TIME TO PICK A SIDE SERGEANT."
"ALL DUE RESPECT, LT? I'VE GOT WOUNDED TO CHECK ON."
I KNOW WHAT YOU'RE THINKING, BUT I AIN'T LETTING IRVING DIE BECAUSE OF SUPERSTITION.
YOU'RE NOT GOING TO MAKE ME SAY THE Z WORD, ARE YOU?
MOFO I SHOT WAS FUCKED UP BAD, NO DOUBT, BUT HE'S PROBABLY HOPPED UP ON THE SAME SHIT YOU ARE.
YOU REALLY SURPRISED ONE OF THE MOOJ WOULD BITE ME?
THE TALIB ARE MANY THINGS, BUT THEY ARE NOT CANNIBALS. AND IF, AFTER YOU LET WILD DOGS FEAST ON OUR CORPSES, YOUR SOLDIER CONTRACTS RABIES?
RIP
RIP
"POETIC JUSTICE."
CHOMP

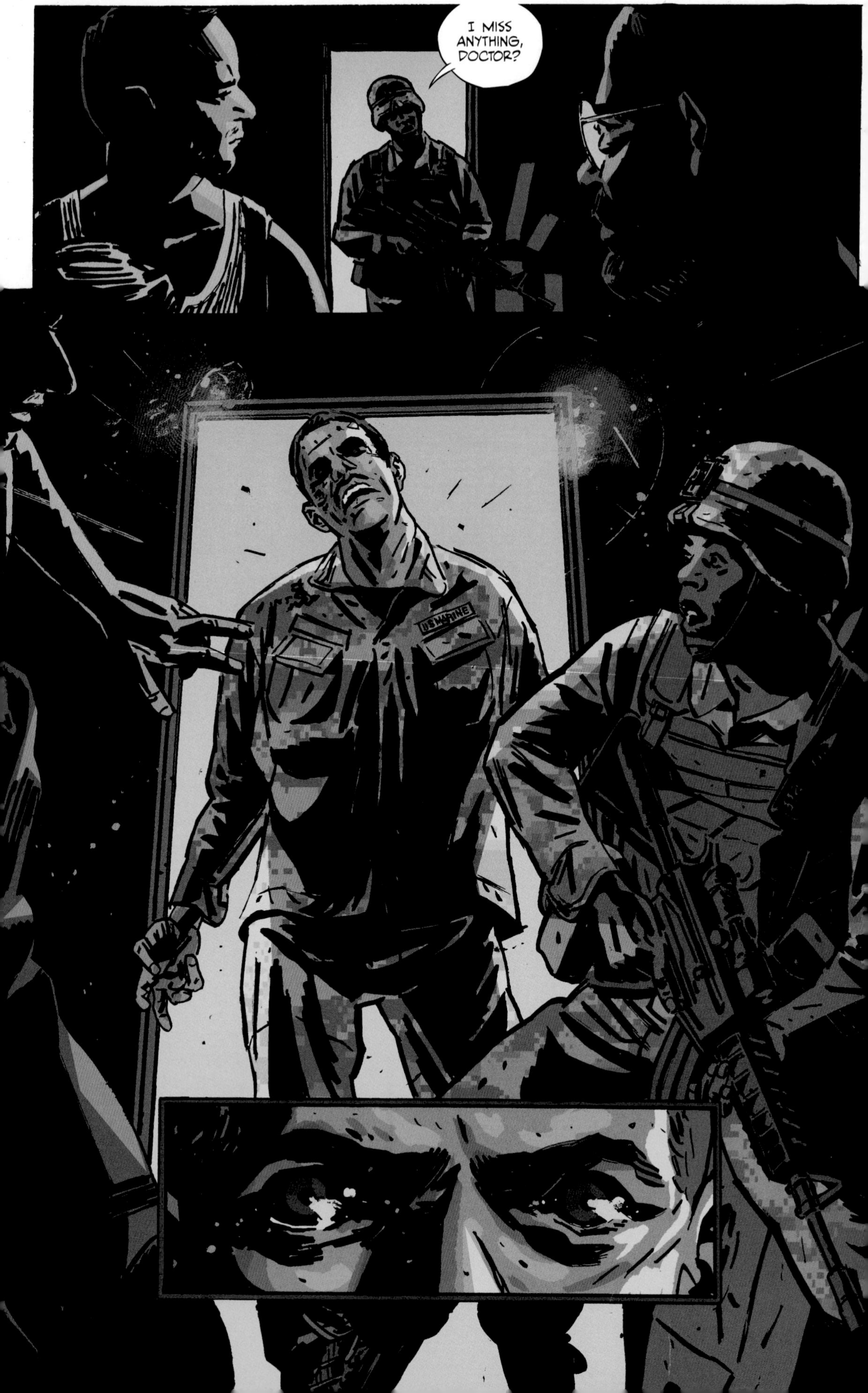
I MISS ANYTHING, DOCTOR?
U.S. MARINE

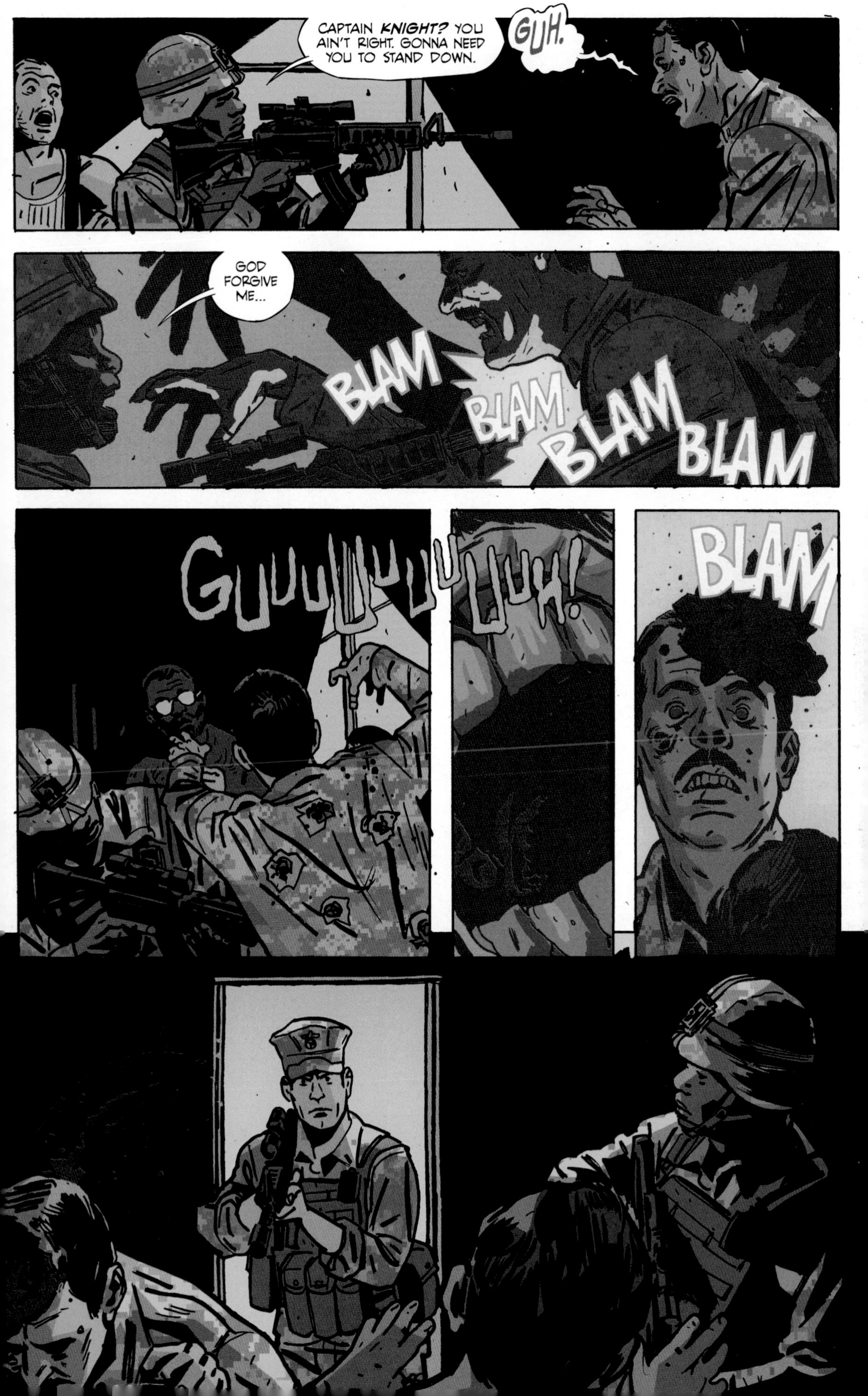
CAPTAIN KNIGHT? YOU AIN'T RIGHT. GONNA NEED YOU TO STAND DOWN.
GUH.
GOD FORGIVE ME...
BLAM
BLAM
BLAM
BLAM
GUUUUUUUUUH!
BLAM

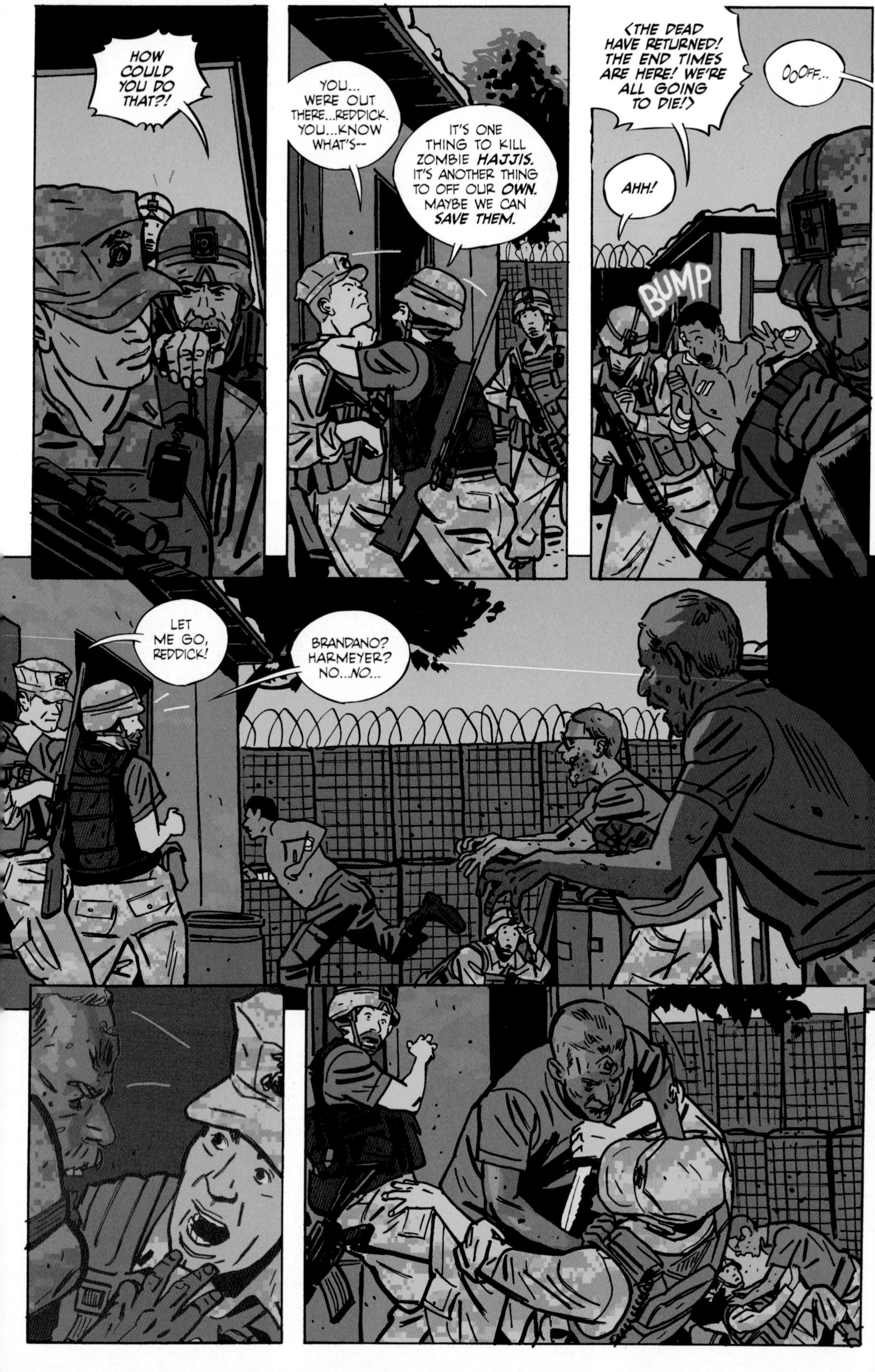
HOW COULD YOU DO THAT?!
YOU... WERE OUT THERE...REDDICK. YOU...KNOW WHAT'S--
IT'S ONE THING TO KILL ZOMBIE HAJJIS. IT'S ANOTHER THING TO OFF OUR OWN. MAYBE WE CAN SAVE THEM.
<THE DEAD HAVE RETURNED! THE END TIMES ARE HERE! WE'RE ALL GOING TO DIE!>
OOOFF...
AHH!
BUMP
LET ME GO, REDDICK!
BRANDANO? HARMEYER? NO...NO...

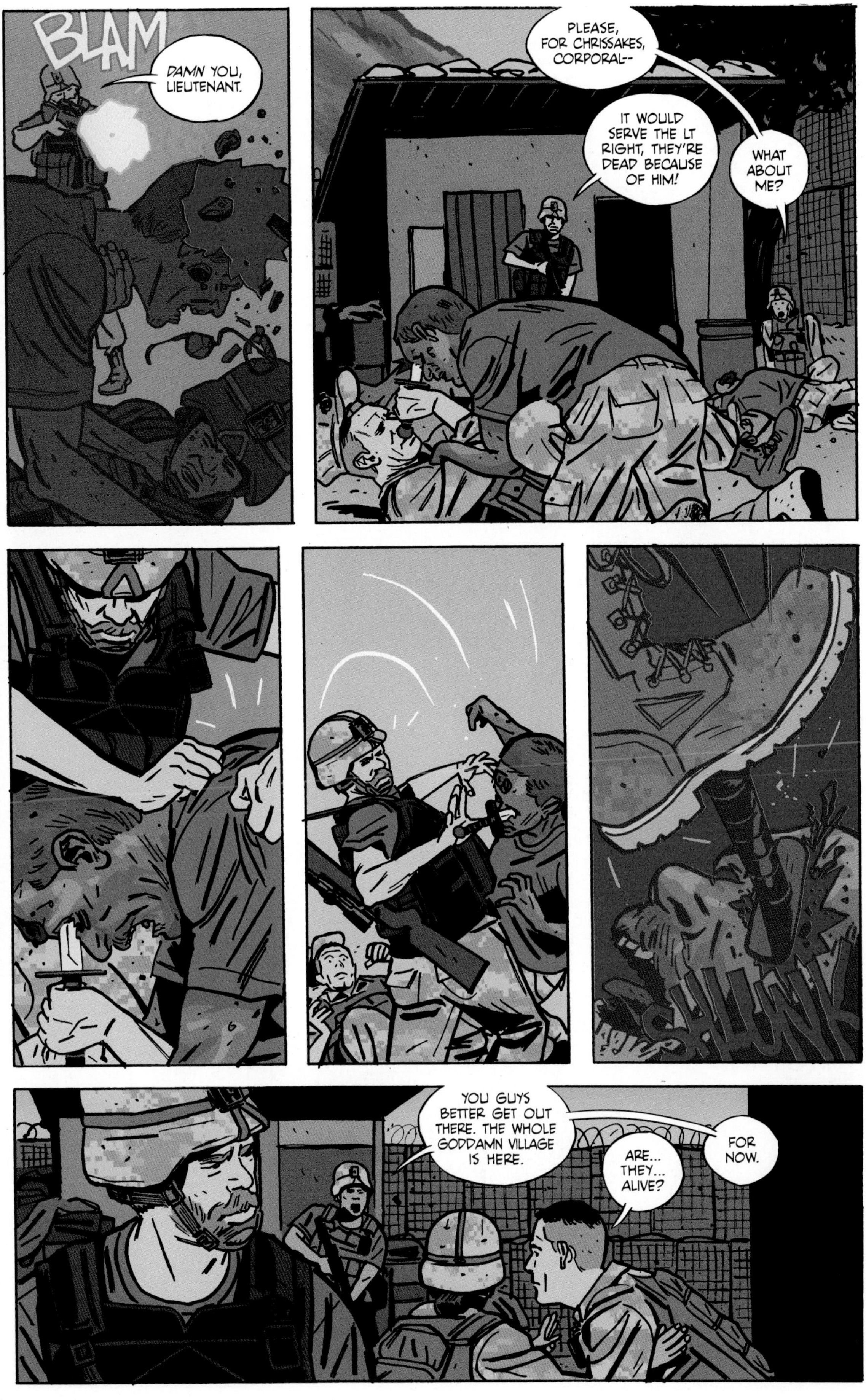
BLAM
DAMN YOU, LIEUTENANT.
PLEASE, FOR CHRISSAKES, CORPORAL--
IT WOULD SERVE THE LT RIGHT, THEY'RE DEAD BECAUSE OF HIM!
WHAT ABOUT ME?
SHUNK
YOU GUYS BETTER GET OUT THERE. THE WHOLE GODDAMN VILLAGE IS HERE.
ARE... THEY... ALIVE?
FOR NOW.

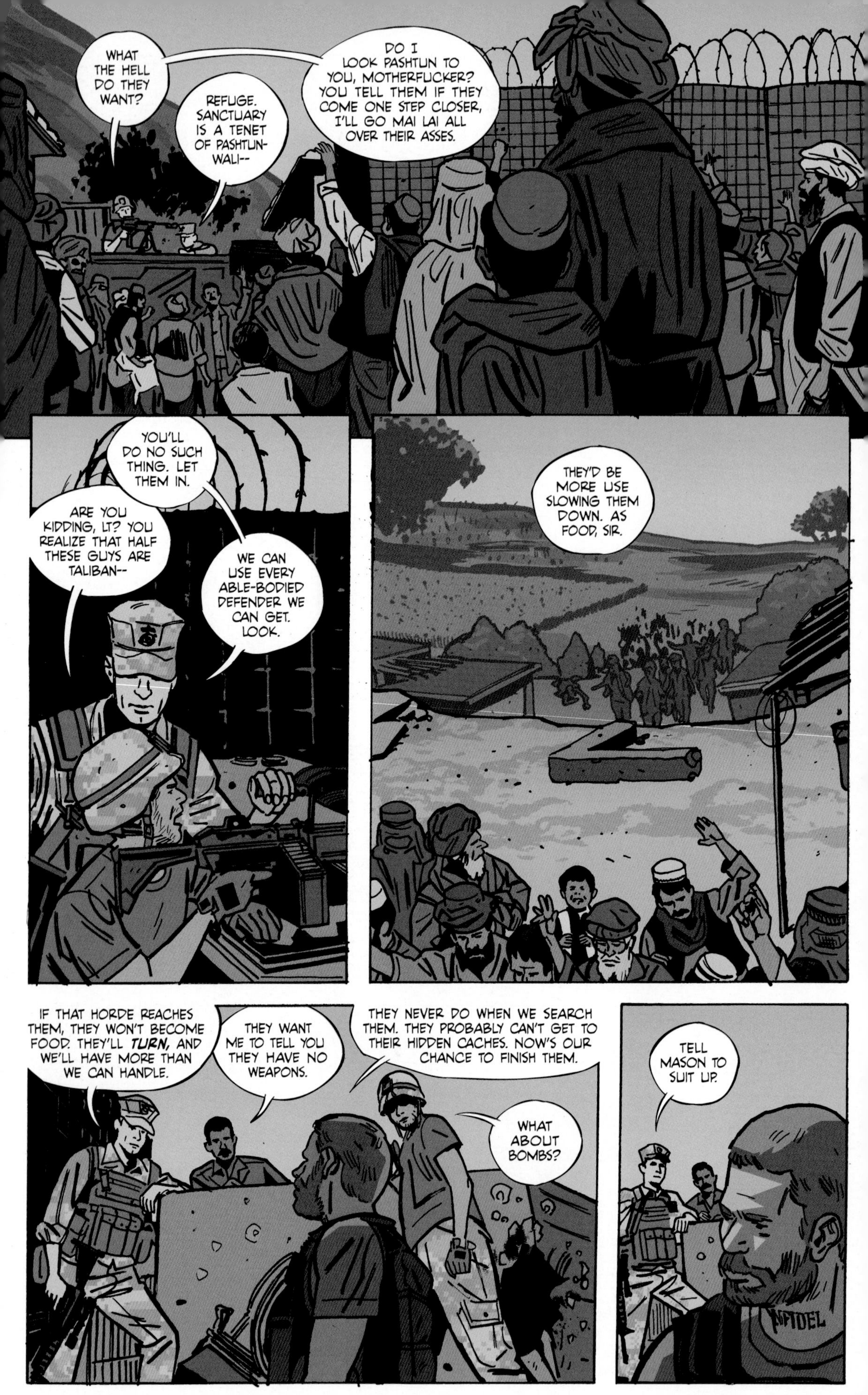
WHAT THE HELL DO THEY WANT?
REFUGE. SANCTUARY IS A TENET OF PASHTUN-WALI--
DO I LOOK PASHTUN TO YOU, MOTHERFUCKER? YOU TELL THEM IF THEY COME ONE STEP CLOSER, I'LL GO MAI LAI ALL OVER THEIR ASSES.
YOU'LL DO NO SUCH THING. LET THEM IN.
ARE YOU KIDDING, LT? YOU REALIZE THAT HALF THESE GUYS ARE TALIBAN--
WE CAN USE EVERY ABLE-BODIED DEFENDER WE CAN GET. LOOK.
THEY'D BE MORE USE SLOWING THEM DOWN. AS FOOD, SIR.
IF THAT HORDE REACHES THEM, THEY WON'T BECOME FOOD. THEY'LL TURN, AND WE'LL HAVE MORE THAN WE CAN HANDLE.
THEY WANT ME TO TELL YOU THEY HAVE NO WEAPONS.
THEY NEVER DO WHEN WE SEARCH THEM. THEY PROBABLY CAN'T GET TO THEIR HIDDEN CACHES. NOW'S OUR CHANCE TO FINISH THEM.
WHAT ABOUT BOMBS?
TELL MASON TO SUIT UP.
INFIDEL

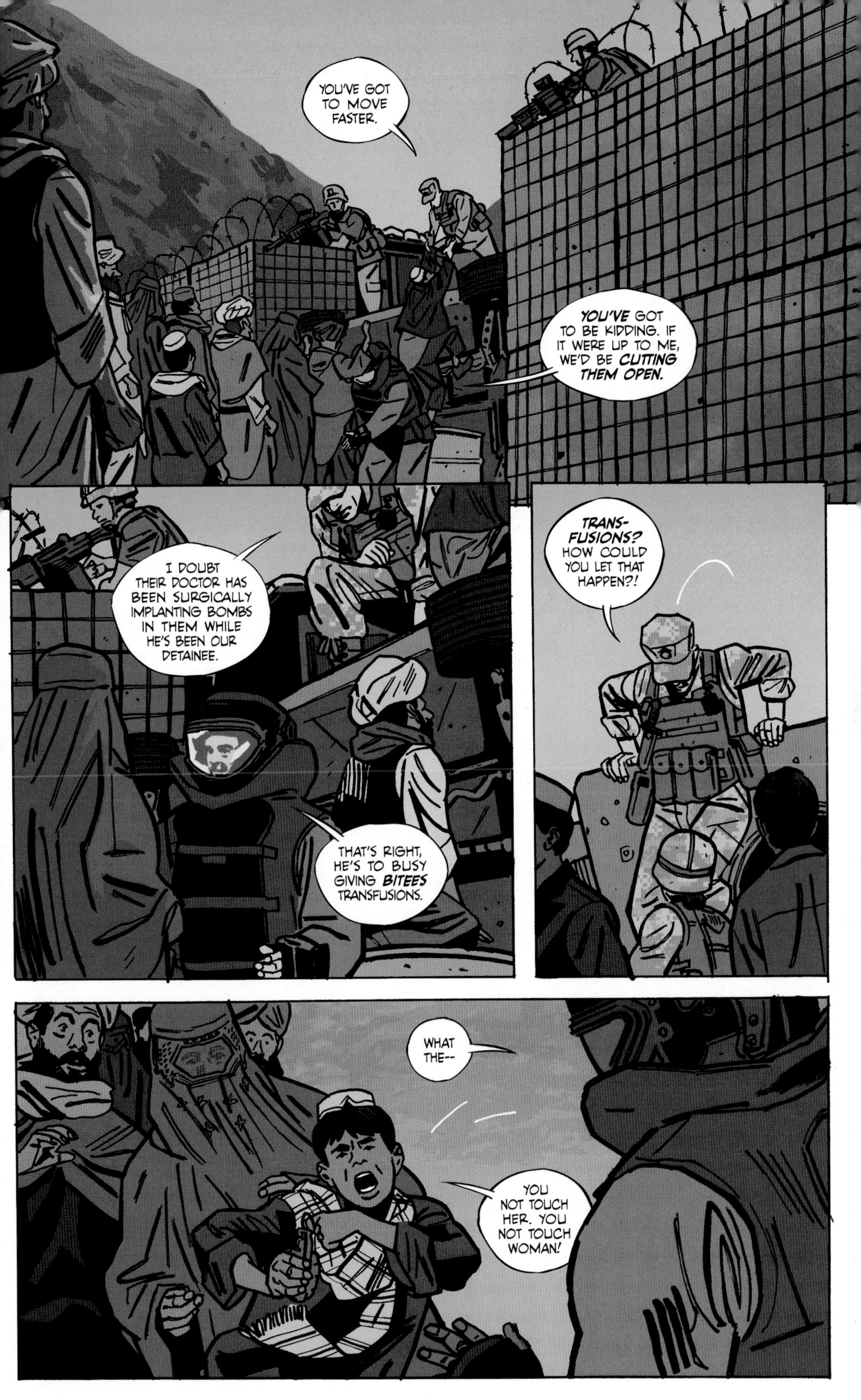
YOU'VE GOT TO MOVE FASTER.
YOU'VE GOT TO BE KIDDING. IF IT WERE UP TO ME, WE'D BE CUTTING THEM OPEN.
I DOUBT THEIR DOCTOR HAS BEEN SURGICALLY IMPLANTING BOMBS IN THEM WHILE HE'S BEEN OUR DETAINEE.
THAT'S RIGHT, HE'S TO BUSY GIVING BITEES TRANSFUSIONS.
TRANS-FUSIONS? HOW COULD YOU LET THAT HAPPEN?!
WHAT THE--
YOU NOT TOUCH HER. YOU NOT TOUCH WOMAN!

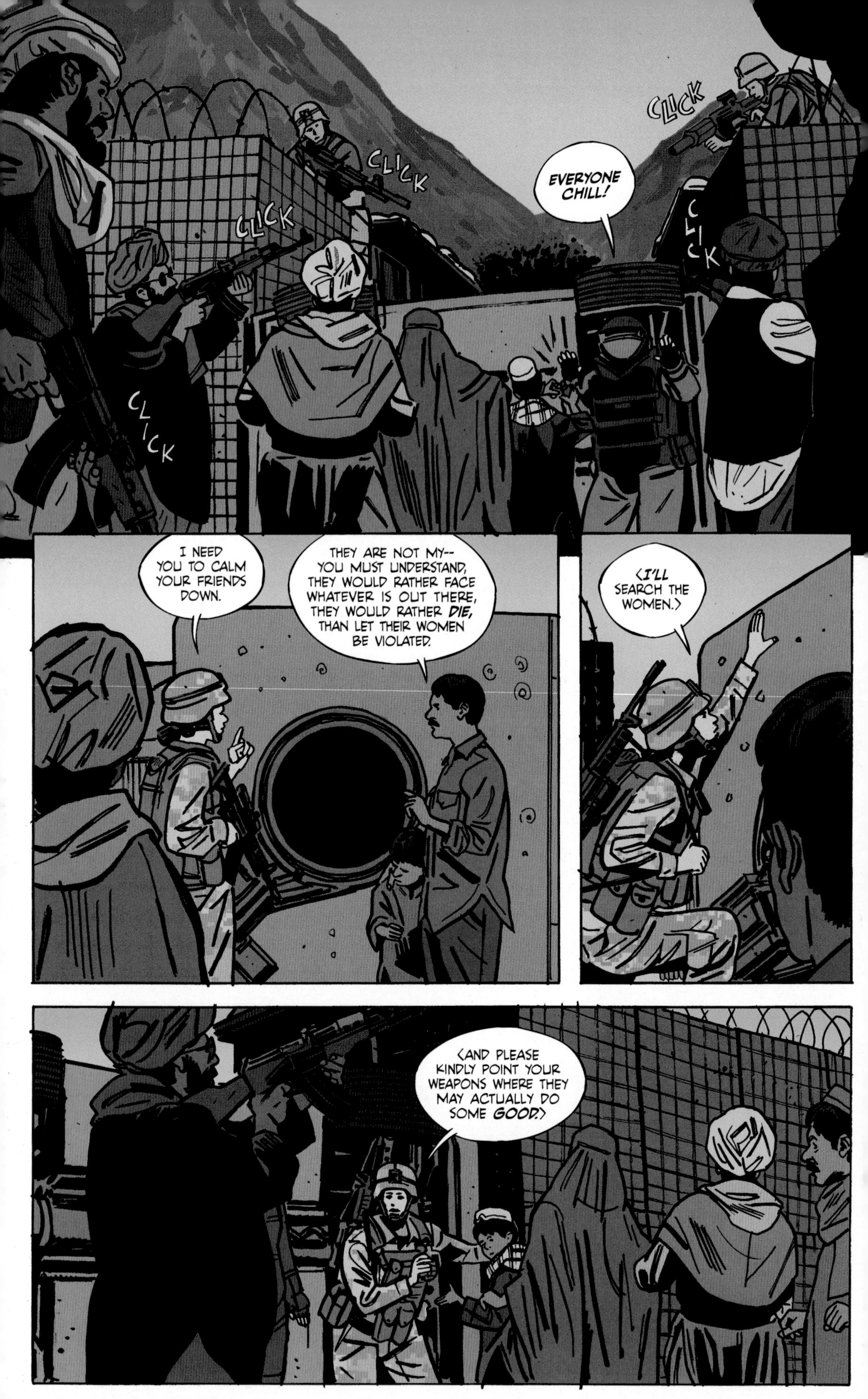
CLICK
CLICK
CLICK
EVERYONE CHILL!
CLICK
CLICK
I NEED YOU TO CALM YOUR FRIENDS DOWN.
THEY ARE NOT MY-- YOU MUST UNDERSTAND, THEY WOULD RATHER FACE WHATEVER IS OUT THERE, THEY WOULD RATHER DIE, THAN LET THEIR WOMEN BE VIOLATED.
<I'LL SEARCH THE WOMEN.>
<AND PLEASE KINDLY POINT YOUR WEAPONS WHERE THEY MAY ACTUALLY DO SOME GOOD.>

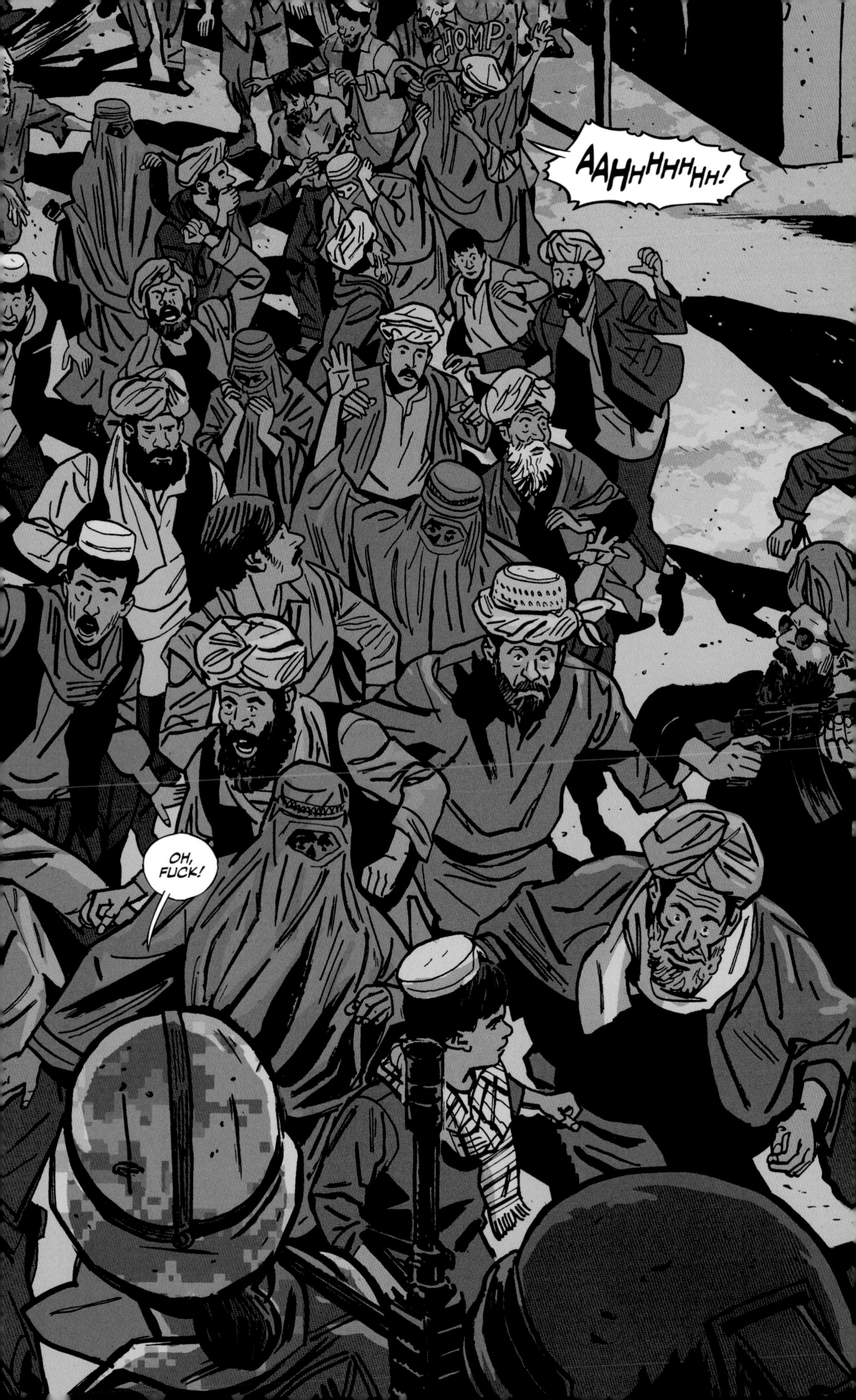
CHOMP
AAHHHHHHH!
OH, FUCK!

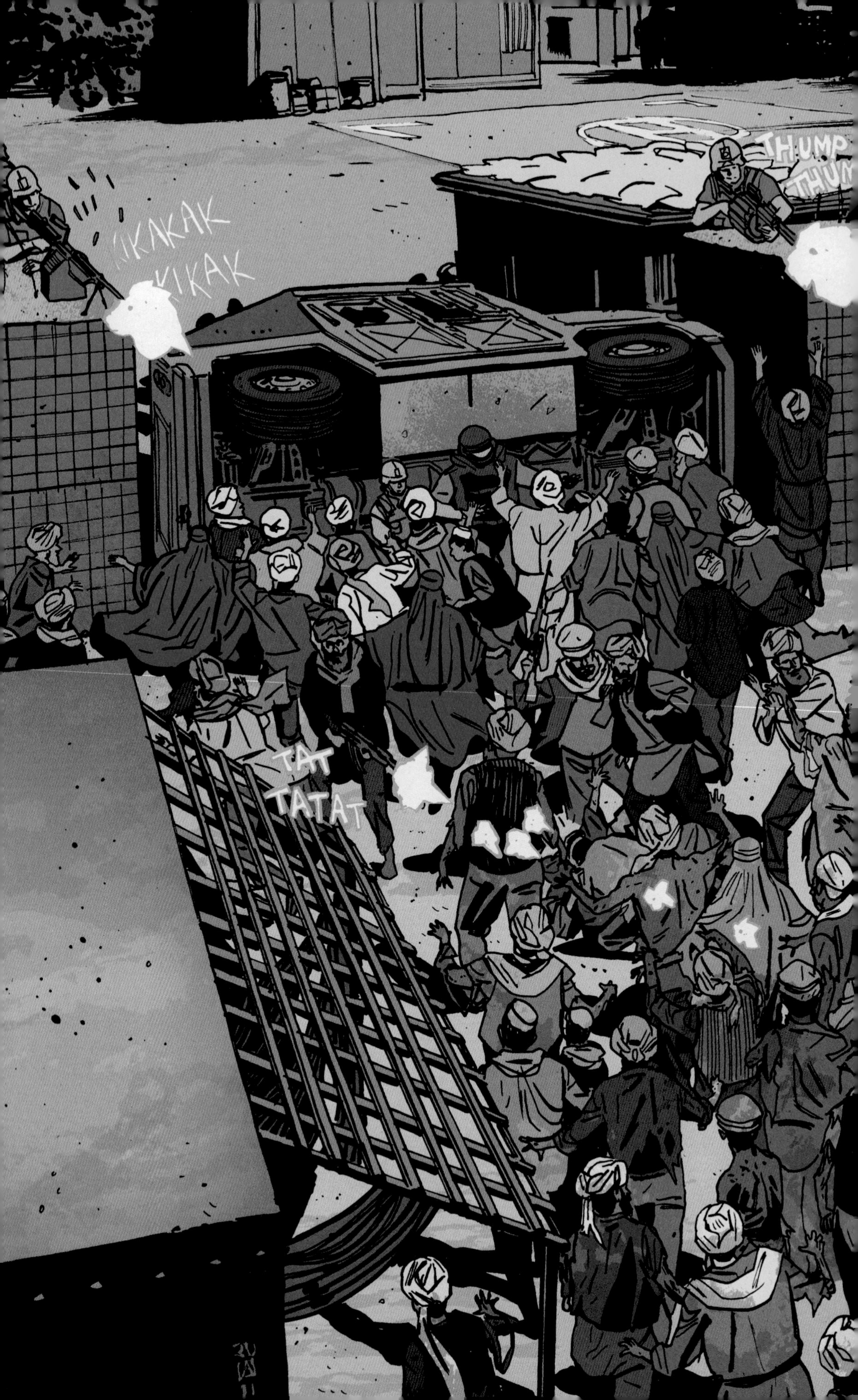

KIKAKAK
KIKAK
THUMP
THUMP
TAT
TATAT

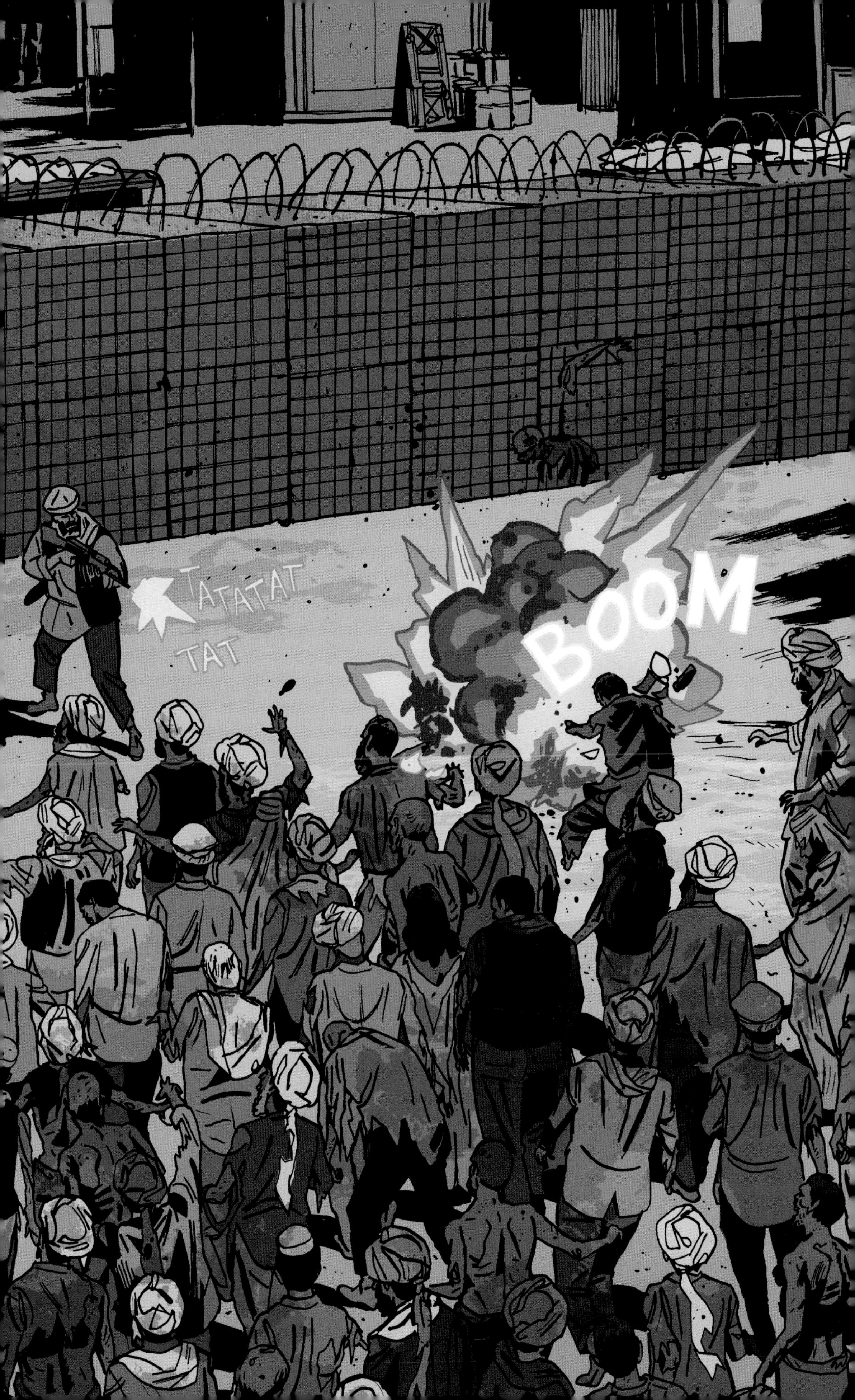
TATATAT
TAT
BOOM

CHAPTER 3

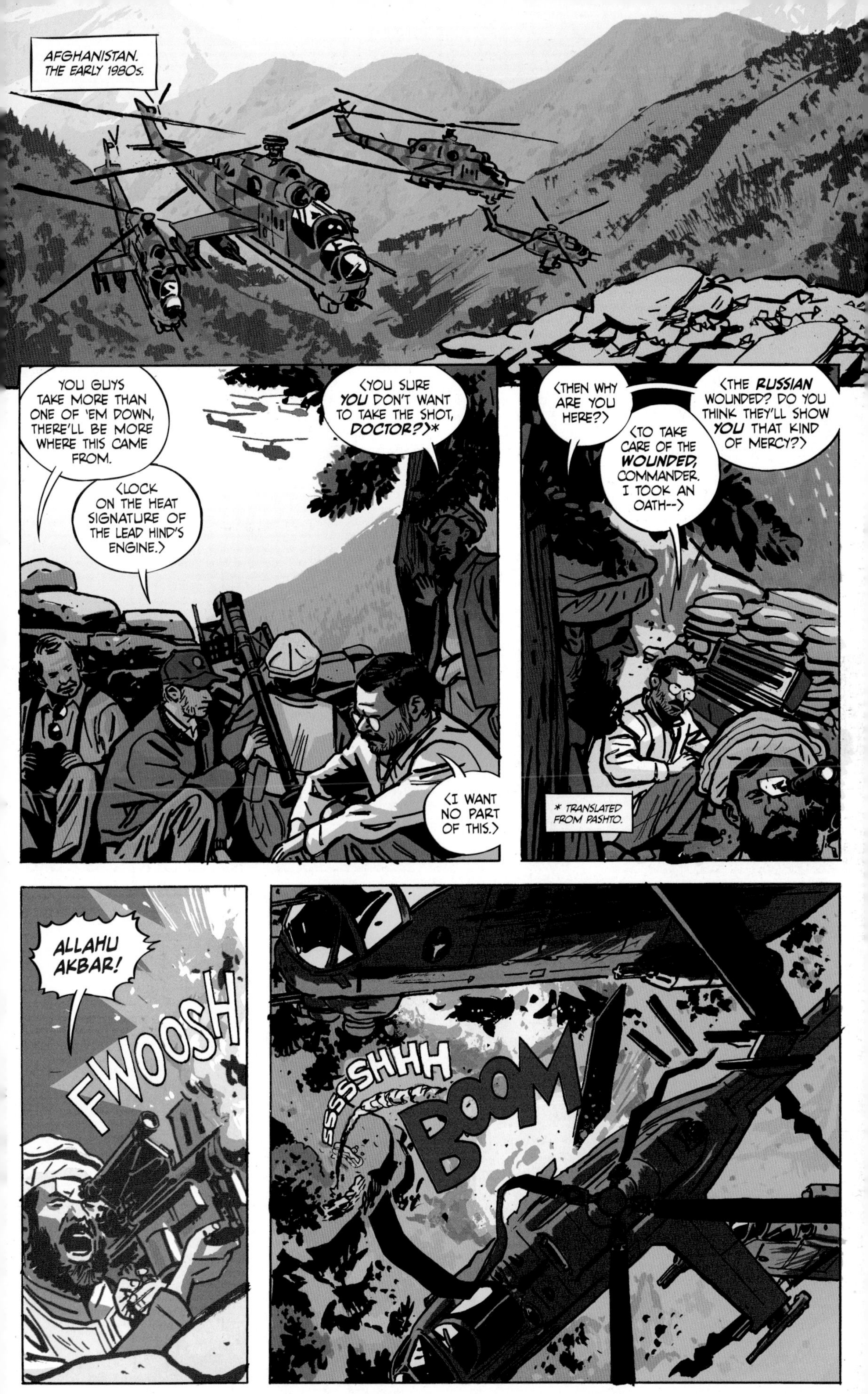
AFGHANISTAN. THE EARLY 1980s.
YOU GUYS TAKE MORE THAN ONE OF 'EM DOWN, THERE'LL BE MORE WHERE THIS CAME FROM.
‹LOCK ON THE HEAT SIGNATURE OF THE LEAD HIND'S ENGINE.›
‹YOU SURE YOU DON'T WANT TO TAKE THE SHOT, DOCTOR?›*
‹I WANT NO PART OF THIS.›
‹THEN WHY ARE YOU HERE?›
‹TO TAKE CARE OF THE WOUNDED, COMMANDER. I TOOK AN OATH--›
‹THE RUSSIAN WOUNDED? DO YOU THINK THEY'LL SHOW YOU THAT KIND OF MERCY?›
* TRANSLATED FROM PASHTO.
ALLAHU AKBAR!
FWOOSH
SSSSSHHH
BOOM

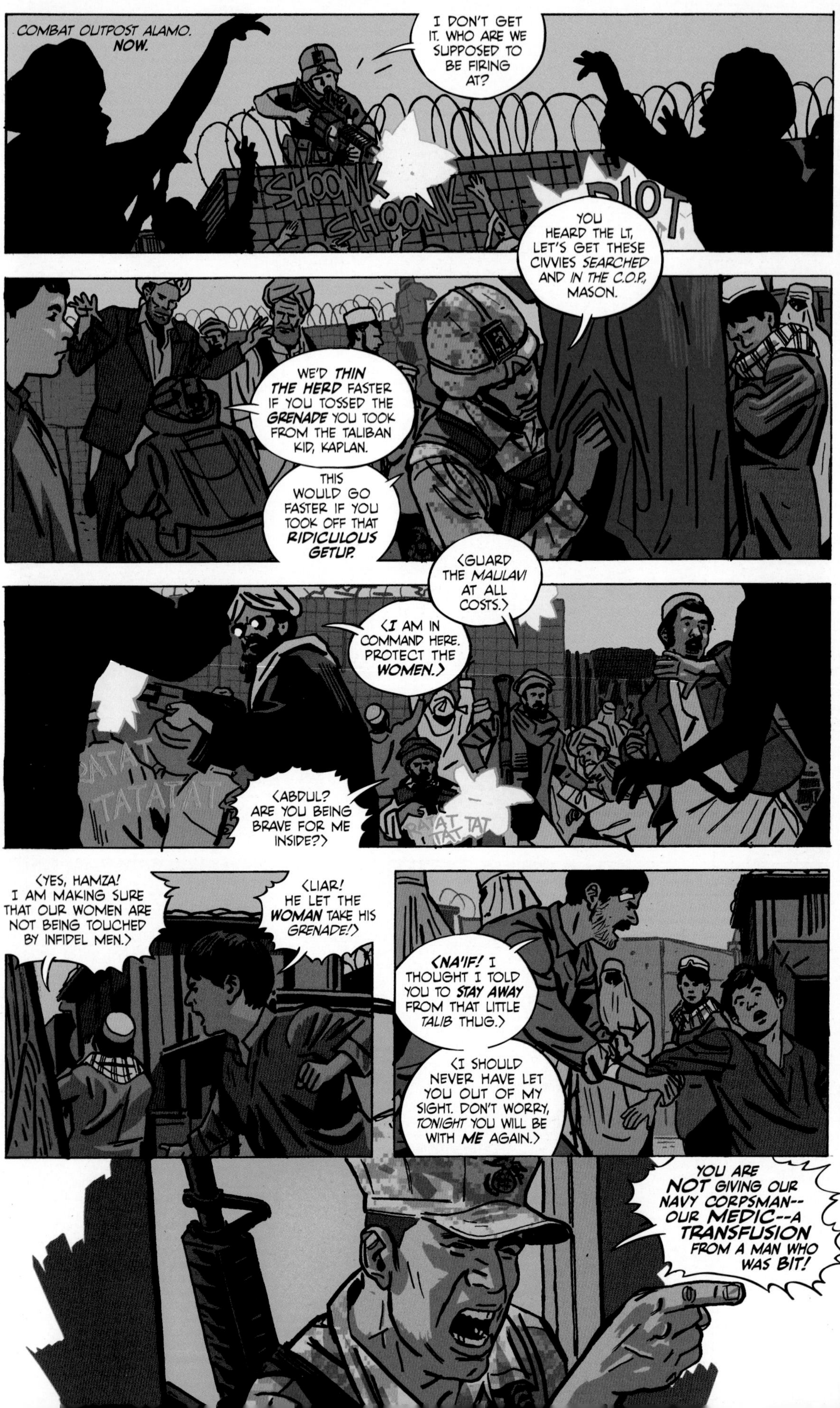
COMBAT OUTPOST ALAMO. NOW.
I DON'T GET IT. WHO ARE WE SUPPOSED TO BE FIRING AT?
SHOONK
SHOONK
RIOT
YOU HEARD THE LT, LET'S GET THESE CIVVIES SEARCHED AND IN THE C.O.P., MASON.
WE'D THIN THE HERD FASTER IF YOU TOSSED THE GRENADE YOU TOOK FROM THE TALIBAN KID, KAPLAN.
THIS WOULD GO FASTER IF YOU TOOK OFF THAT RIDICULOUS GETUP.
<GUARD THE MAULAVI AT ALL COSTS.>
<I AM IN COMMAND HERE. PROTECT THE WOMEN.>
RATAT TATATAT
<ABDUL? ARE YOU BEING BRAVE FOR ME INSIDE?>
RATAT TAT TATAT
<YES, HAMZA! I AM MAKING SURE THAT OUR WOMEN ARE NOT BEING TOUCHED BY INFIDEL MEN.>
<LIAR! HE LET THE WOMAN TAKE HIS GRENADE!>
<NA'IF! I THOUGHT I TOLD YOU TO STAY AWAY FROM THAT LITTLE TALIB THUG.>
<I SHOULD NEVER HAVE LET YOU OUT OF MY SIGHT. DON'T WORRY, TONIGHT YOU WILL BE WITH ME AGAIN.>
YOU ARE NOT GIVING OUR NAVY CORPSMAN--OUR MEDIC--A TRANSFUSION FROM A MAN WHO WAS BIT!

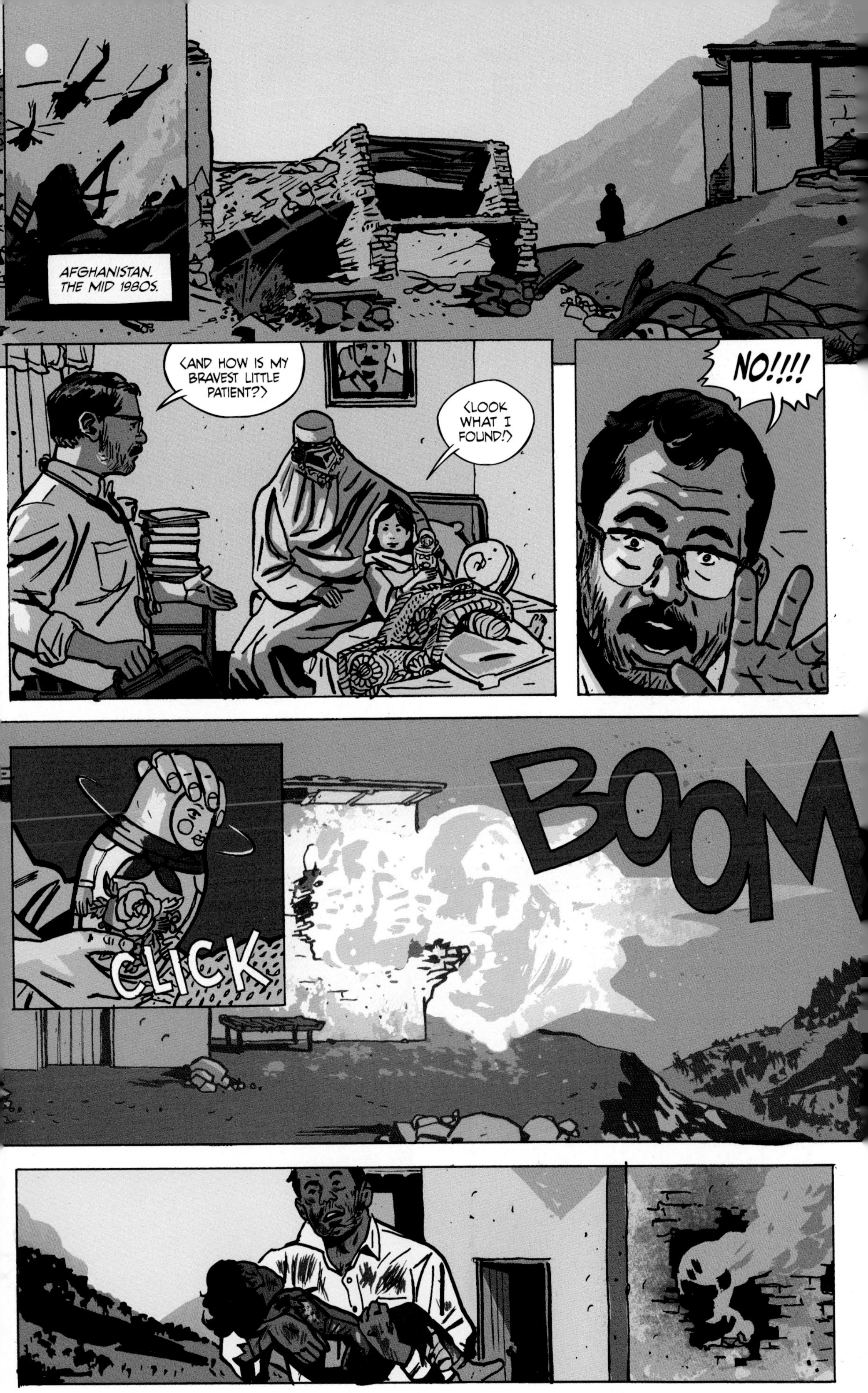

AFGHANISTAN. THE MID 1980S.
<AND HOW IS MY BRAVEST LITTLE PATIENT?>
<LOOK WHAT I FOUND!>
NO!!!!
CLICK
BOOM

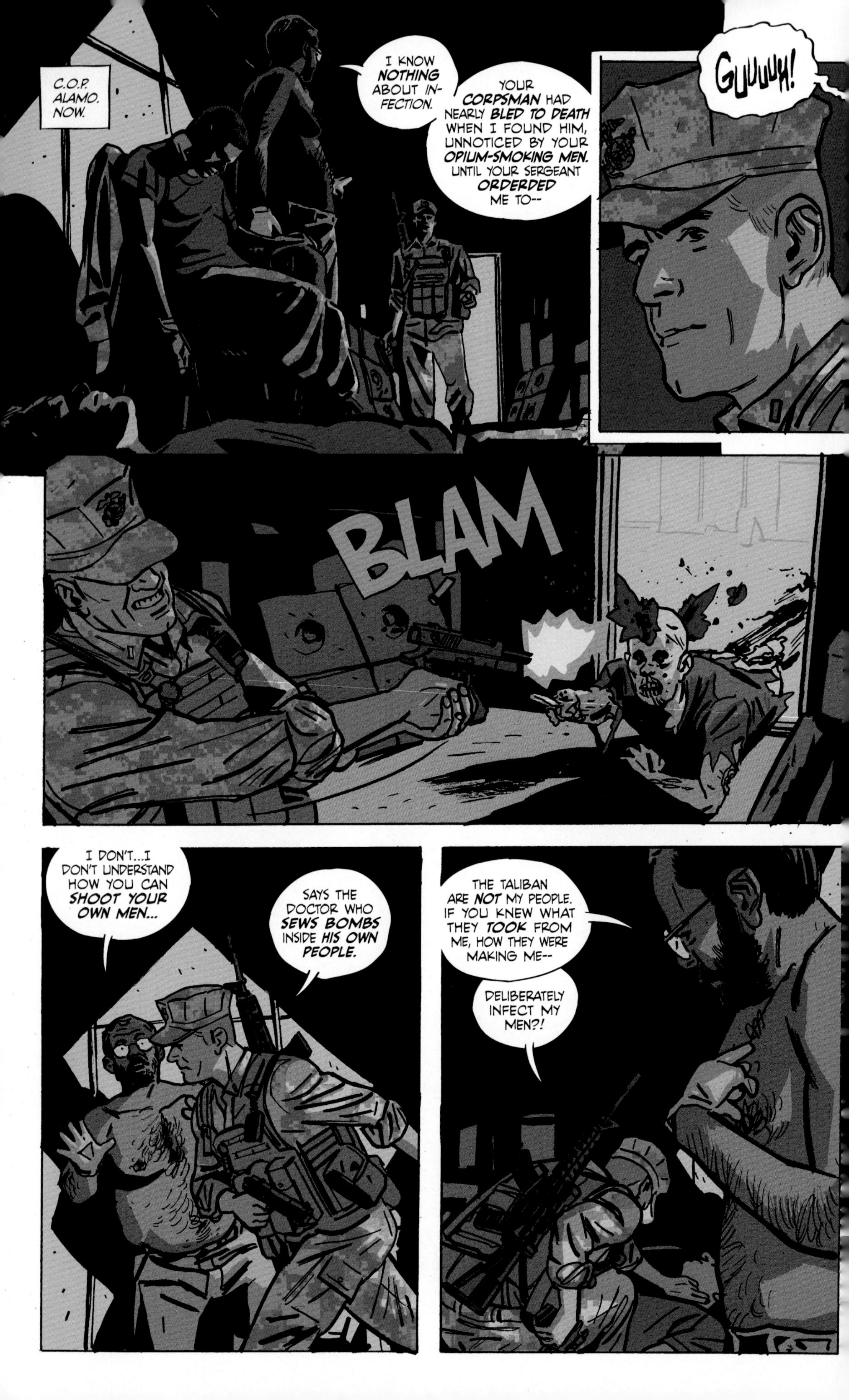

C.O.P. ALAMO. NOW.
I KNOW NOTHING ABOUT IN-FECTION.
YOUR CORPSMAN HAD NEARLY BLED TO DEATH WHEN I FOUND HIM, UNNOTICED BY YOUR OPIUM-SMOKING MEN. UNTIL YOUR SERGEANT ORDERDED ME TO--
GUUUUH!
BLAM
I DON'T...I DON'T UNDERSTAND HOW YOU CAN SHOOT YOUR OWN MEN...
SAYS THE DOCTOR WHO SEWS BOMBS INSIDE HIS OWN PEOPLE.
THE TALIBAN ARE NOT MY PEOPLE. IF YOU KNEW WHAT THEY TOOK FROM ME, HOW THEY WERE MAKING ME--
DELIBERATELY INFECT MY MEN?!

THE "DURAND LINE": THE AFGHAN-PAKISTAN BORDER. THE LATE 1980s.

THAT'S OKAY, COMRADE. ENJOY THE VODKA, ANYWAY. YOU'LL NEED IT.

HE WON'T GIVE UP THE COMBO AND I CAN'T CUT THROUGH THE CHAIN. WILL YOU DO THE HONORS, DOCTOR?

I...

TOOK AN *OATH?* THEY TOOK SOME-THING *MUCH* WORSE.

YOU ALREADY PASSED UP *ONE* CHANCE TO TAKE SOMETHING IN RETURN. YOU WON'T GET *ANOTHER.*

GOD FORGIVE ME...

AAAHHHHH!!!

DRESSING THE WOUND *YOU* INFLICTED?

DOC, I'M MOVED BY YOUR *COMPASSION*, BUT YOU ARE ONLY DELAYING THE *IN-EVITABLE.* DEAD OR ALIVE--

"--WE CAN'T HAVE SOVIETS ON THIS SIDE OF THE BORDER."

HYUK

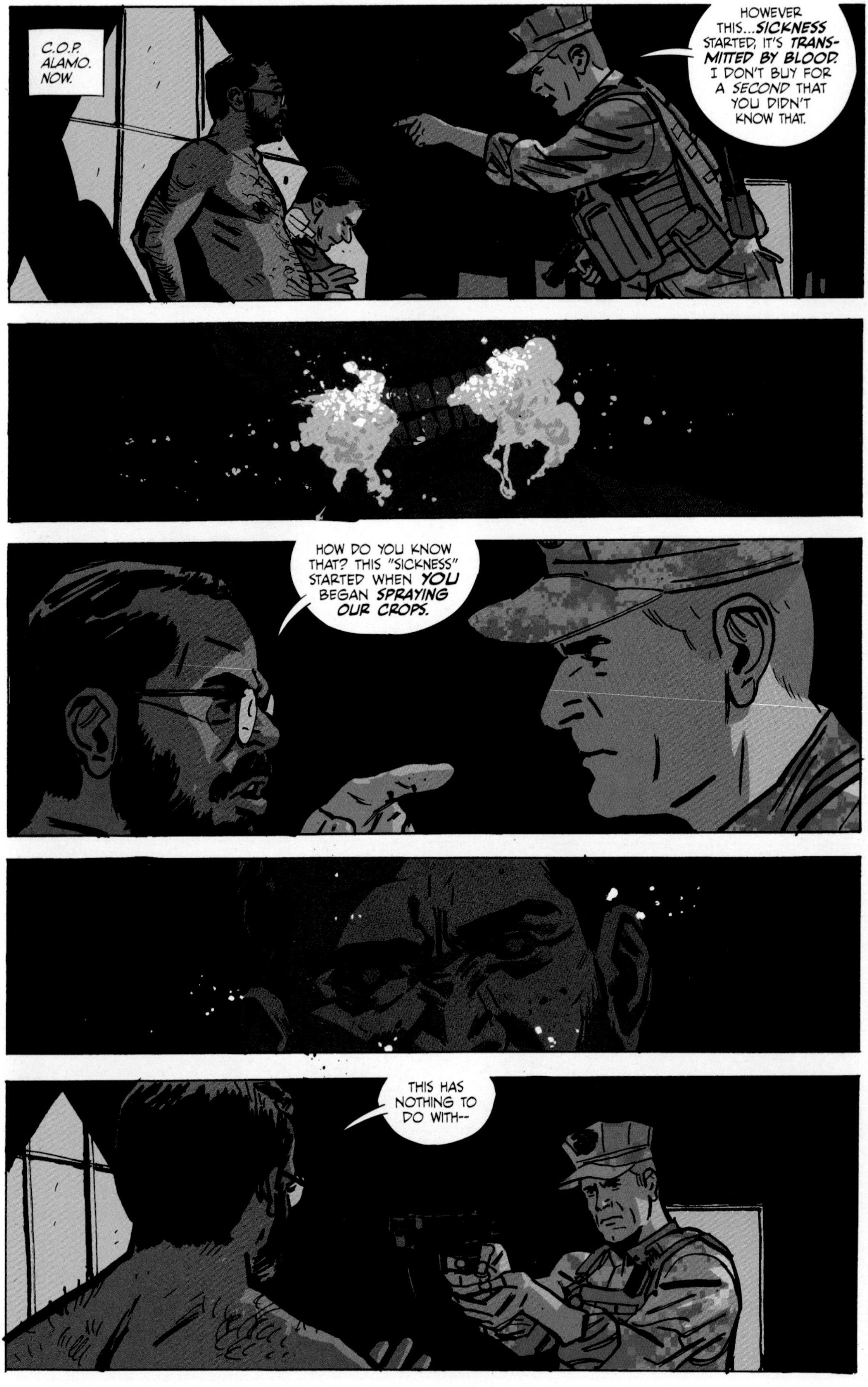
C.O.P. ALAMO. NOW.
HOWEVER THIS...SICKNESS STARTED, IT'S TRANS-MITTED BY BLOOD. I DON'T BUY FOR A SECOND THAT YOU DIDN'T KNOW THAT.
HOW DO YOU KNOW THAT? THIS "SICKNESS" STARTED WHEN YOU BEGAN SPRAYING OUR CROPS.
THIS HAS NOTHING TO DO WITH--

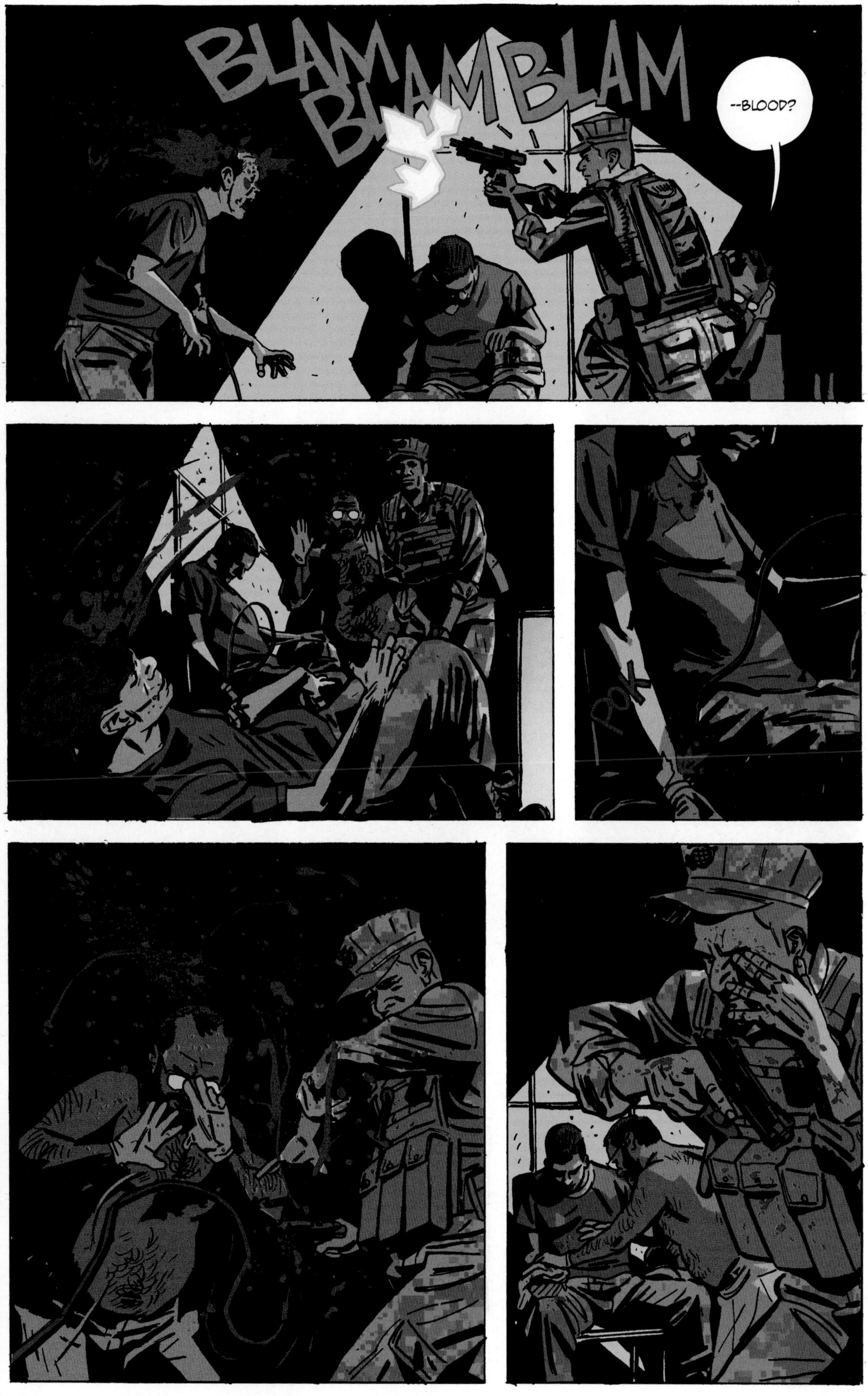
BLAM
BLAM
BLAM
--BLOOD?
POK

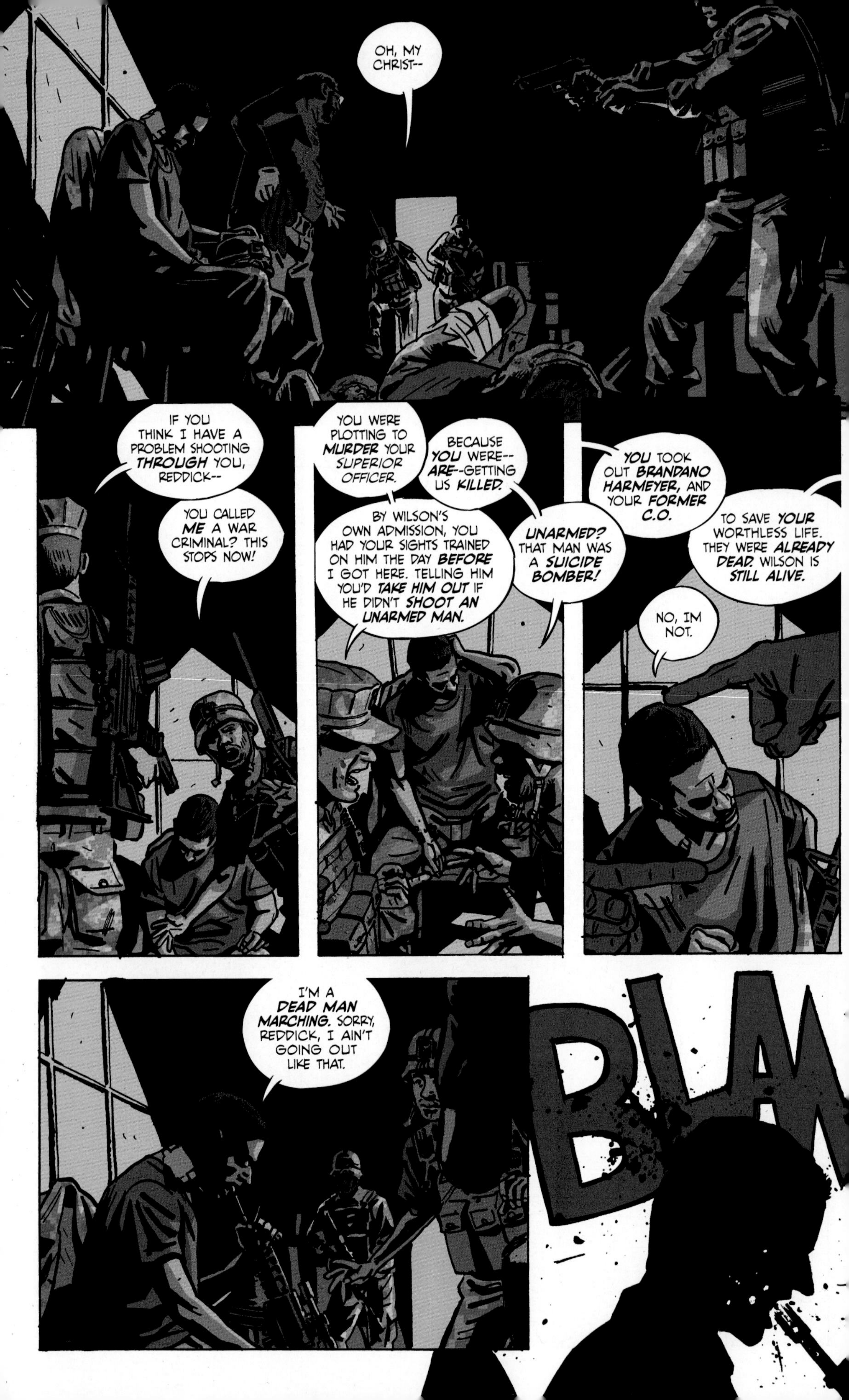
OH, MY CHRIST--
IF YOU THINK I HAVE A PROBLEM SHOOTING THROUGH YOU, REDDICK--
YOU CALLED ME A WAR CRIMINAL? THIS STOPS NOW!
YOU WERE PLOTTING TO MURDER YOUR SUPERIOR OFFICER.
BECAUSE YOU WERE--ARE--GETTING US KILLED.
BY WILSON'S OWN ADMISSION, YOU HAD YOUR SIGHTS TRAINED ON HIM THE DAY BEFORE I GOT HERE. TELLING HIM YOU'D TAKE HIM OUT IF HE DIDN'T SHOOT AN UNARMED MAN.
UNARMED? THAT MAN WAS A SUICIDE BOMBER!
YOU TOOK OUT BRANDANO HARMEYER, AND YOUR FORMER C.O.
TO SAVE YOUR WORTHLESS LIFE. THEY WERE ALREADY DEAD. WILSON IS STILL ALIVE.
NO, IM NOT.
I'M A DEAD MAN MARCHING. SORRY, REDDICK, I AIN'T GOING OUT LIKE THAT.
BLAM

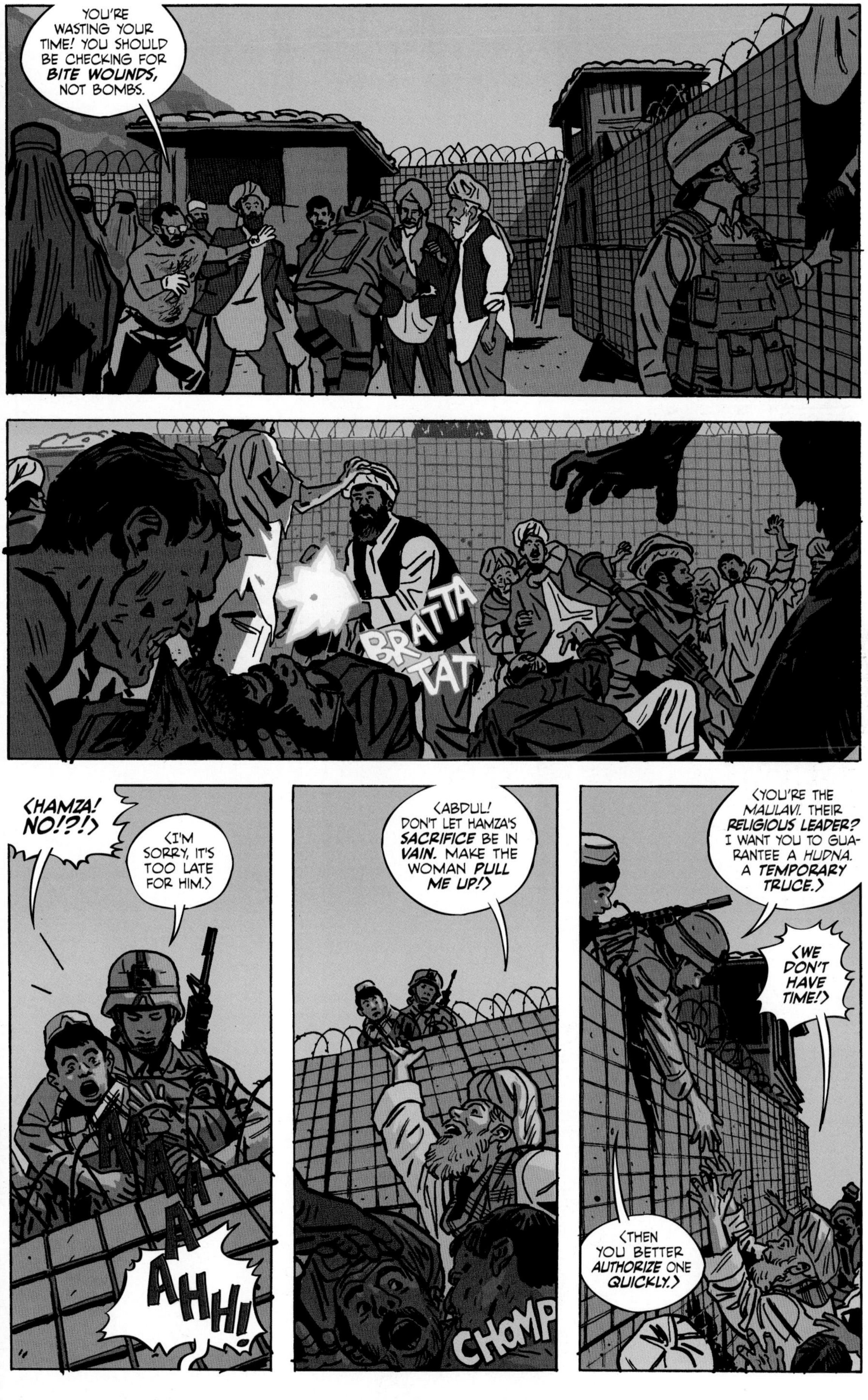
YOU'RE WASTING YOUR TIME! YOU SHOULD BE CHECKING FOR BITE WOUNDS, NOT BOMBS.
BRATTA TAT
<HAMZA! NO!?!>
<I'M SORRY, IT'S TOO LATE FOR HIM.>
AAAAAAHH!
<ABDUL! DON'T LET HAMZA'S SACRIFICE BE IN VAIN. MAKE THE WOMAN PULL ME UP!>
CHOMP
<YOU'RE THE MAULAVI. THEIR RELIGIOUS LEADER? I WANT YOU TO GUARANTEE A HUDNA. A TEMPORARY TRUCE.>
<WE DON'T HAVE TIME!>
<THEN YOU BETTER AUTHORIZE ONE QUICKLY.>

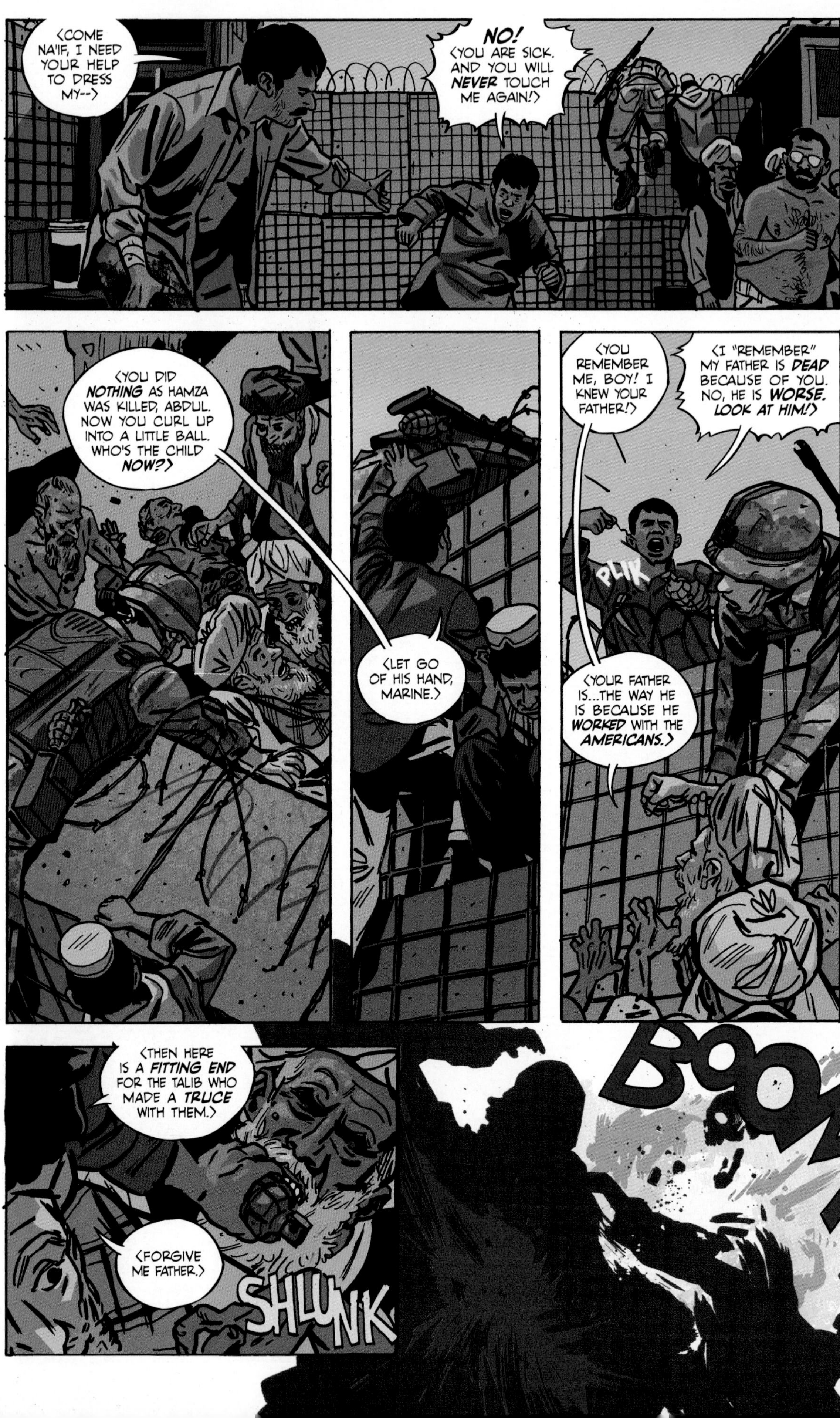
<COME NA'IF, I NEED YOUR HELP TO DRESS MY-->
NO!
<YOU ARE SICK. AND YOU WILL NEVER TOUCH ME AGAIN!>
<YOU DID NOTHING AS HAMZA WAS KILLED, ABDUL. NOW YOU CURL UP INTO A LITTLE BALL. WHO'S THE CHILD NOW?>
<LET GO OF HIS HAND, MARINE.>
<YOU REMEMBER ME, BOY! I KNEW YOUR FATHER!>
<I "REMEMBER" MY FATHER IS DEAD BECAUSE OF YOU. NO, HE IS WORSE. LOOK AT HIM!>
PLIK
<YOUR FATHER IS...THE WAY HE IS BECAUSE HE WORKED WITH THE AMERICANS.>
<THEN HERE IS A FITTING END FOR THE TALIB WHO MADE A TRUCE WITH THEM.>
<FORGIVE ME FATHER.>
SHLUNK
BOOM

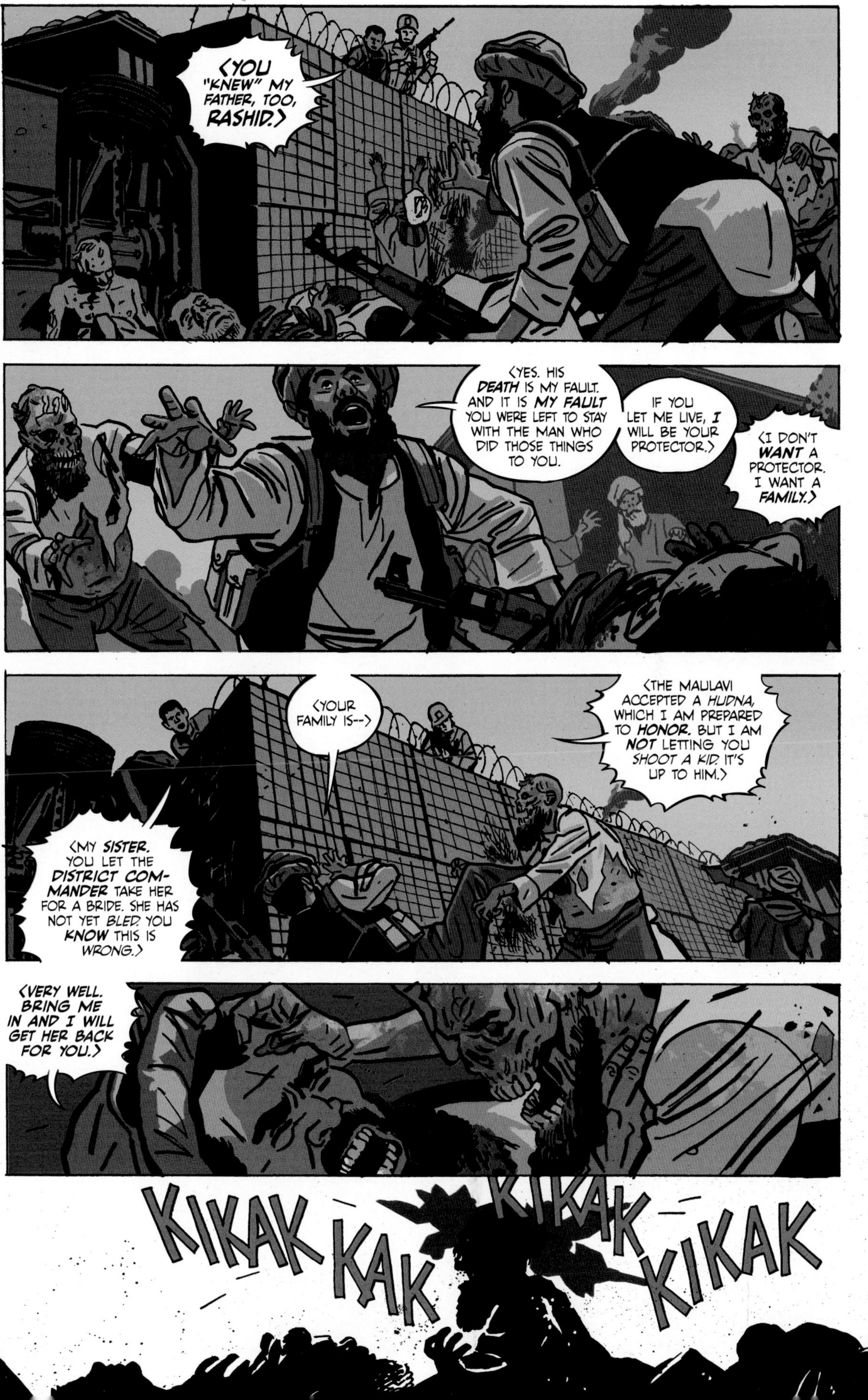

‹YOU "KNEW" MY FATHER, TOO, RASHID.›
‹YES. HIS DEATH IS MY FAULT. AND IT IS MY FAULT YOU WERE LEFT TO STAY WITH THE MAN WHO DID THOSE THINGS TO YOU.
IF YOU LET ME LIVE, I WILL BE YOUR PROTECTOR.›
‹I DON'T WANT A PROTECTOR. I WANT A FAMILY.›
‹YOUR FAMILY IS--›
‹THE MAULAVI ACCEPTED A HUDNA, WHICH I AM PREPARED TO HONOR. BUT I AM NOT LETTING YOU SHOOT A KID. IT'S UP TO HIM.›
‹MY SISTER. YOU LET THE DISTRICT COMMANDER TAKE HER FOR A BRIDE. SHE HAS NOT YET BLED. YOU KNOW THIS IS WRONG.›
‹VERY WELL. BRING ME IN AND I WILL GET HER BACK FOR YOU.›
KIKAK
KAK
KIKAK
KIKAK

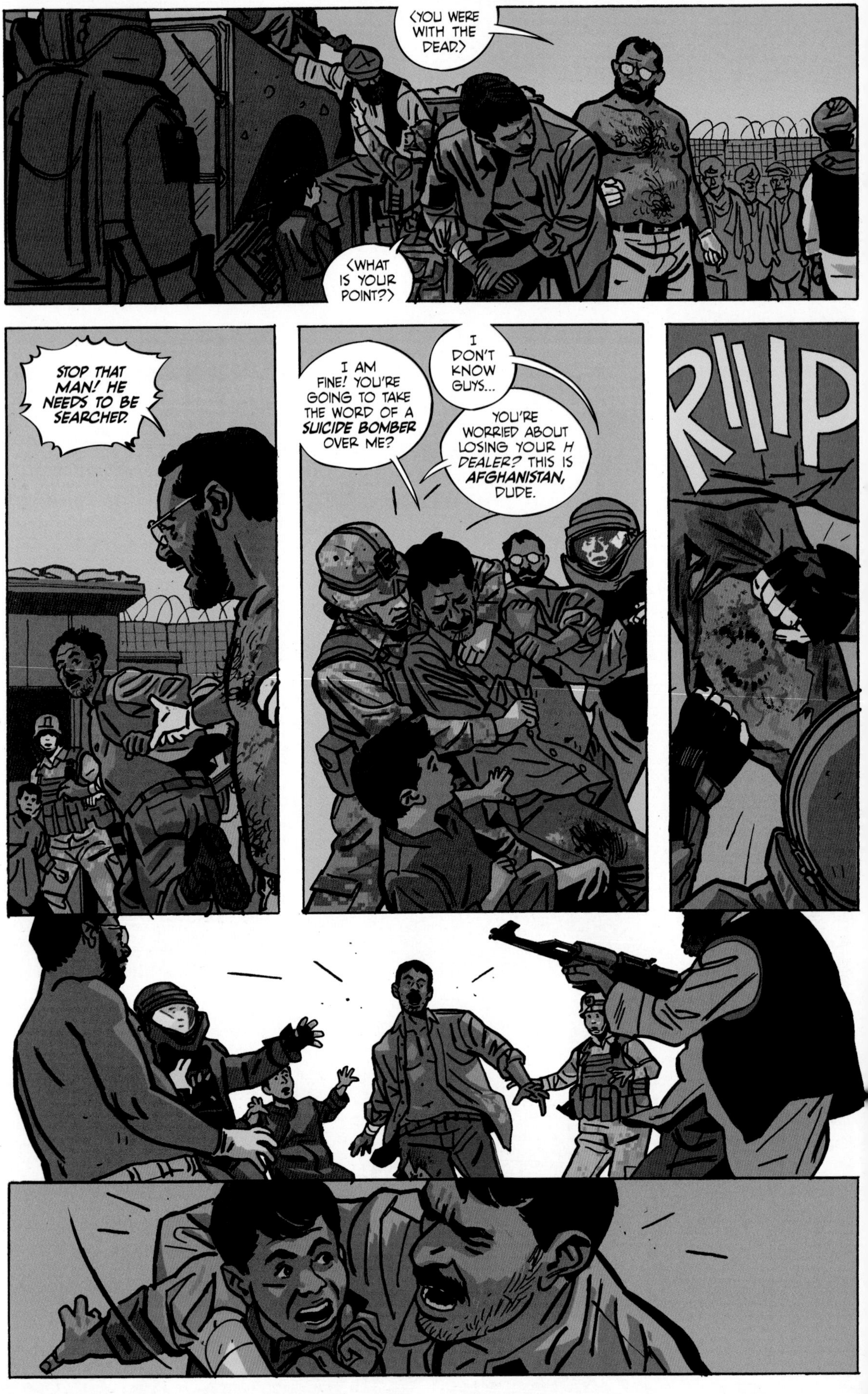

<YOU WERE WITH THE DEAD.>
<WHAT IS YOUR POINT?>
STOP THAT MAN! HE NEEDS TO BE SEARCHED.
I AM FINE! YOU'RE GOING TO TAKE THE WORD OF A SUICIDE BOMBER OVER ME?
I DON'T KNOW GUYS...
YOU'RE WORRIED ABOUT LOSING YOUR H DEALER? THIS IS AFGHANISTAN, DUDE.
RIIIP

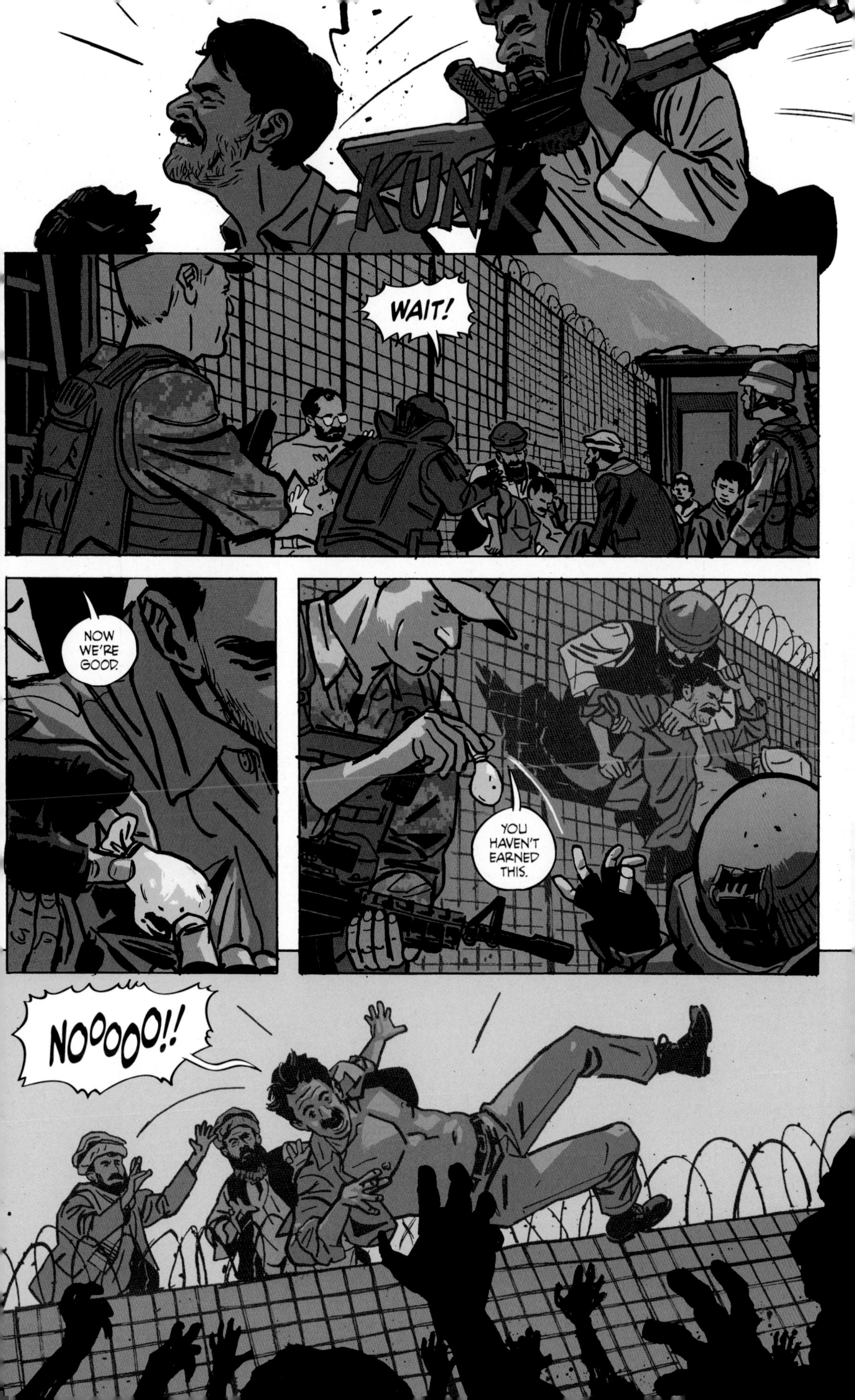
KUNK
WAIT!
NOW WE'RE GOOD.
YOU HAVEN'T EARNED THIS.
NOOOOO!!

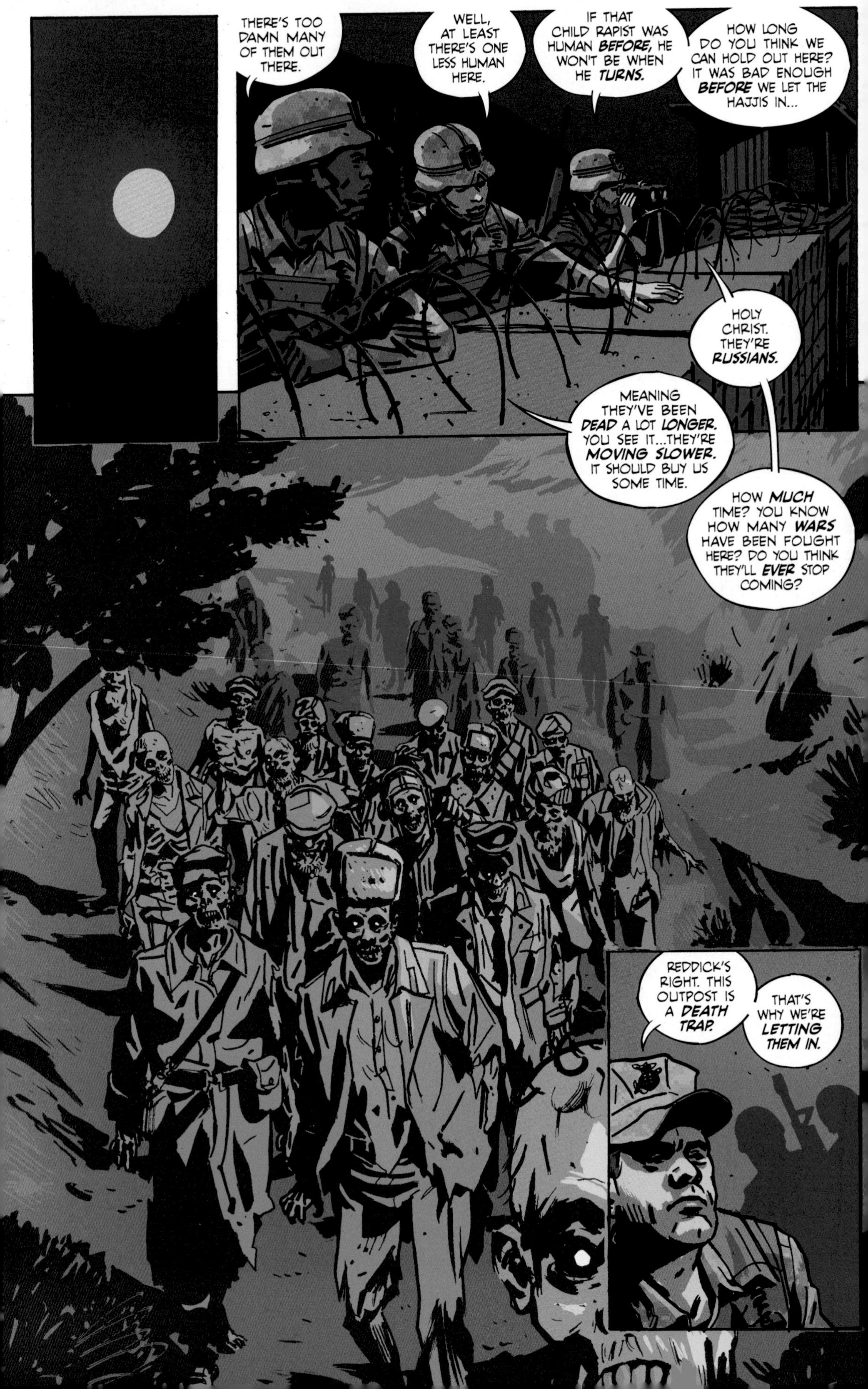
THERE'S TOO DAMN MANY OF THEM OUT THERE.
WELL, AT LEAST THERE'S ONE LESS HUMAN HERE.
IF THAT CHILD RAPIST WAS HUMAN BEFORE, HE WON'T BE WHEN HE TURNS.
HOW LONG DO YOU THINK WE CAN HOLD OUT HERE? IT WAS BAD ENOUGH BEFORE WE LET THE HAJJIS IN...
HOLY CHRIST. THEY'RE RUSSIANS.
MEANING THEY'VE BEEN DEAD A LOT LONGER. YOU SEE IT...THEY'RE MOVING SLOWER. IT SHOULD BUY US SOME TIME.
HOW MUCH TIME? YOU KNOW HOW MANY WARS HAVE BEEN FOUGHT HERE? DO YOU THINK THEY'LL EVER STOP COMING?
REDDICK'S RIGHT. THIS OUTPOST IS A DEATH TRAP.
THAT'S WHY WE'RE LETTING THEM IN.

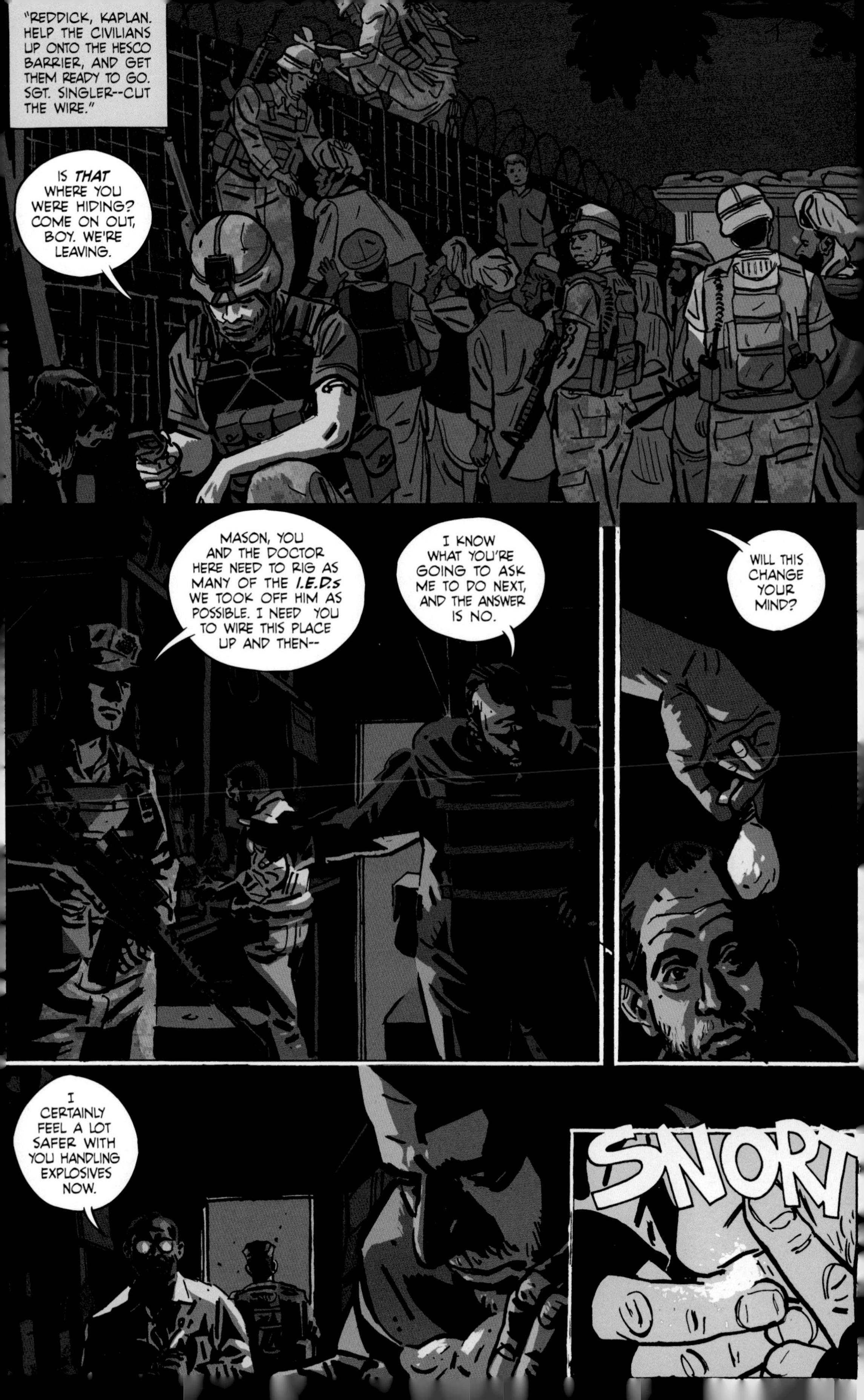
"REDDICK, KAPLAN. HELP THE CIVILIANS UP ONTO THE HESCO BARRIER, AND GET THEM READY TO GO. SGT. SINGLER--CUT THE WIRE."
IS *THAT* WHERE YOU WERE HIDING? COME ON OUT, BOY. WE'RE LEAVING.
MASON, YOU AND THE DOCTOR HERE NEED TO RIG AS MANY OF THE *I.E.D.s* WE TOOK OFF HIM AS POSSIBLE. I NEED YOU TO WIRE THIS PLACE UP AND THEN--
I KNOW WHAT YOU'RE GOING TO ASK ME TO DO NEXT, AND THE ANSWER IS NO.
WILL THIS CHANGE YOUR MIND?
I CERTAINLY FEEL A LOT SAFER WITH YOU HANDLING EXPLOSIVES NOW.
SNORT

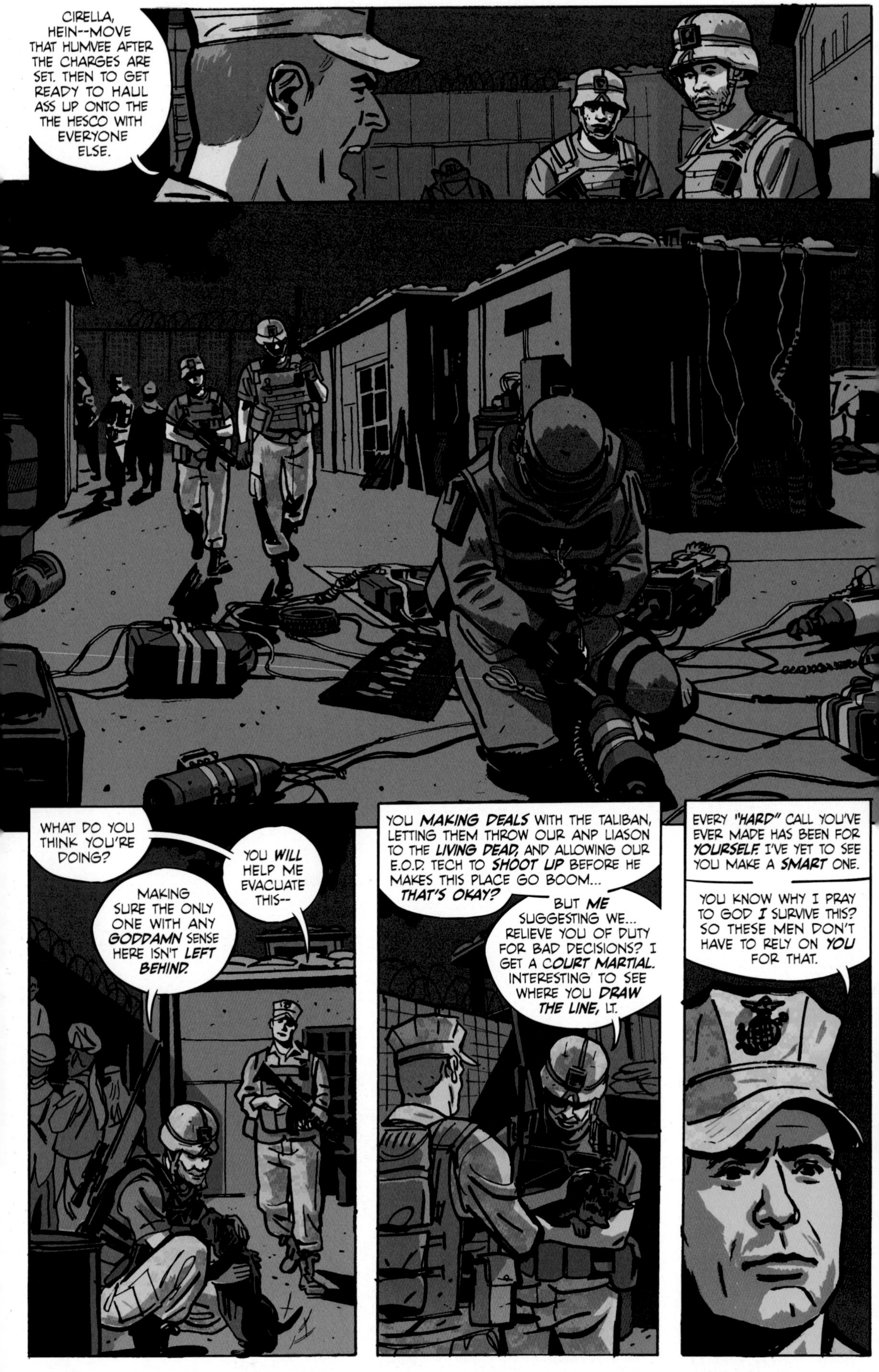
CIRELLA, HEIN--MOVE THAT HUMVEE AFTER THE CHARGES ARE SET. THEN TO GET READY TO HAUL ASS UP ONTO THE THE HESCO WITH EVERYONE ELSE.
WHAT DO YOU THINK YOU'RE DOING?
YOU *WILL* HELP ME EVACUATE THIS--
MAKING SURE THE ONLY ONE WITH ANY *GODDAMN* SENSE HERE ISN'T *LEFT BEHIND.*
YOU *MAKING DEALS* WITH THE TALIBAN, LETTING THEM THROW OUR ANP LIASON TO THE *LIVING DEAD,* AND ALLOWING OUR E.O.D. TECH TO *SHOOT UP* BEFORE HE MAKES THIS PLACE GO BOOM... *THAT'S OKAY?*
BUT *ME* SUGGESTING WE... RELIEVE YOU OF DUTY FOR BAD DECISIONS? I GET A *COURT MARTIAL.* INTERESTING TO SEE WHERE YOU *DRAW THE LINE,* LT.
EVERY *"HARD"* CALL YOU'VE EVER MADE HAS BEEN FOR *YOURSELF.* I'VE YET TO SEE YOU MAKE A *SMART* ONE.
YOU KNOW WHY I PRAY TO GOD *I* SURVIVE THIS? SO THESE MEN DON'T HAVE TO RELY ON *YOU* FOR THAT.

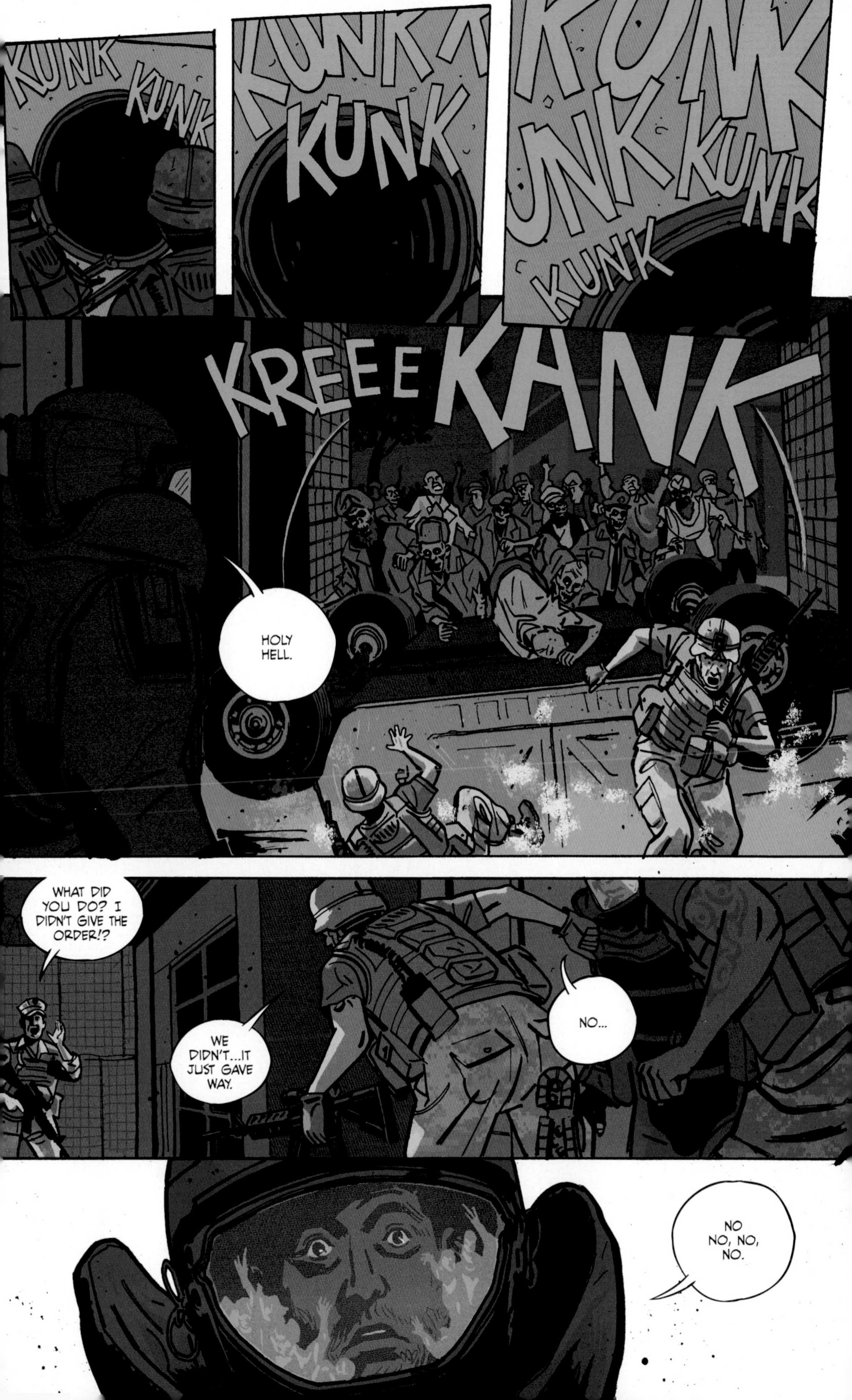
KUNK
KUNK
KUNK
KUNK
KUNK
KUNK
KUNK
KREEEKANK
HOLY HELL.
WHAT DID YOU DO? I DIDN'T GIVE THE ORDER!?
WE DIDN'T...IT JUST GAVE WAY.
NO...
NO NO, NO, NO.

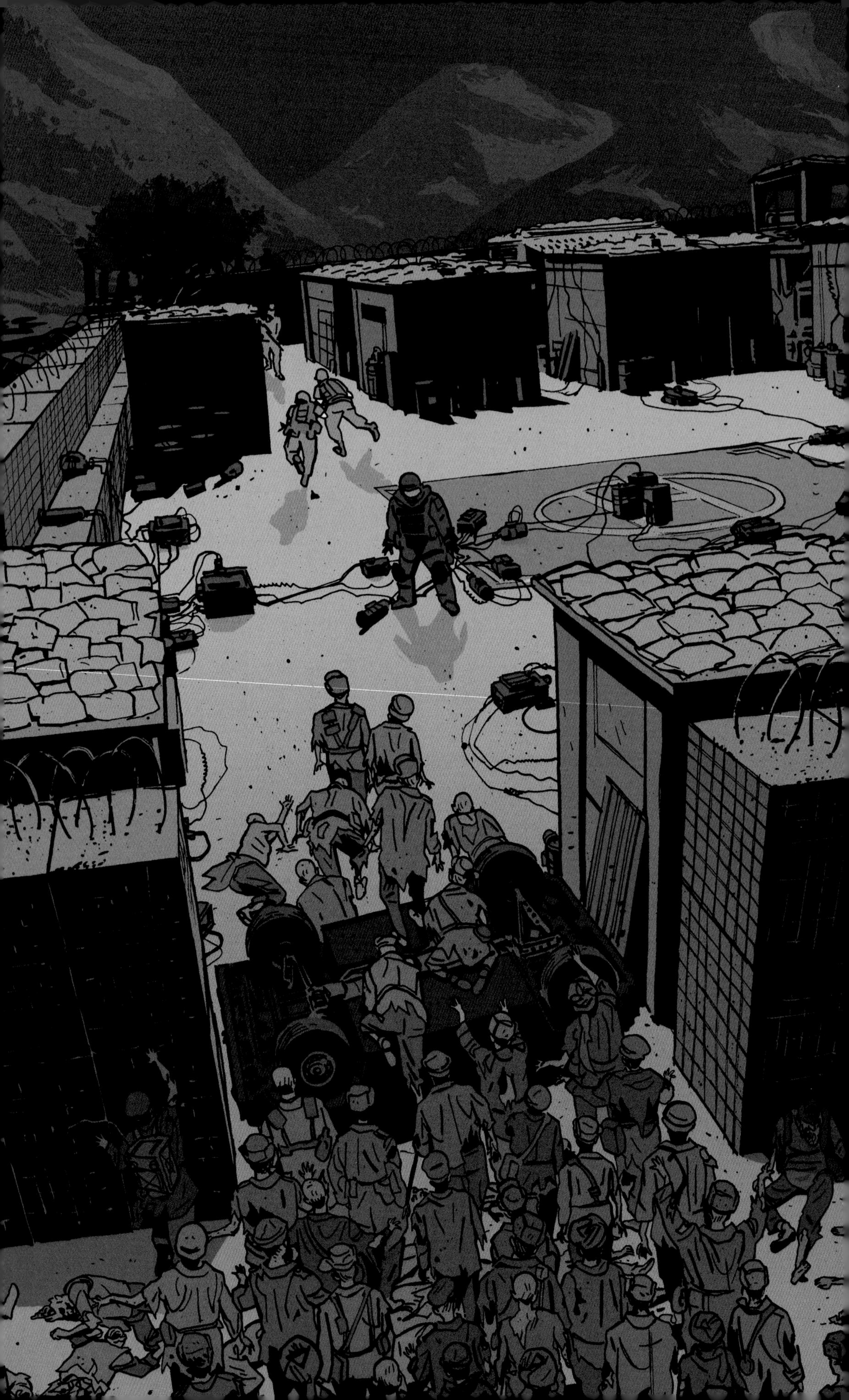

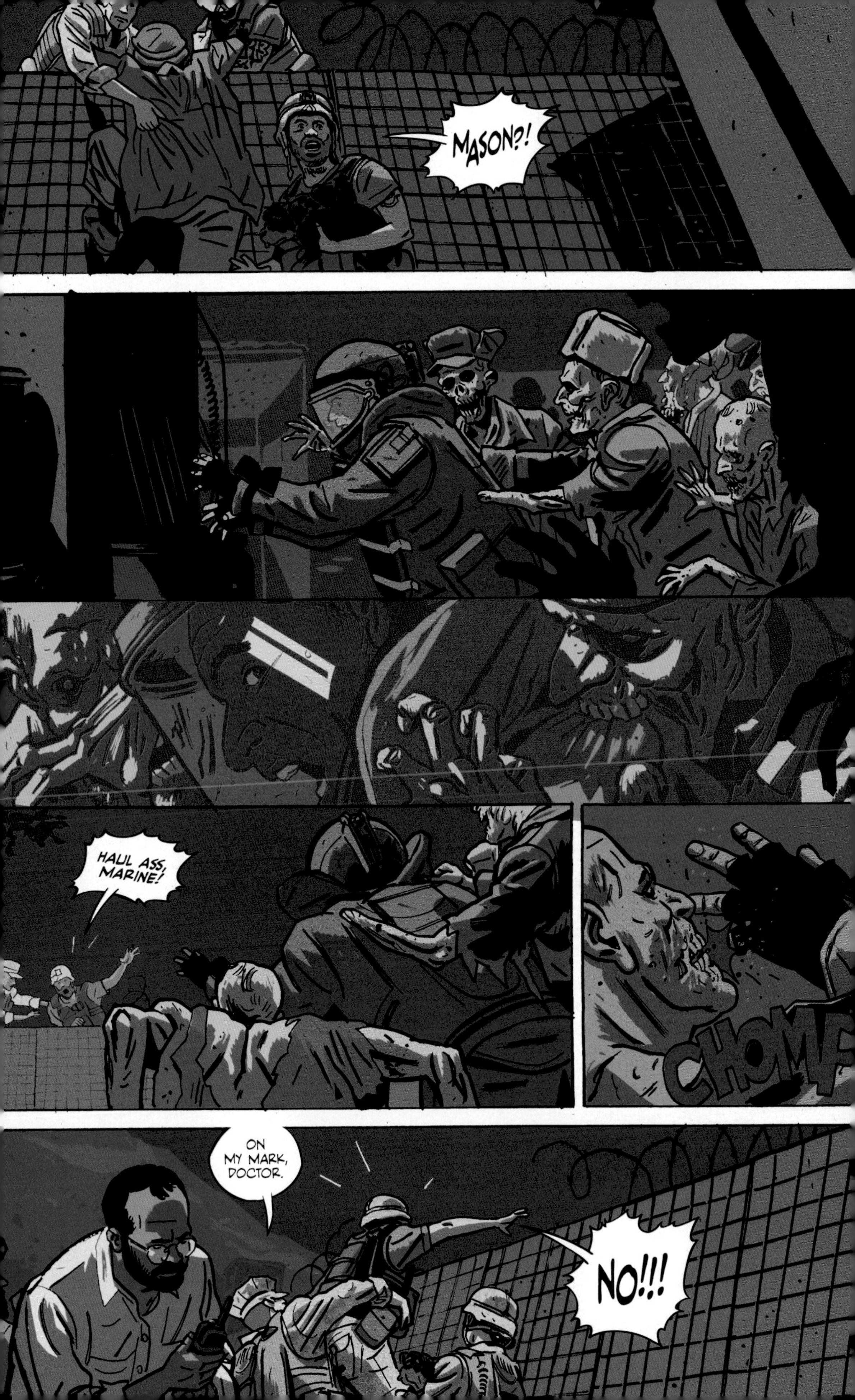
MASON?!
HAUL ASS, MARINE!
CHOMP
ON MY MARK, DOCTOR.
NO!!!

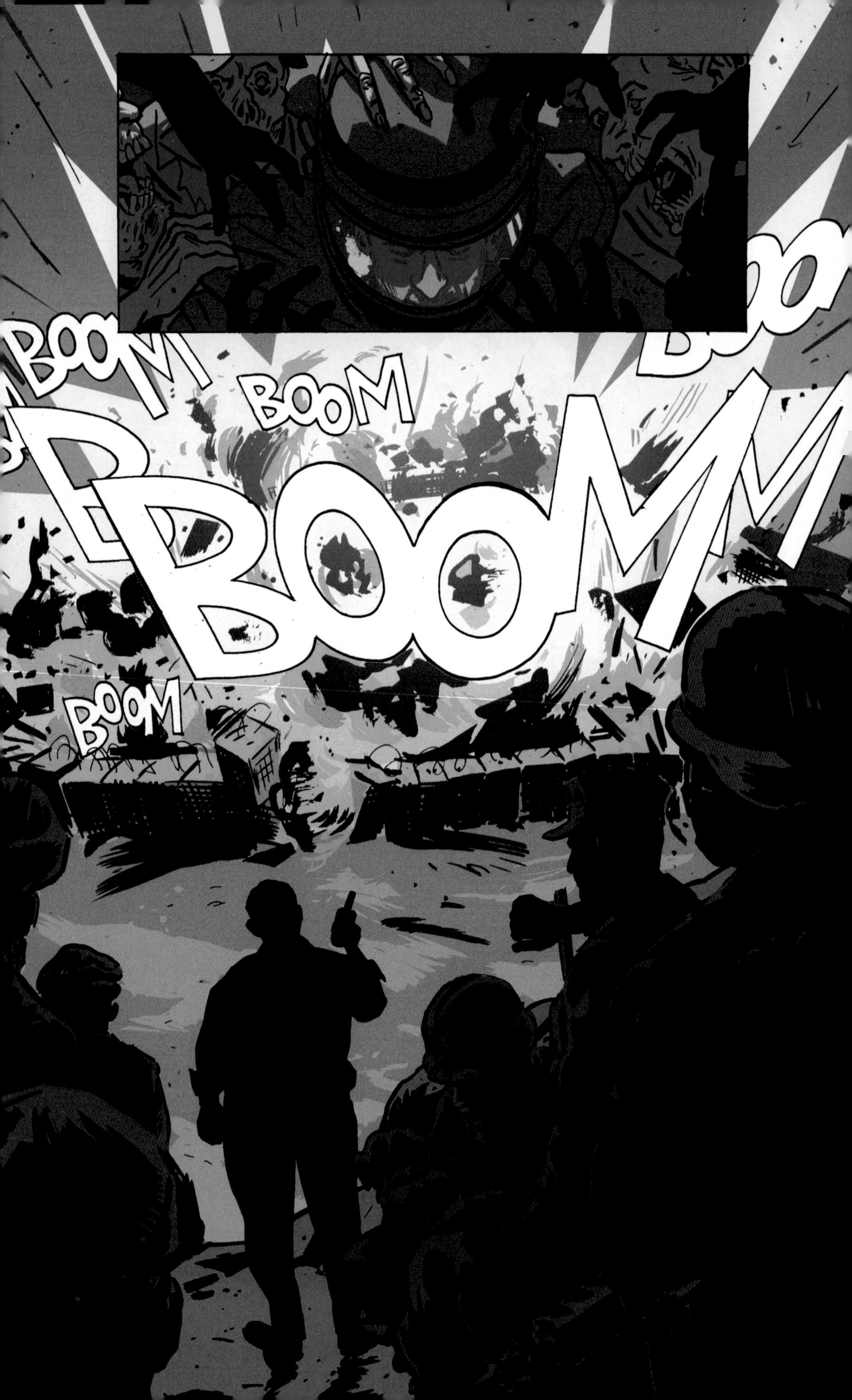
BOOM
BOOM
BOOM
BOOM
BOOM
BOOM

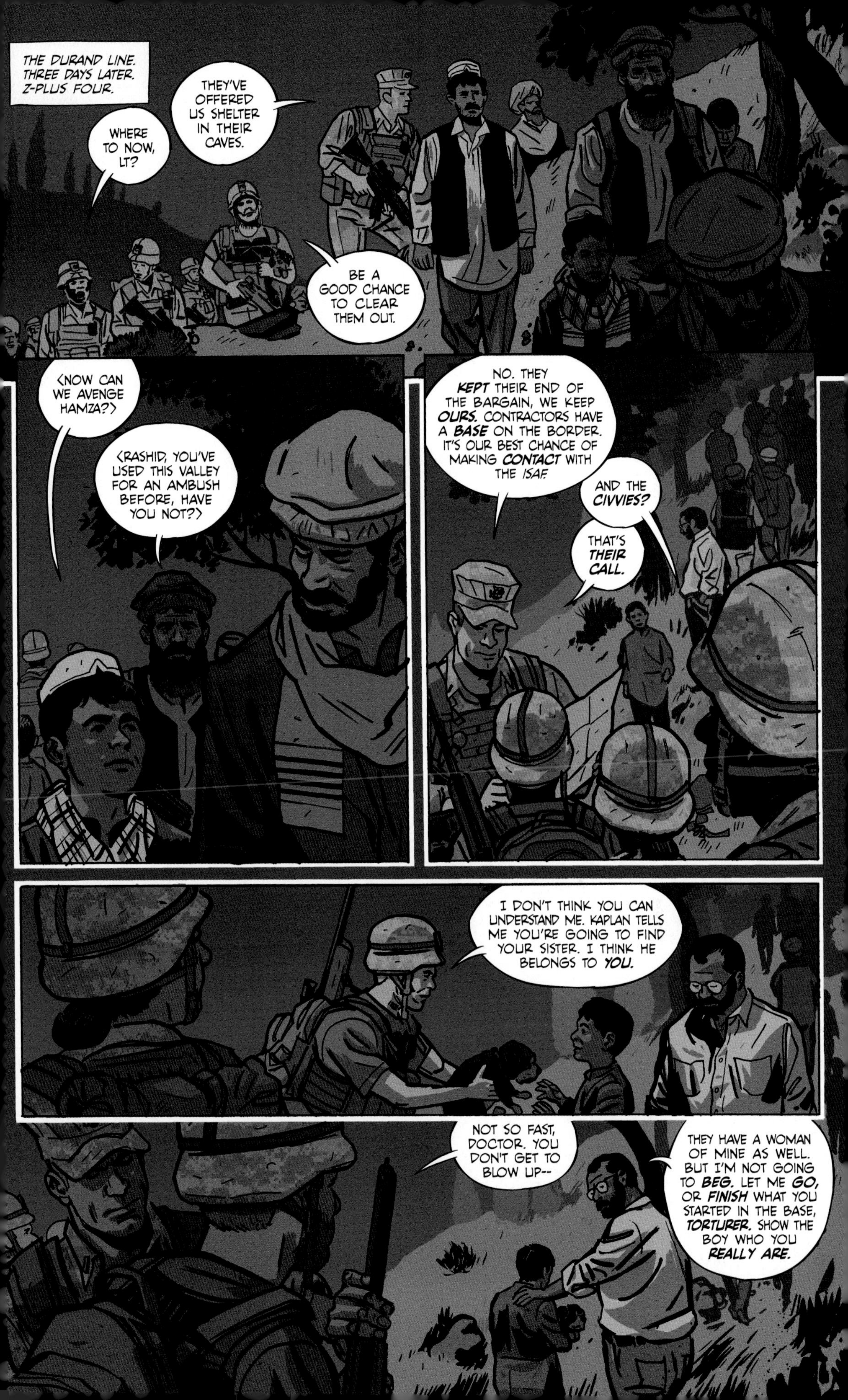
THE DURAND LINE. THREE DAYS LATER. Z-PLUS FOUR.
WHERE TO NOW, LT?
THEY'VE OFFERED US SHELTER IN THEIR CAVES.
BE A GOOD CHANCE TO CLEAR THEM OUT.
<NOW CAN WE AVENGE HAMZA?>
<RASHID, YOU'VE USED THIS VALLEY FOR AN AMBUSH BEFORE, HAVE YOU NOT?>
NO. THEY KEPT THEIR END OF THE BARGAIN, WE KEEP OURS. CONTRACTORS HAVE A BASE ON THE BORDER. IT'S OUR BEST CHANCE OF MAKING CONTACT WITH THE ISAF.
AND THE CIVVIES?
THAT'S THEIR CALL.
I DON'T THINK YOU CAN UNDERSTAND ME. KAPLAN TELLS ME YOU'RE GOING TO FIND YOUR SISTER. I THINK HE BELONGS TO YOU.
NOT SO FAST, DOCTOR. YOU DON'T GET TO BLOW UP--
THEY HAVE A WOMAN OF MINE AS WELL. BUT I'M NOT GOING TO BEG. LET ME GO, OR FINISH WHAT YOU STARTED IN THE BASE, TORTURER. SHOW THE BOY WHO YOU REALLY ARE.

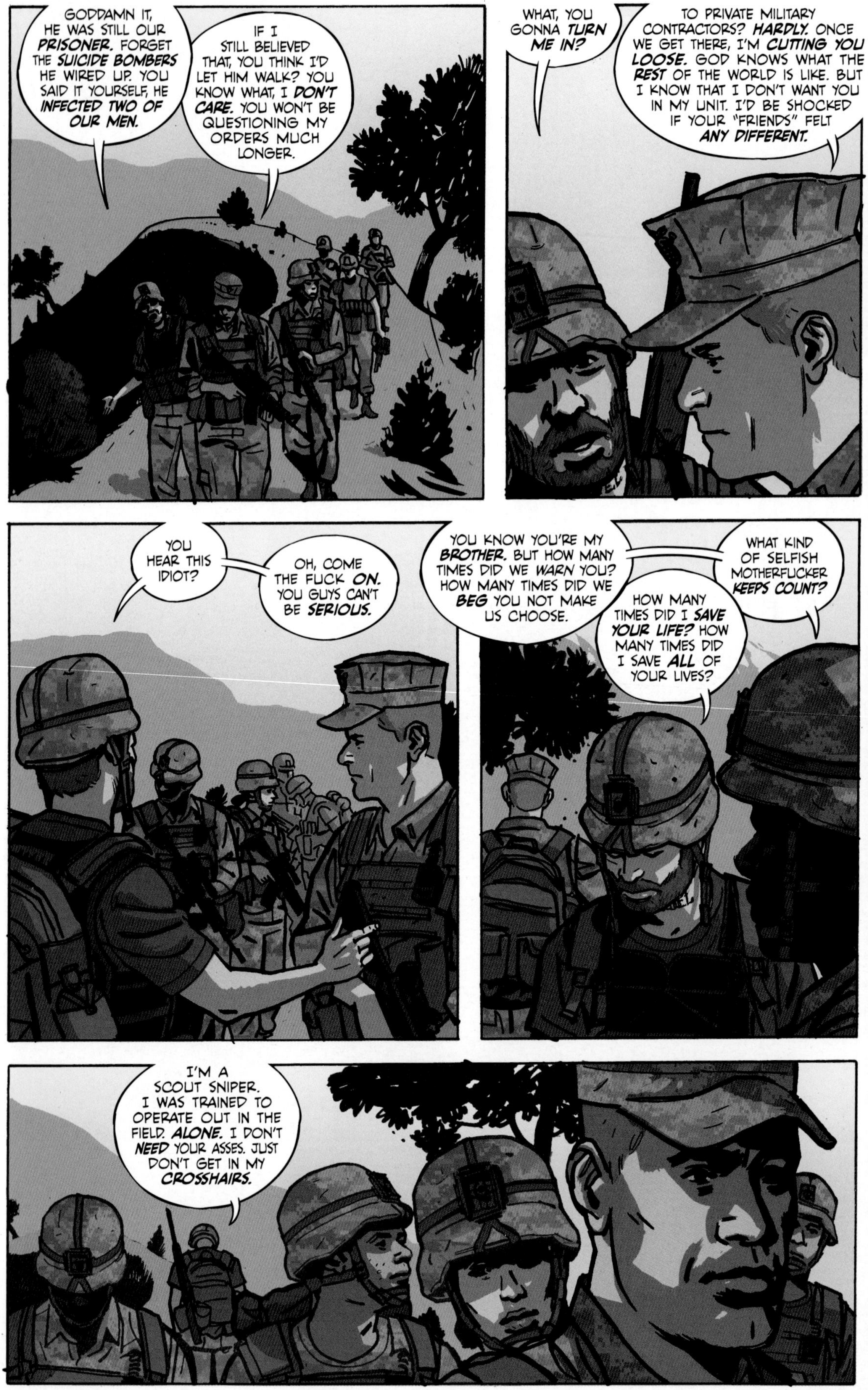
GODDAMN IT, HE WAS STILL OUR PRISONER. FORGET THE SUICIDE BOMBERS HE WIRED UP. YOU SAID IT YOURSELF, HE INFECTED TWO OF OUR MEN.
IF I STILL BELIEVED THAT, YOU THINK I'D LET HIM WALK? YOU KNOW WHAT, I DON'T CARE. YOU WON'T BE QUESTIONING MY ORDERS MUCH LONGER.
WHAT, YOU GONNA TURN ME IN?
TO PRIVATE MILITARY CONTRACTORS? HARDLY. ONCE WE GET THERE, I'M CUTTING YOU LOOSE. GOD KNOWS WHAT THE REST OF THE WORLD IS LIKE. BUT I KNOW THAT I DON'T WANT YOU IN MY UNIT. I'D BE SHOCKED IF YOUR "FRIENDS" FELT ANY DIFFERENT.
YOU HEAR THIS IDIOT?
OH, COME THE FUCK ON. YOU GUYS CAN'T BE SERIOUS.
YOU KNOW YOU'RE MY BROTHER. BUT HOW MANY TIMES DID WE WARN YOU? HOW MANY TIMES DID WE BEG YOU NOT MAKE US CHOOSE.
WHAT KIND OF SELFISH MOTHERFUCKER KEEPS COUNT?
HOW MANY TIMES DID I SAVE YOUR LIFE? HOW MANY TIMES DID I SAVE ALL OF YOUR LIVES?
I'M A SCOUT SNIPER. I WAS TRAINED TO OPERATE OUT IN THE FIELD. ALONE. I DON'T NEED YOUR ASSES. JUST DON'T GET IN MY CROSSHAIRS.

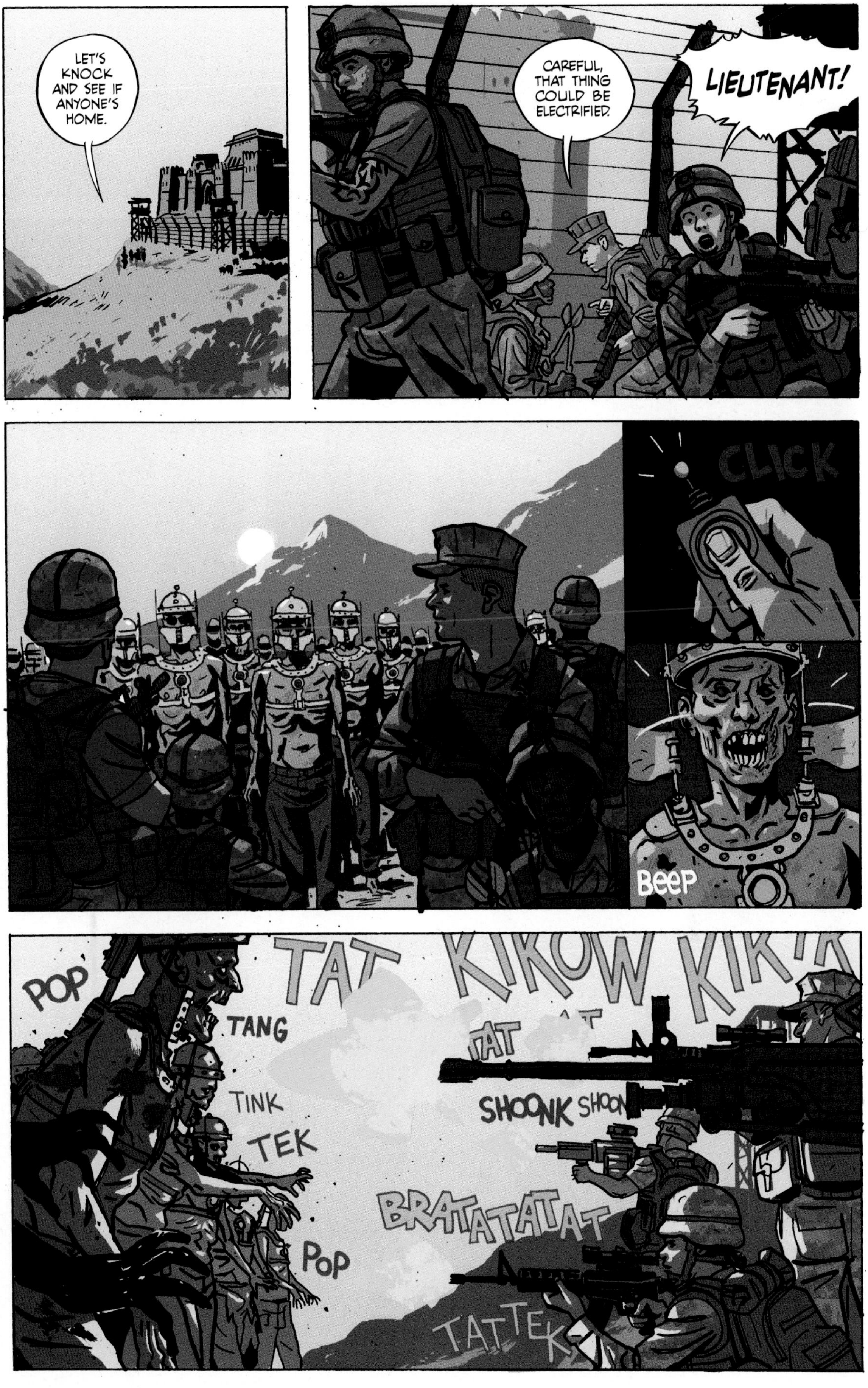
LET'S KNOCK AND SEE IF ANYONE'S HOME.
CAREFUL, THAT THING COULD BE ELECTRIFIED.
LIEUTENANT!
CLICK
BEEP
POP
TAT
KIKOW
TANG
TAT
TINK
SHOONK
TEK
BRATATATAT
POP

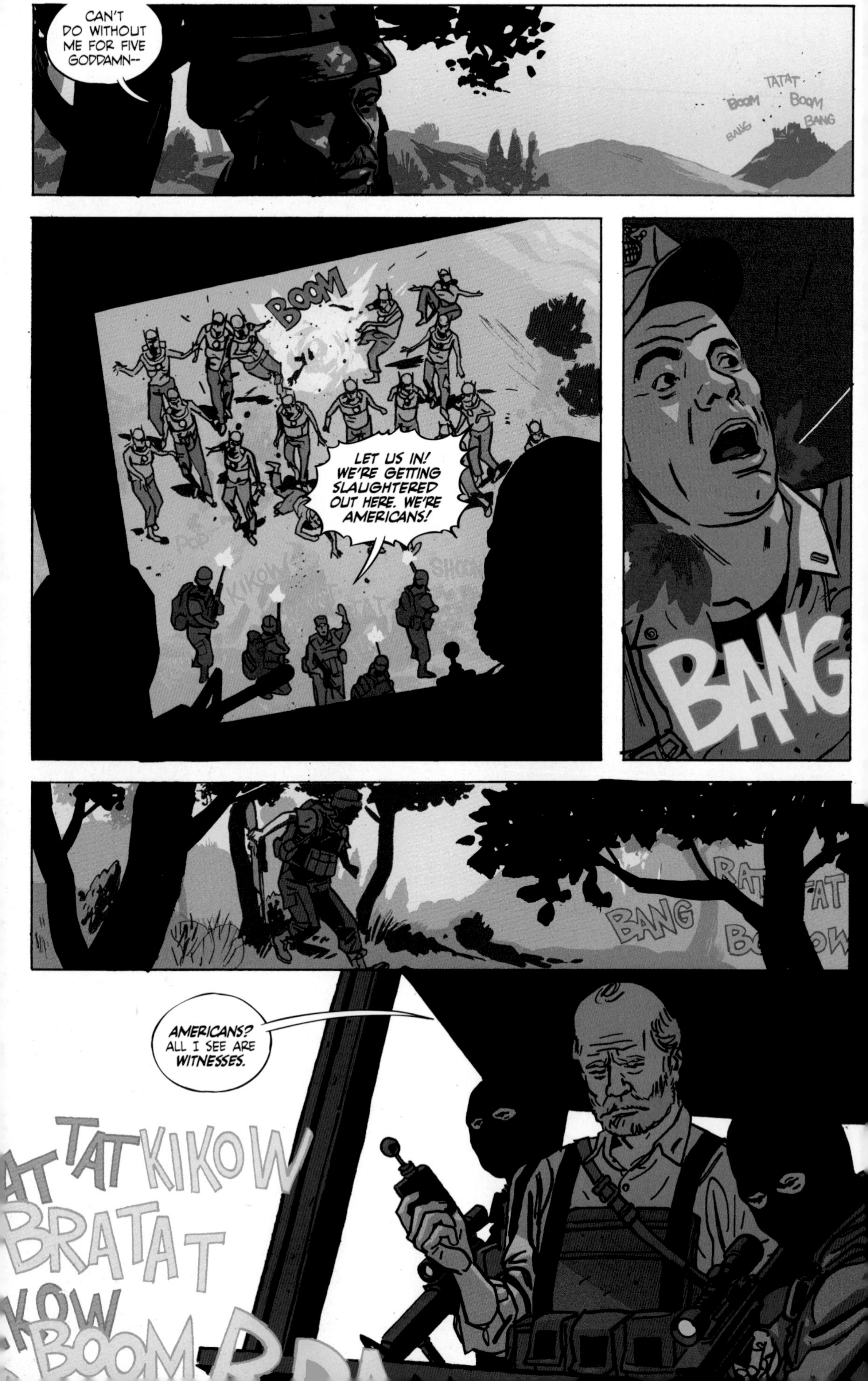
CAN'T DO WITHOUT ME FOR FIVE GODDAMN--
TATAT
BOOM
BOOM
BANG
BANG
BOOM
LET US IN! WE'RE GETTING SLAUGHTERED OUT HERE. WE'RE AMERICANS!
KIKOW
BANG
BANG
AMERICANS? ALL I SEE ARE WITNESSES.
TAT KIKOW
BRATAT
BOOM

CHAPTER 4

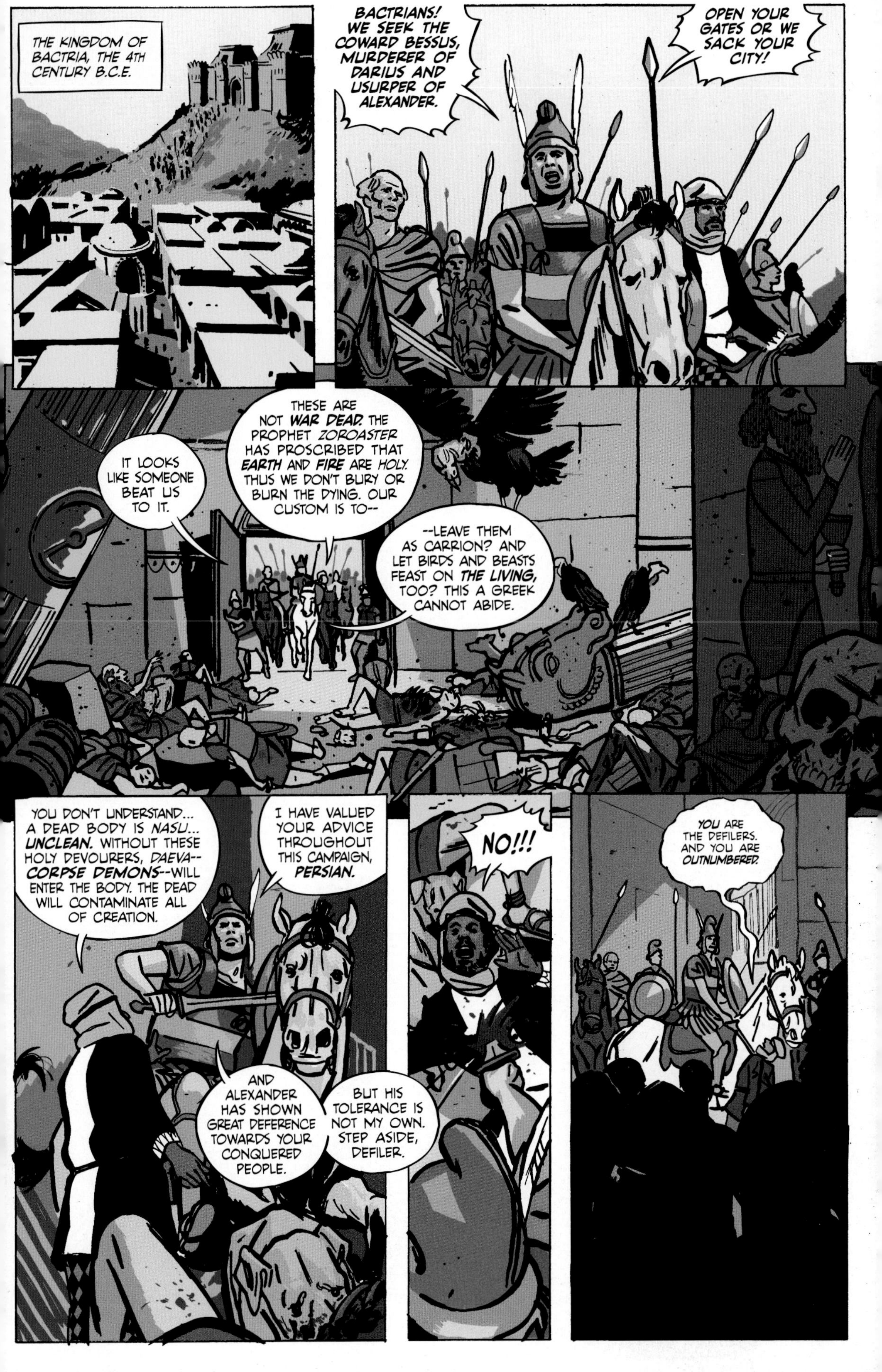
THE KINGDOM OF BACTRIA, THE 4TH CENTURY B.C.E.
BACTRIANS! WE SEEK THE COWARD BESSUS, MURDERER OF DARIUS AND USURPER OF ALEXANDER.
OPEN YOUR GATES OR WE SACK YOUR CITY!
IT LOOKS LIKE SOMEONE BEAT US TO IT.
THESE ARE NOT WAR DEAD. THE PROPHET ZOROASTER HAS PROSCRIBED THAT EARTH AND FIRE ARE HOLY. THUS WE DON'T BURY OR BURN THE DYING. OUR CUSTOM IS TO--
--LEAVE THEM AS CARRION? AND LET BIRDS AND BEASTS FEAST ON THE LIVING, TOO? THIS A GREEK CANNOT ABIDE.
YOU DON'T UNDERSTAND... A DEAD BODY IS NASU... UNCLEAN. WITHOUT THESE HOLY DEVOURERS, DAEVA--CORPSE DEMONS--WILL ENTER THE BODY. THE DEAD WILL CONTAMINATE ALL OF CREATION.
I HAVE VALUED YOUR ADVICE THROUGHOUT THIS CAMPAIGN, PERSIAN.
AND ALEXANDER HAS SHOWN GREAT DEFERENCE TOWARDS YOUR CONQUERED PEOPLE.
BUT HIS TOLERANCE IS NOT MY OWN. STEP ASIDE, DEFILER.
NO!!!
YOU ARE THE DEFILERS. AND YOU ARE OUTNUMBERED.

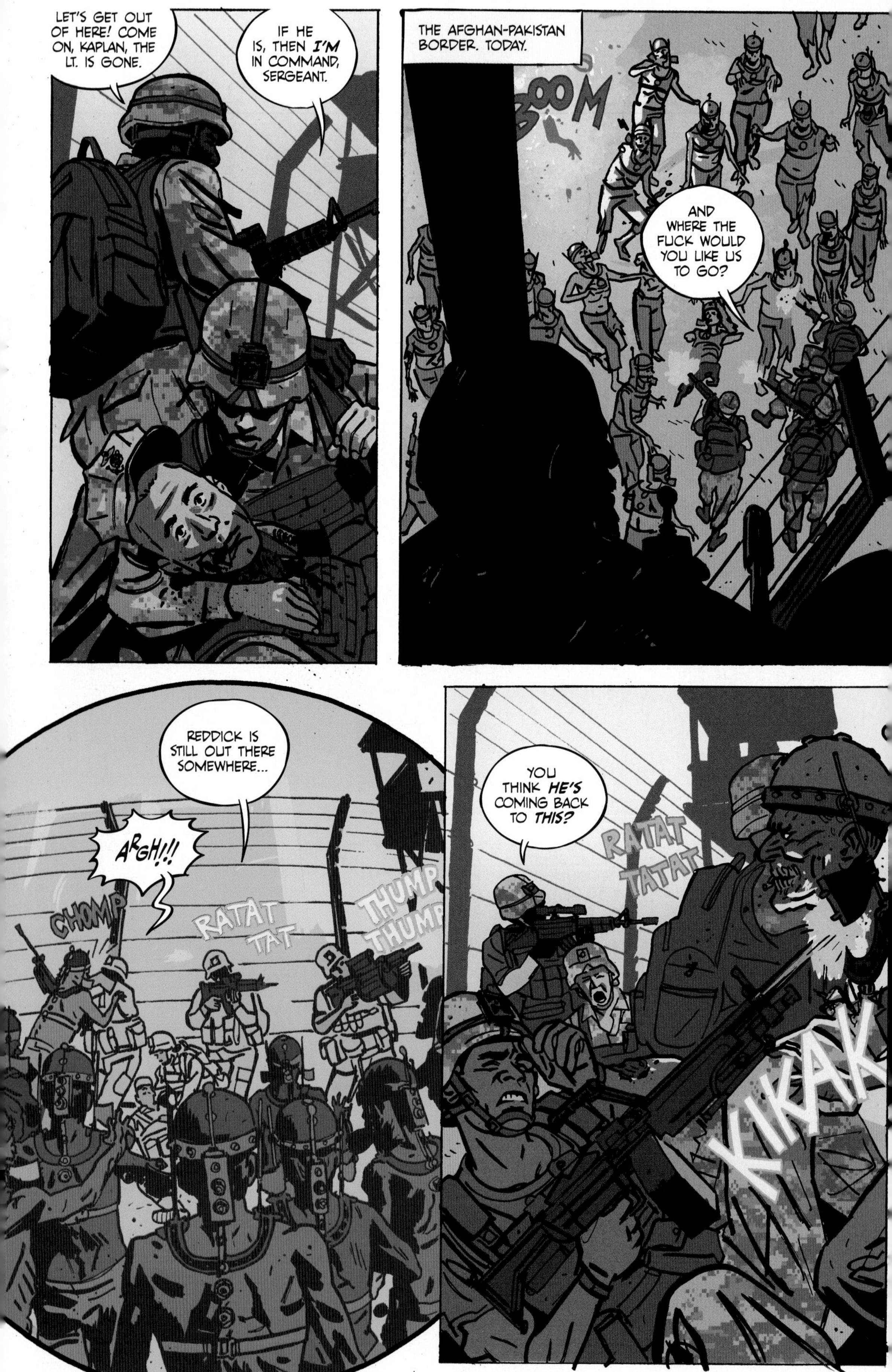

LET'S GET OUT OF HERE! COME ON, KAPLAN, THE LT. IS GONE.
IF HE IS, THEN I'M IN COMMAND, SERGEANT.
THE AFGHAN-PAKISTAN BORDER. TODAY.
BOOM
AND WHERE THE FUCK WOULD YOU LIKE US TO GO?
REDDICK IS STILL OUT THERE SOMEWHERE...
ARGH!!!
CHOMP
RATAT TAT
THUMP THUMP
YOU THINK HE'S COMING BACK TO THIS?
RATAT TATAT
KIKAK

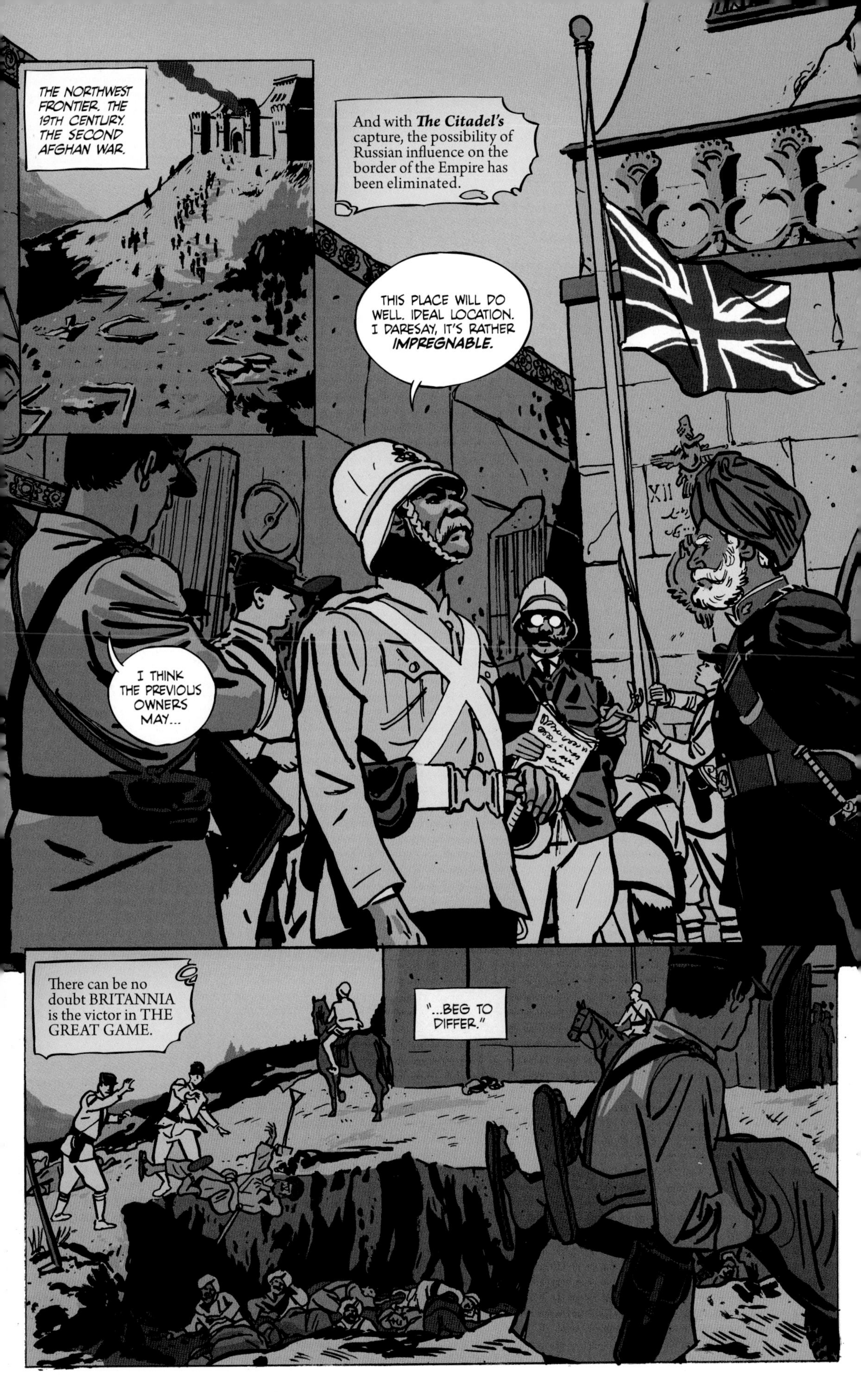
THE NORTHWEST FRONTIER. THE 19TH CENTURY. THE SECOND AFGHAN WAR.
And with The Citadel's capture, the possibility of Russian influence on the border of the Empire has been eliminated.
THIS PLACE WILL DO WELL. IDEAL LOCATION. I DARESAY, IT'S RATHER IMPREGNABLE.
I THINK THE PREVIOUS OWNERS MAY...
There can be no doubt BRITANNIA is the victor in THE GREAT GAME.
"...BEG TO DIFFER."

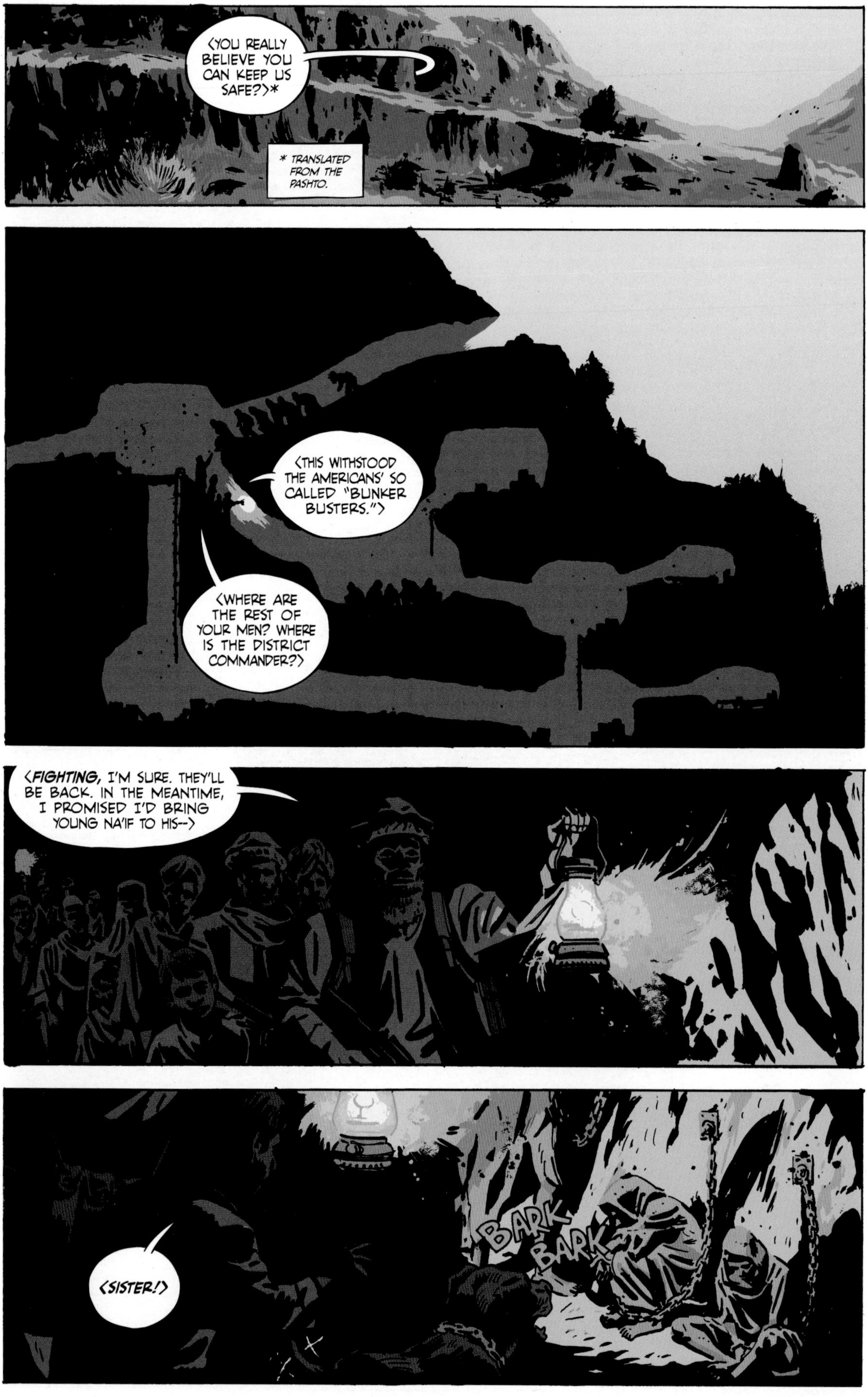

<YOU REALLY BELIEVE YOU CAN KEEP US SAFE?>*
* TRANSLATED FROM THE PASHTO.
<THIS WITHSTOOD THE AMERICANS' SO CALLED "BUNKER BUSTERS.">
<WHERE ARE THE REST OF YOUR MEN? WHERE IS THE DISTRICT COMMANDER?>
<FIGHTING, I'M SURE. THEY'LL BE BACK. IN THE MEANTIME, I PROMISED I'D BRING YOUNG NA'IF TO HIS-->
BARK BARK
<SISTER!>

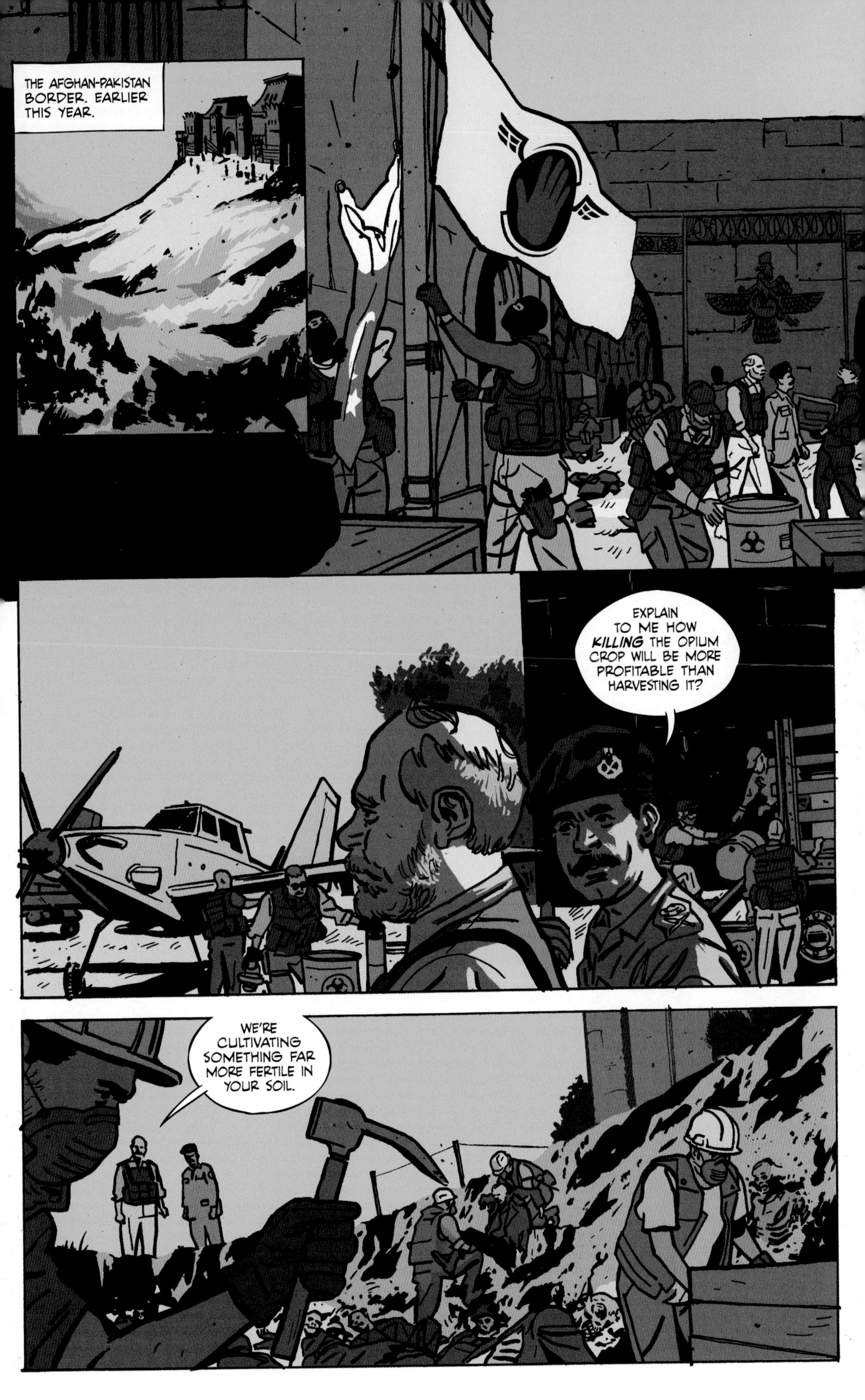
THE AFGHAN-PAKISTAN BORDER. EARLIER THIS YEAR.
EXPLAIN TO ME HOW KILLING THE OPIUM CROP WILL BE MORE PROFITABLE THAN HARVESTING IT?
WE'RE CULTIVATING SOMETHING FAR MORE FERTILE IN YOUR SOIL.

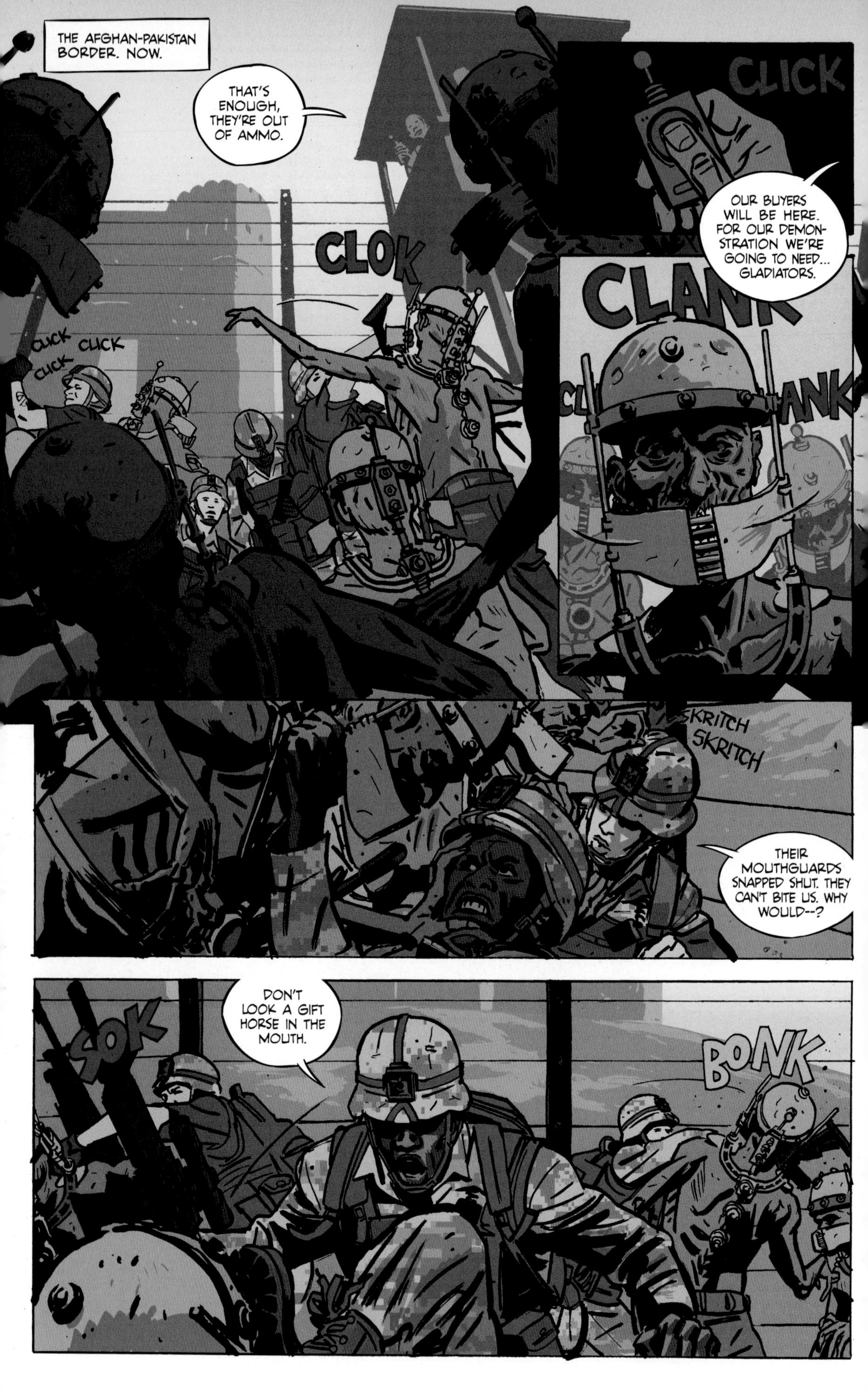
THE AFGHAN-PAKISTAN BORDER. NOW.
THAT'S ENOUGH, THEY'RE OUT OF AMMO.
CLOK
CLICK CLICK CLICK
CLICK
OUR BUYERS WILL BE HERE. FOR OUR DEMONSTRATION WE'RE GOING TO NEED... GLADIATORS.
CLANK
SKRITCH SKRITCH
THEIR MOUTHGUARDS SNAPPED SHUT. THEY CAN'T BITE US. WHY WOULD--?
SOK
DON'T LOOK A GIFT HORSE IN THE MOUTH.
BONK

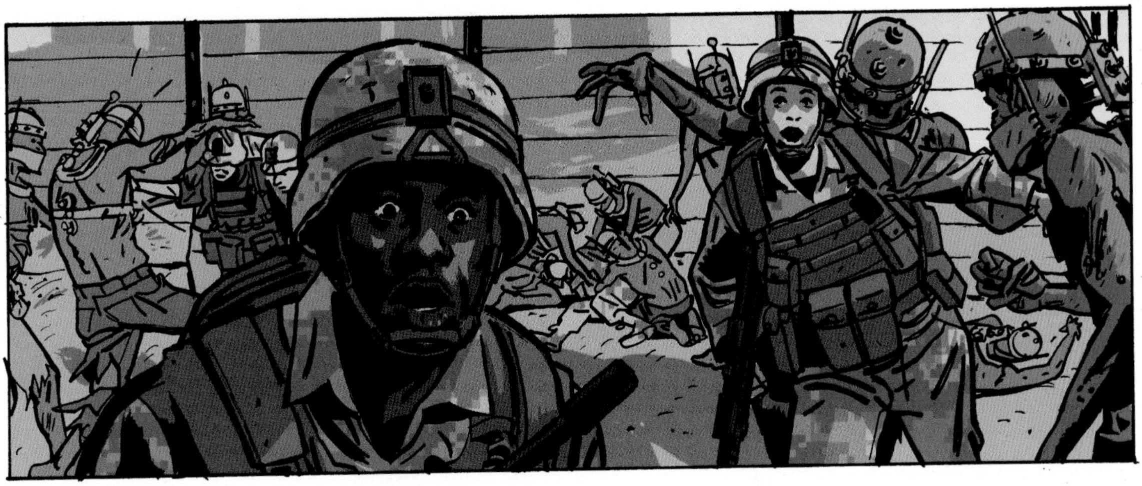

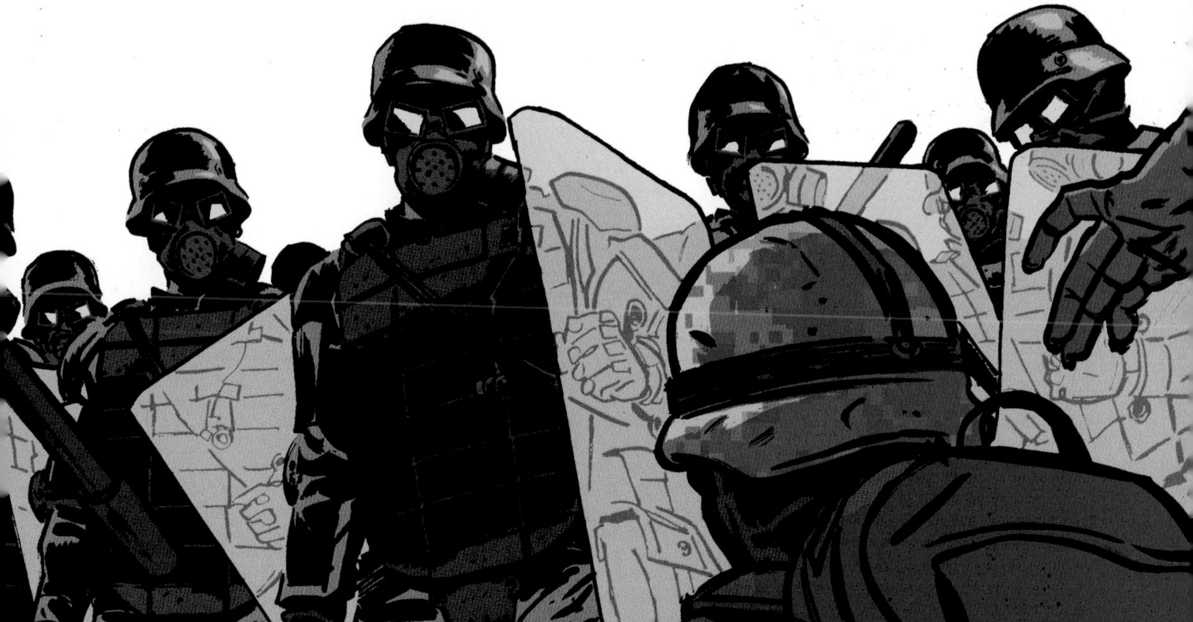

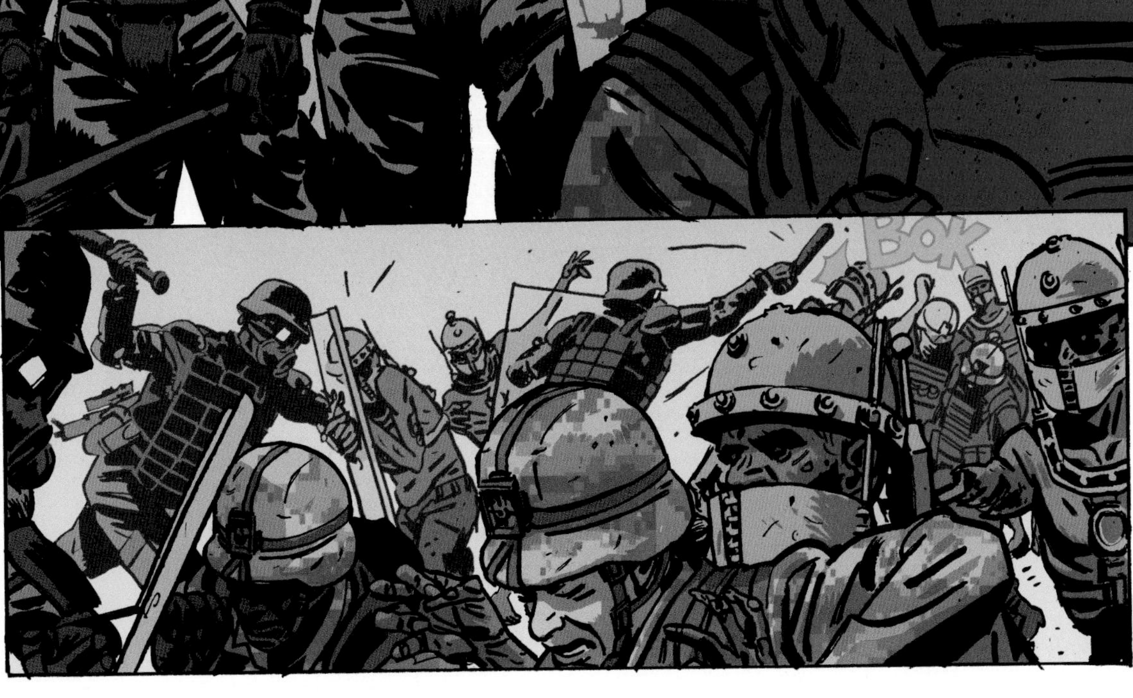
BOK

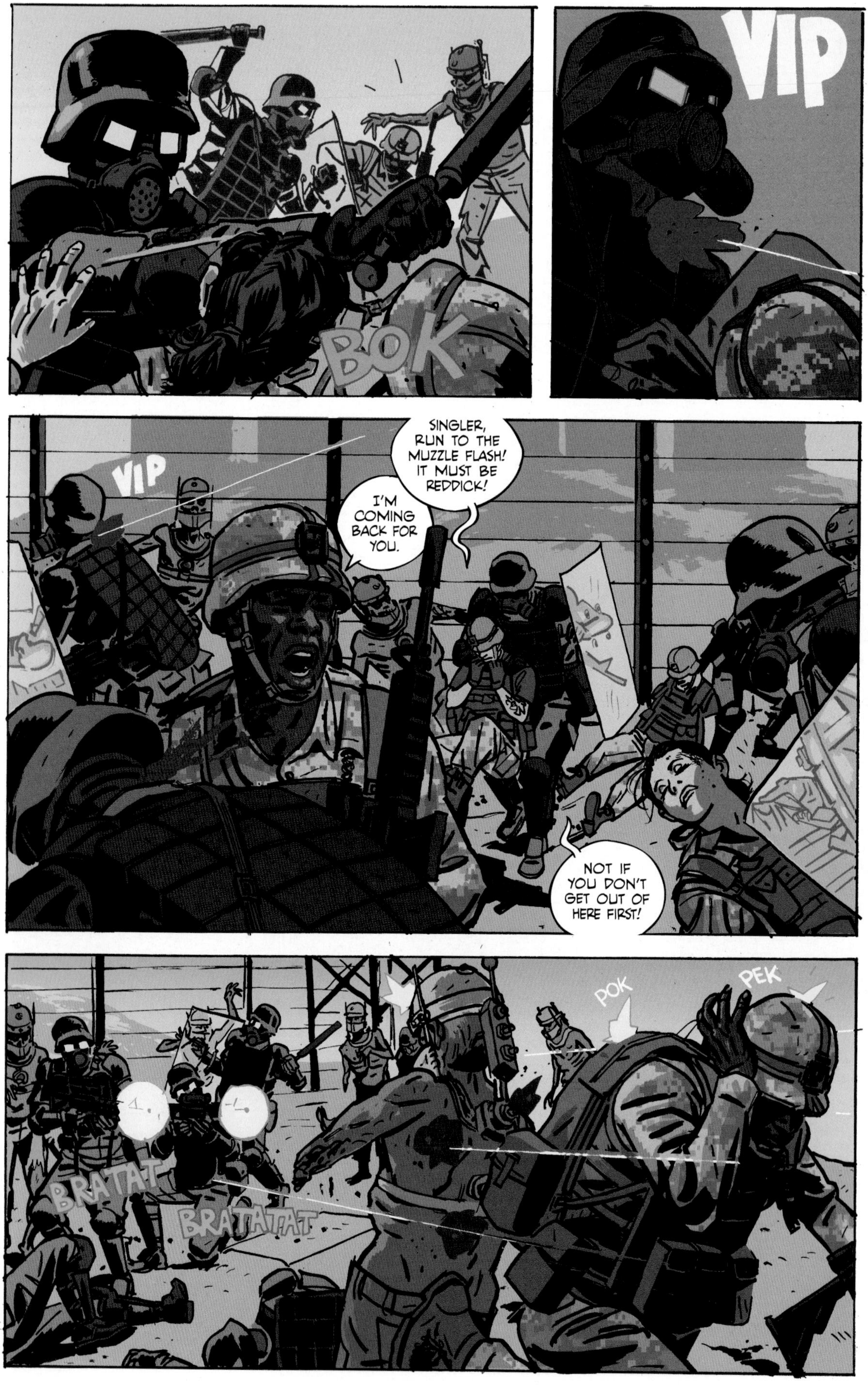
BOK
VIP
VIP
I'M COMING BACK FOR YOU.
SINGLER, RUN TO THE MUZZLE FLASH! IT MUST BE REDDICK!
NOT IF YOU DON'T GET OUT OF HERE FIRST!
POK
PEK
BRATAT
BRATATAT

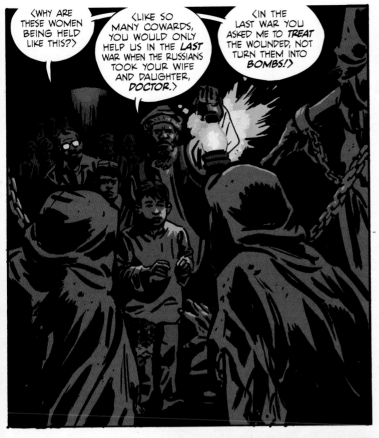

‹WHY ARE THESE WOMEN BEING HELD LIKE THIS?›

‹LIKE SO MANY COWARDS, YOU WOULD ONLY HELP US IN THE *LAST* WAR WHEN THE RUSSIANS TOOK YOUR WIFE AND DAUGHTER, *DOCTOR.*›

‹IN THE LAST WAR YOU ASKED ME TO *TREAT* THE WOUNDED, NOT TURN THEM INTO *BOMBS!*›

‹LET ME GO!›

‹ABDUL, DO AS HE SAYS. I PROMISED NA'IF!›

‹YOU DID NOT NEED TO *CHAIN* THE WOMEN IN MY FAMILY TO ENSURE MY COOPERATION!›

‹I DID NOT KNOW ABOUT THE CHAINS. ALL I CAN ASSUME IS THEY ARE NOT--›

‹BOY, NO!›

GRRRRRR

BARK BARK BARK BARK BARK

‹YOUR SISTER WAS PROMISED TO ME AS A BRIDE!›

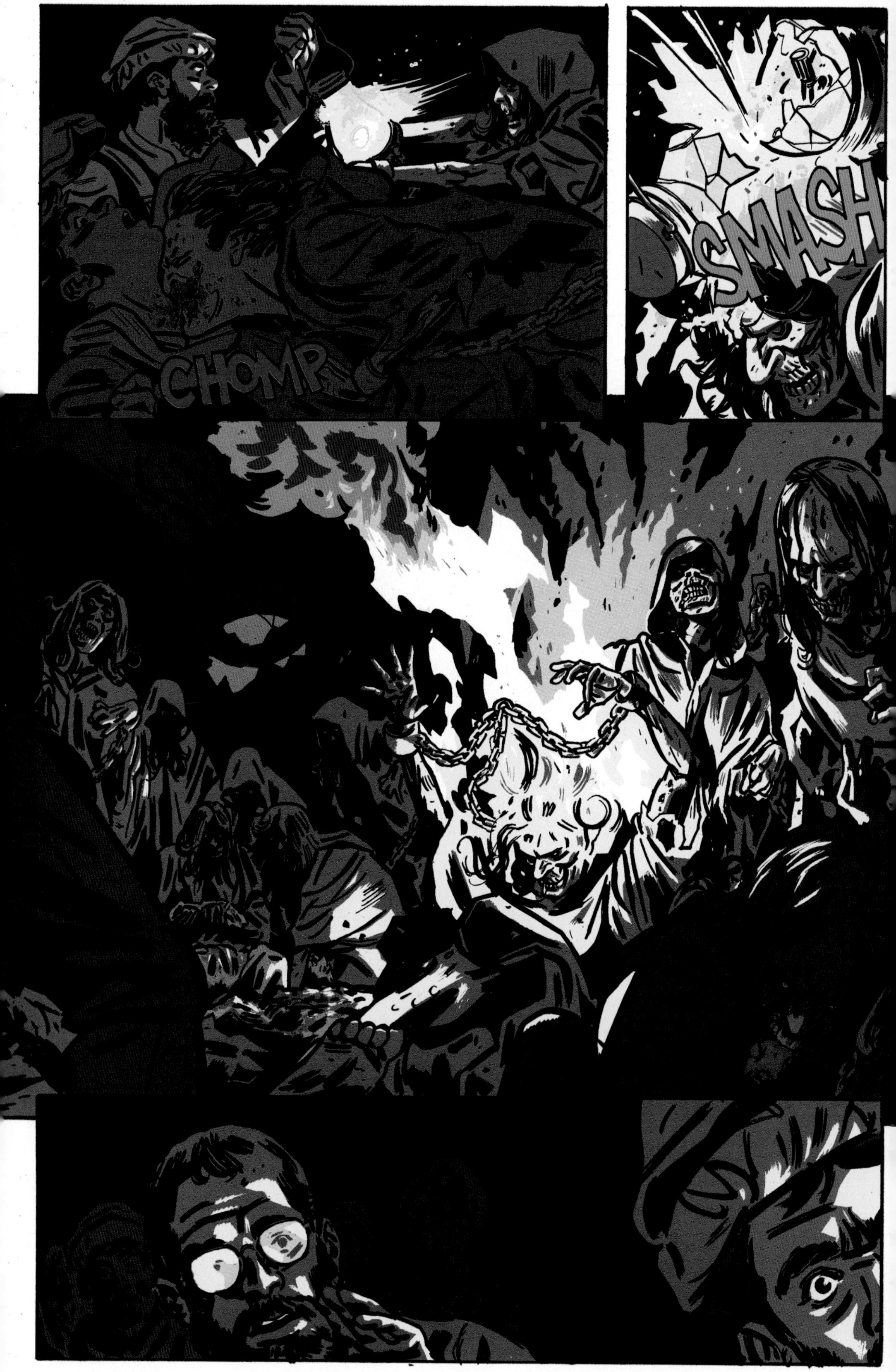
CHOMP
SMASH

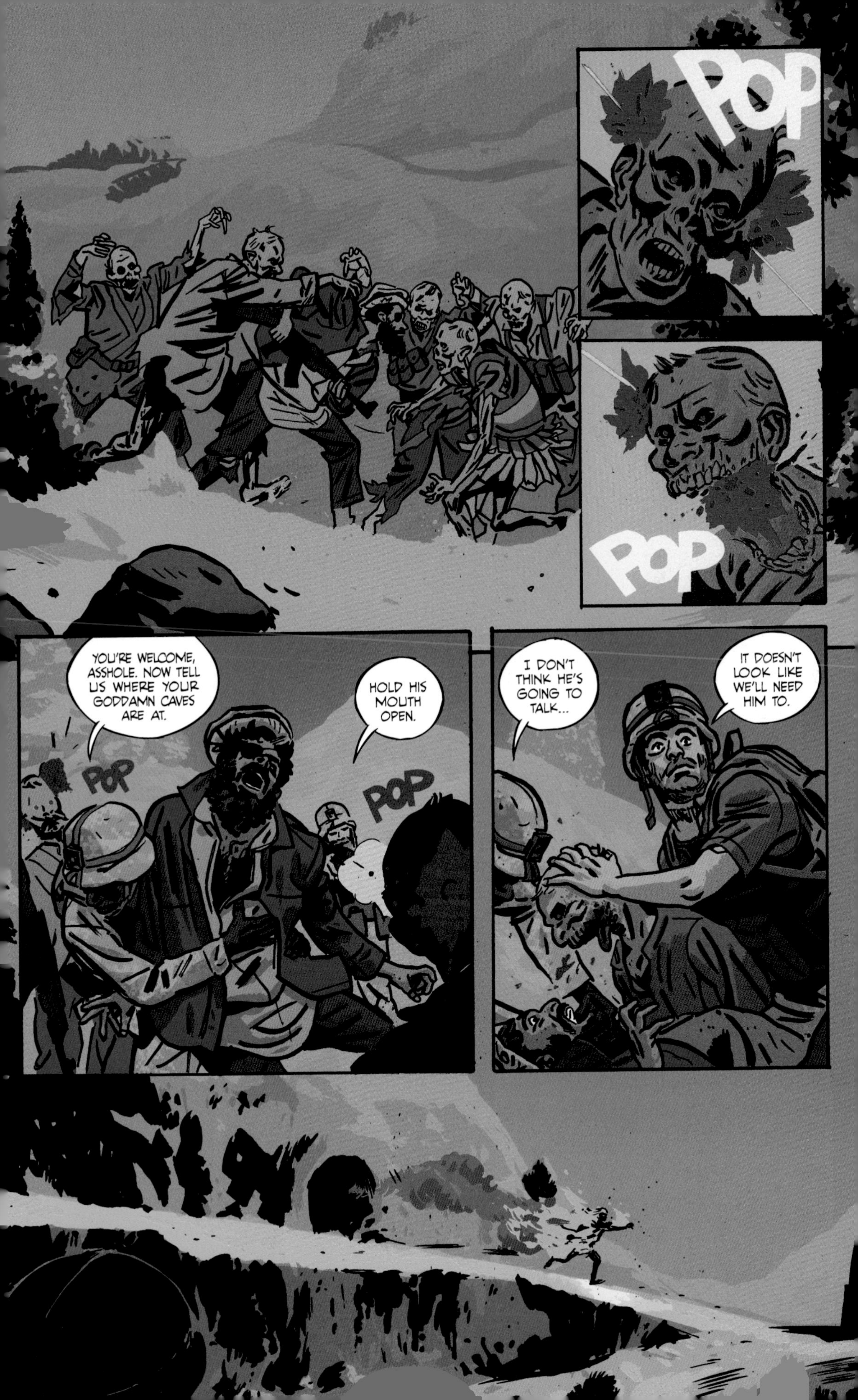
POP
POP
YOU'RE WELCOME, ASSHOLE. NOW TELL US WHERE YOUR GODDAMN CAVES ARE AT.
POP
HOLD HIS MOUTH OPEN.
POP
I DON'T THINK HE'S GOING TO TALK...
IT DOESN'T LOOK LIKE WE'LL NEED HIM TO.

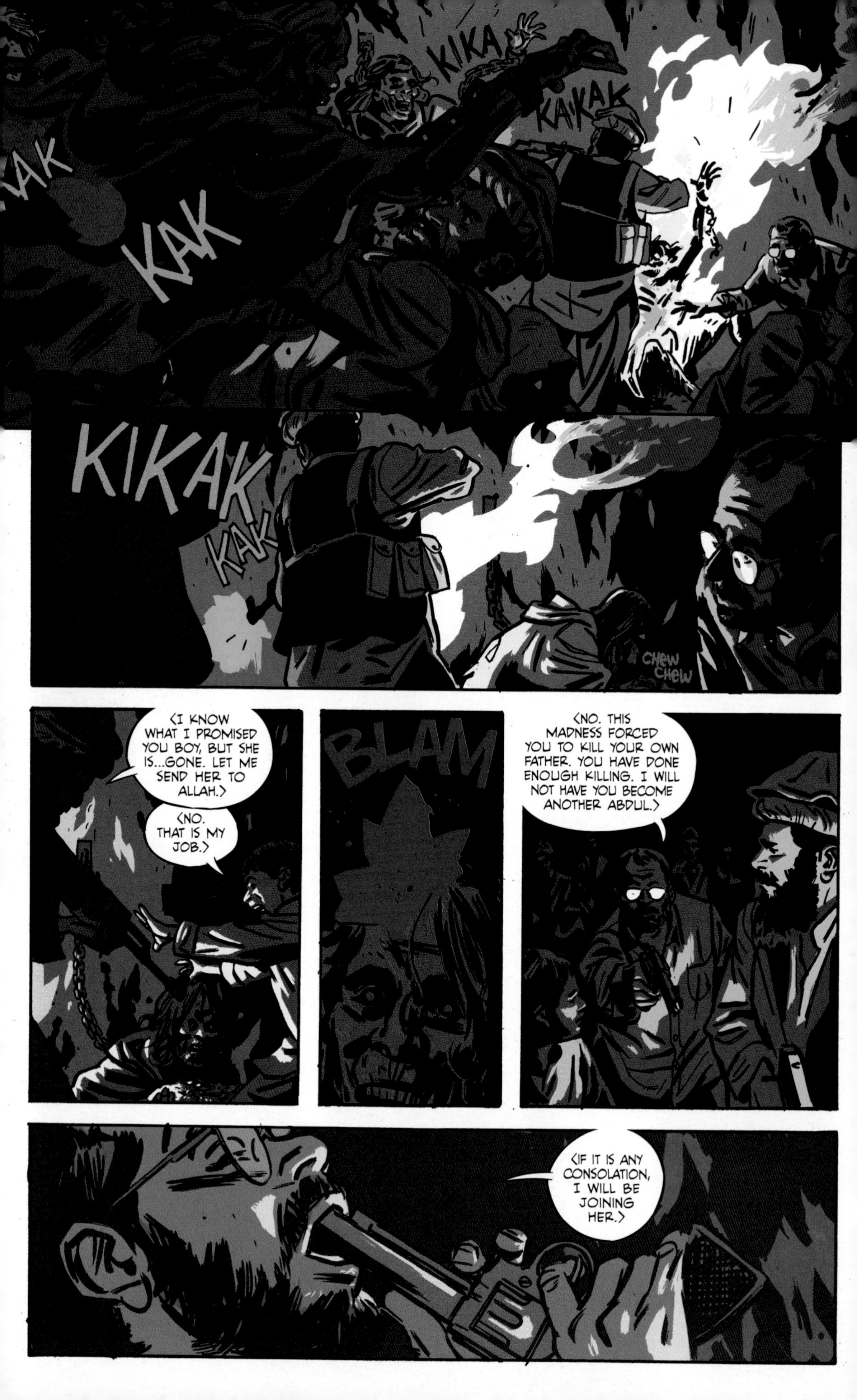
KIKA
KAKAK
KAK
KAK
KIKAK
KAK
CHEW CHEW
<I KNOW WHAT I PROMISED YOU BOY, BUT SHE IS...GONE. LET ME SEND HER TO ALLAH.>
<NO. THAT IS MY JOB.>
BLAM
<NO. THIS MADNESS FORCED YOU TO KILL YOUR OWN FATHER. YOU HAVE DONE ENOUGH KILLING. I WILL NOT HAVE YOU BECOME ANOTHER ABDUL.>
<IF IT IS ANY CONSOLATION, I WILL BE JOINING HER.>

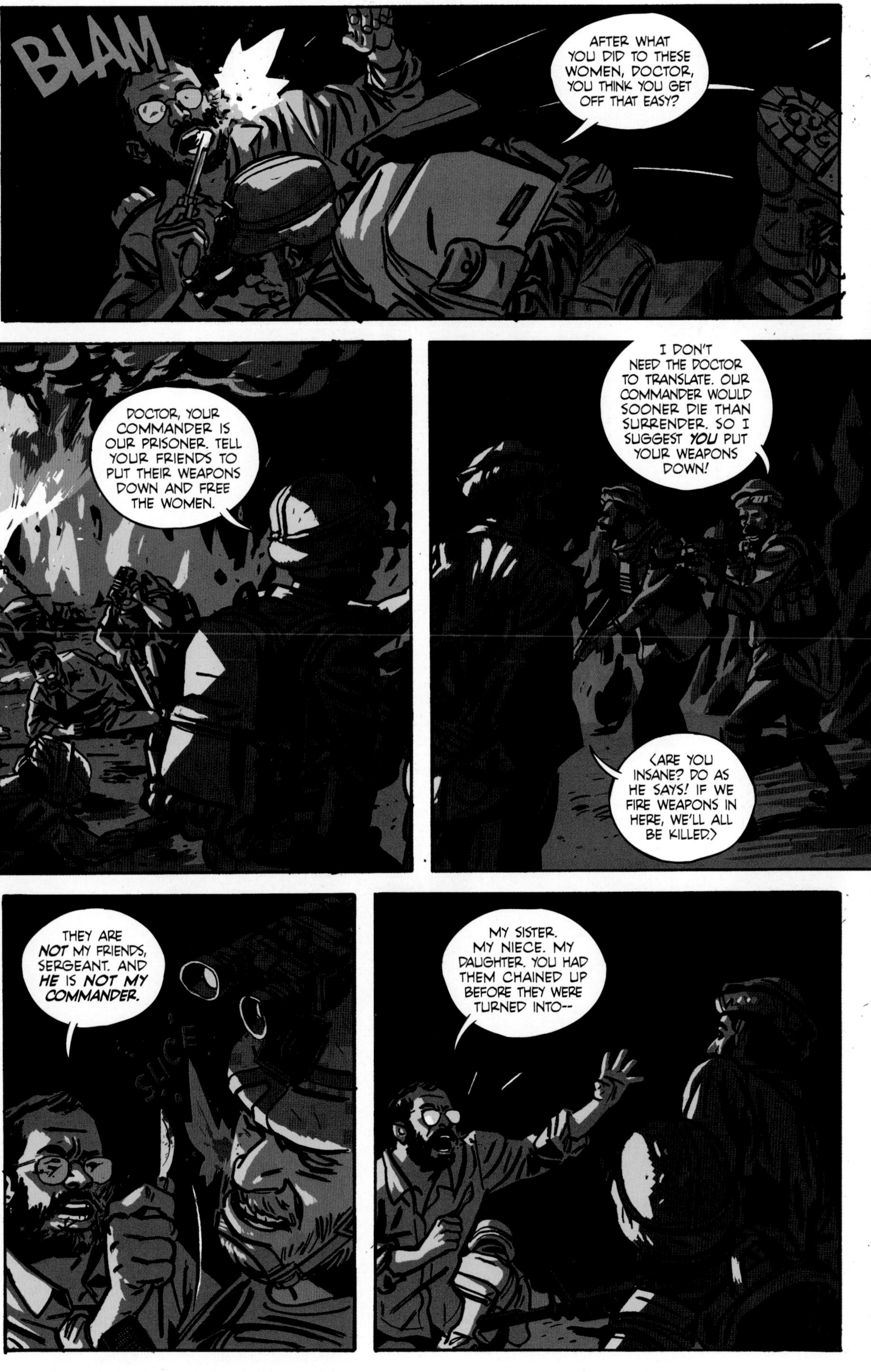
BLAM
AFTER WHAT YOU DID TO THESE WOMEN, DOCTOR, YOU THINK YOU GET OFF THAT EASY?
DOCTOR, YOUR COMMANDER IS OUR PRISONER. TELL YOUR FRIENDS TO PUT THEIR WEAPONS DOWN AND FREE THE WOMEN.
I DON'T NEED THE DOCTOR TO TRANSLATE. OUR COMMANDER WOULD SOONER DIE THAN SURRENDER. SO I SUGGEST *YOU* PUT YOUR WEAPONS DOWN!
<ARE YOU INSANE? DO AS HE SAYS! IF WE FIRE WEAPONS IN HERE, WE'LL ALL BE KILLED.>
THEY ARE *NOT* MY FRIENDS, SERGEANT. AND *HE* IS *NOT MY COMMANDER.*
MY SISTER. MY NIECE. MY DAUGHTER. YOU HAD THEM CHAINED UP BEFORE THEY WERE TURNED INTO--

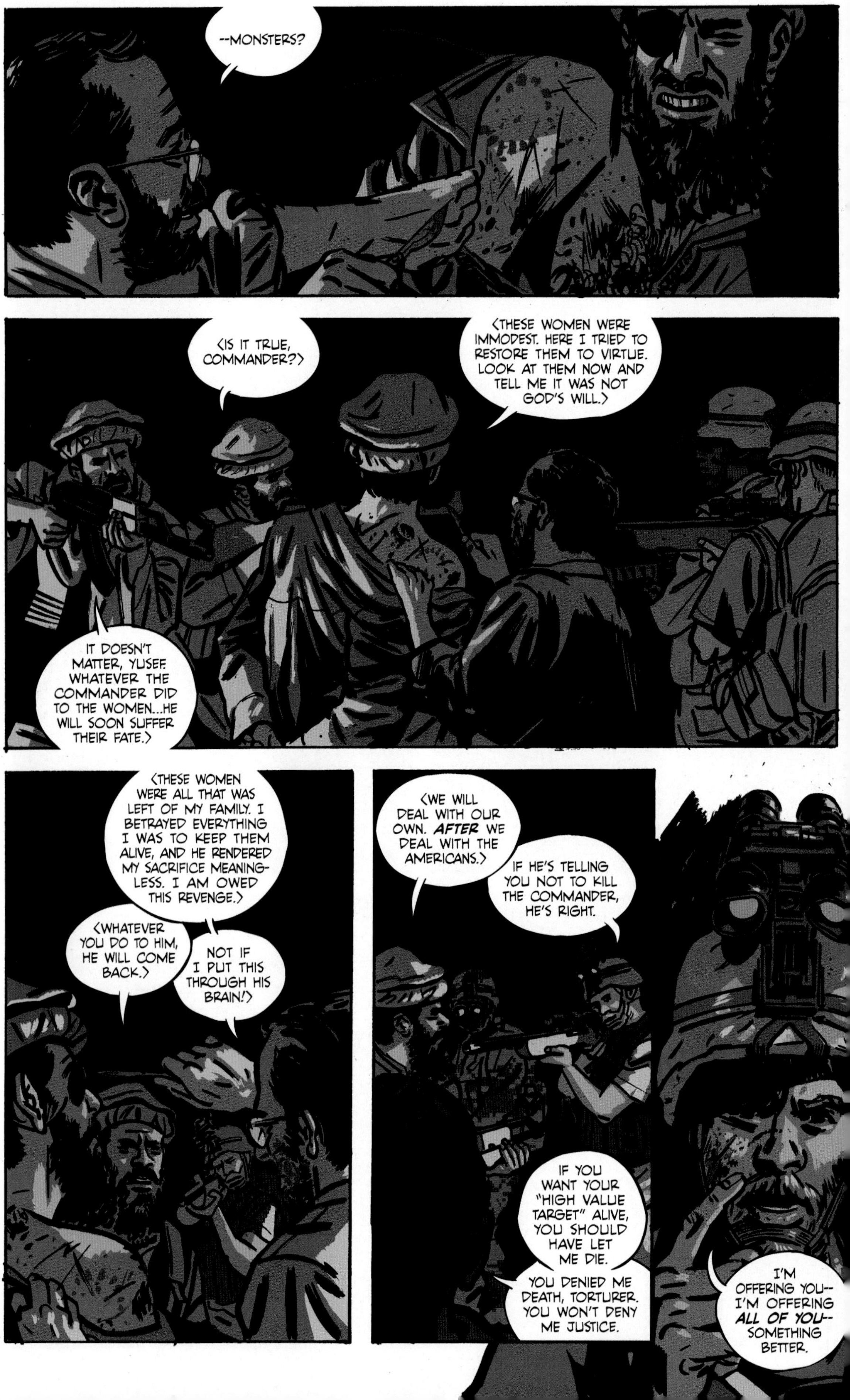
--MONSTERS?
<IS IT TRUE, COMMANDER?>
<THESE WOMEN WERE IMMODEST. HERE I TRIED TO RESTORE THEM TO VIRTUE. LOOK AT THEM NOW AND TELL ME IT WAS NOT GOD'S WILL.>
IT DOESN'T MATTER, YUSEF. WHATEVER THE COMMANDER DID TO THE WOMEN...HE WILL SOON SUFFER THEIR FATE.>
<THESE WOMEN WERE ALL THAT WAS LEFT OF MY FAMILY. I BETRAYED EVERYTHING I WAS TO KEEP THEM ALIVE, AND HE RENDERED MY SACRIFICE MEANINGLESS. I AM OWED THIS REVENGE.>
<WHATEVER YOU DO TO HIM, HE WILL COME BACK.>
NOT IF I PUT THIS THROUGH HIS BRAIN!>
<WE WILL DEAL WITH OUR OWN. *AFTER* WE DEAL WITH THE AMERICANS.>
IF HE'S TELLING YOU NOT TO KILL THE COMMANDER, HE'S RIGHT.
IF YOU WANT YOUR "HIGH VALUE TARGET" ALIVE, YOU SHOULD HAVE LET ME DIE.
YOU DENIED ME DEATH, TORTURER. YOU WON'T DENY ME JUSTICE.
I'M OFFERING YOU-- I'M OFFERING *ALL OF YOU*-- SOMETHING BETTER.

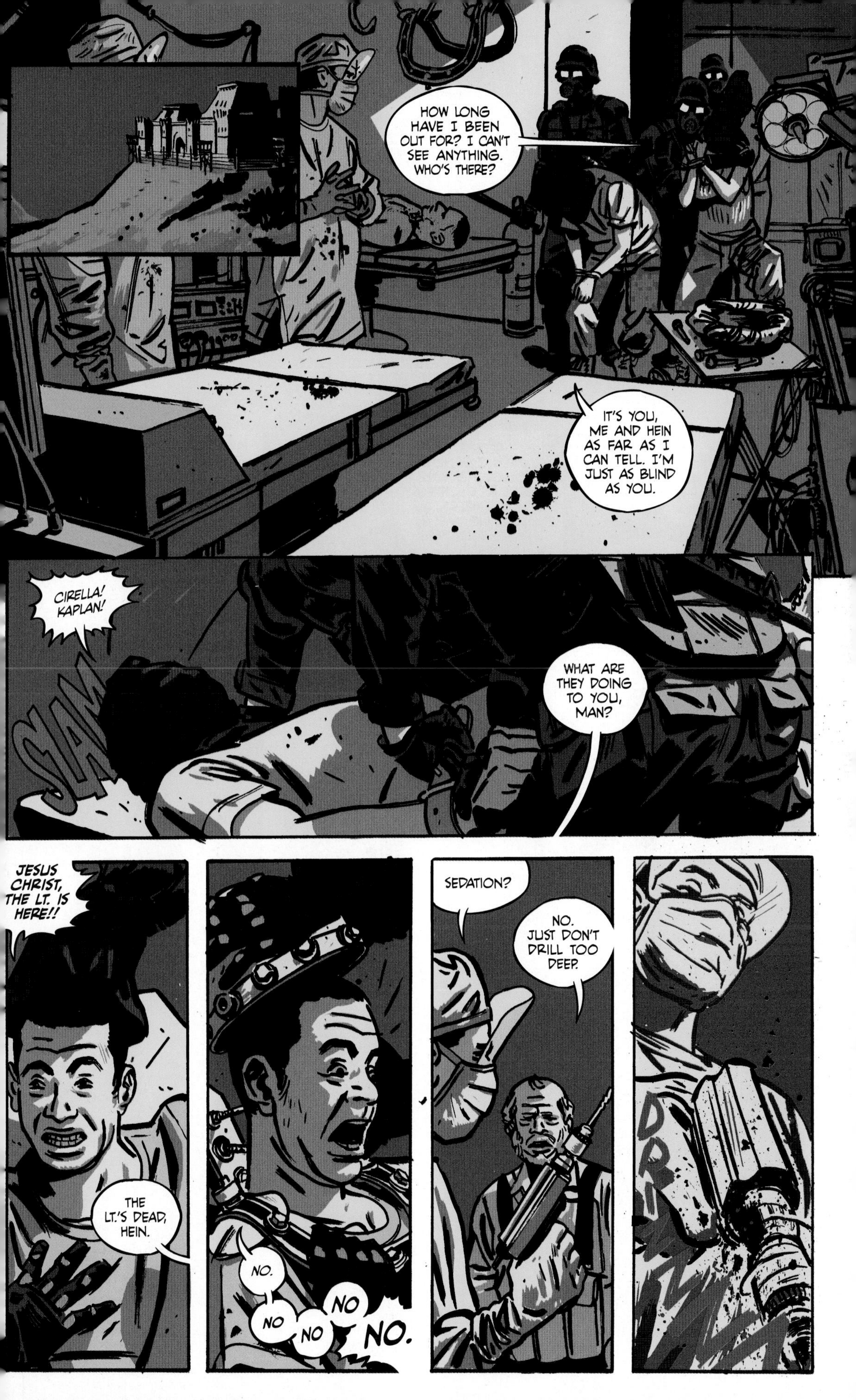
HOW LONG HAVE I BEEN OUT FOR? I CAN'T SEE ANYTHING. WHO'S THERE?
IT'S YOU, ME AND HEIN AS FAR AS I CAN TELL. I'M JUST AS BLIND AS YOU.
CIRELLA! KAPLAN!
SLAM
WHAT ARE THEY DOING TO YOU, MAN?
JESUS CHRIST, THE LT. IS HERE!!
THE LT.'S DEAD, HEIN.
NO.
NO
NO
NO
NO.
SEDATION?
NO. JUST DON'T DRILL TOO DEEP.

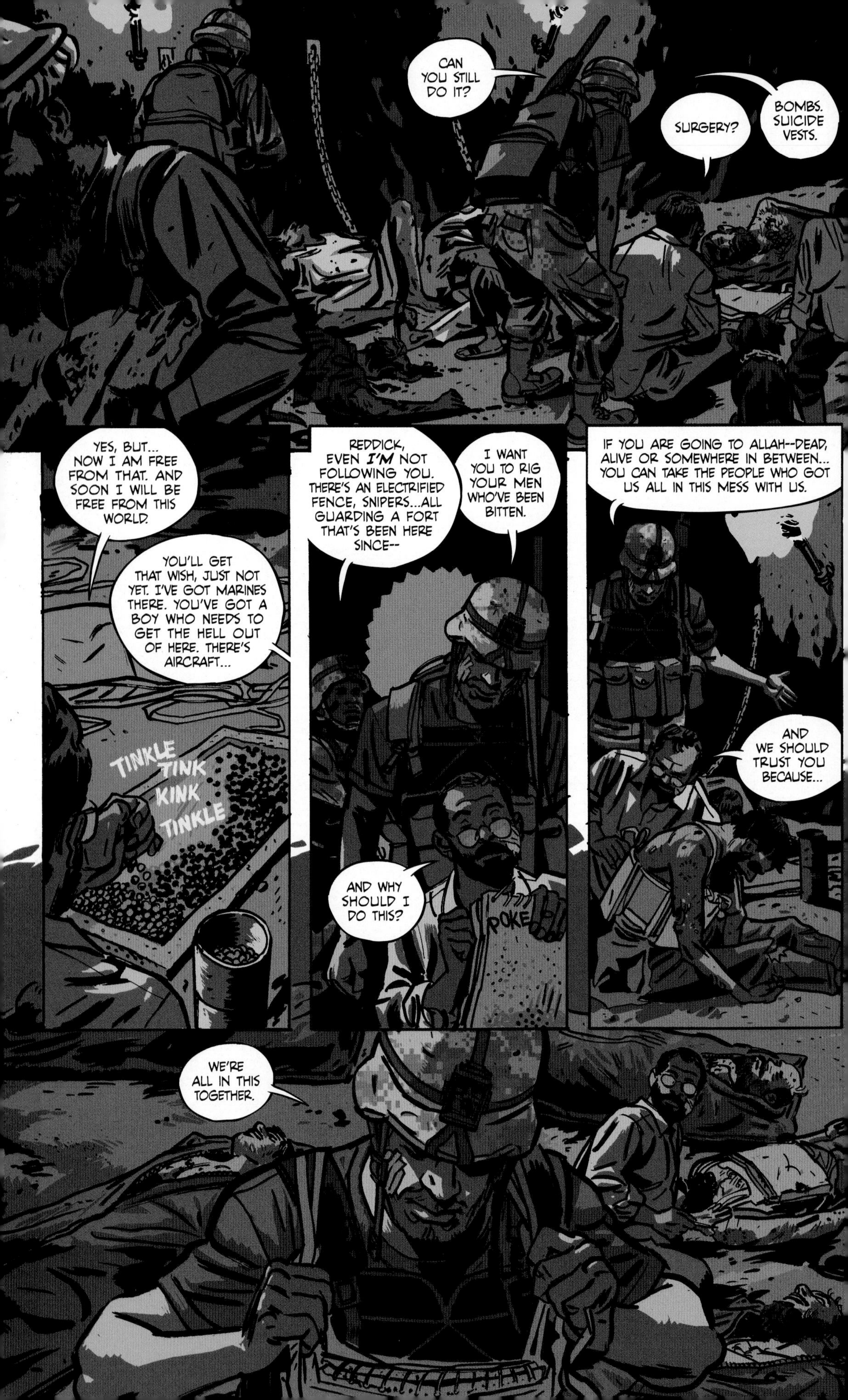
CAN YOU STILL DO IT?
SURGERY?
BOMBS. SUICIDE VESTS.
YES, BUT... NOW I AM FREE FROM THAT. AND SOON I WILL BE FREE FROM THIS WORLD.
YOU'LL GET THAT WISH, JUST NOT YET. I'VE GOT MARINES THERE. YOU'VE GOT A BOY WHO NEEDS TO GET THE HELL OUT OF HERE. THERE'S AIRCRAFT...
TINKLE TINK KINK TINKLE
REDDICK, EVEN I'M NOT FOLLOWING YOU. THERE'S AN ELECTRIFIED FENCE, SNIPERS...ALL GUARDING A FORT THAT'S BEEN HERE SINCE--
I WANT YOU TO RIG YOUR MEN WHO'VE BEEN BITTEN.
AND WHY SHOULD I DO THIS?
POKE
IF YOU ARE GOING TO ALLAH--DEAD, ALIVE OR SOMEWHERE IN BETWEEN... YOU CAN TAKE THE PEOPLE WHO GOT US ALL IN THIS MESS WITH US.
AND WE SHOULD TRUST YOU BECAUSE...
WE'RE ALL IN THIS TOGETHER.

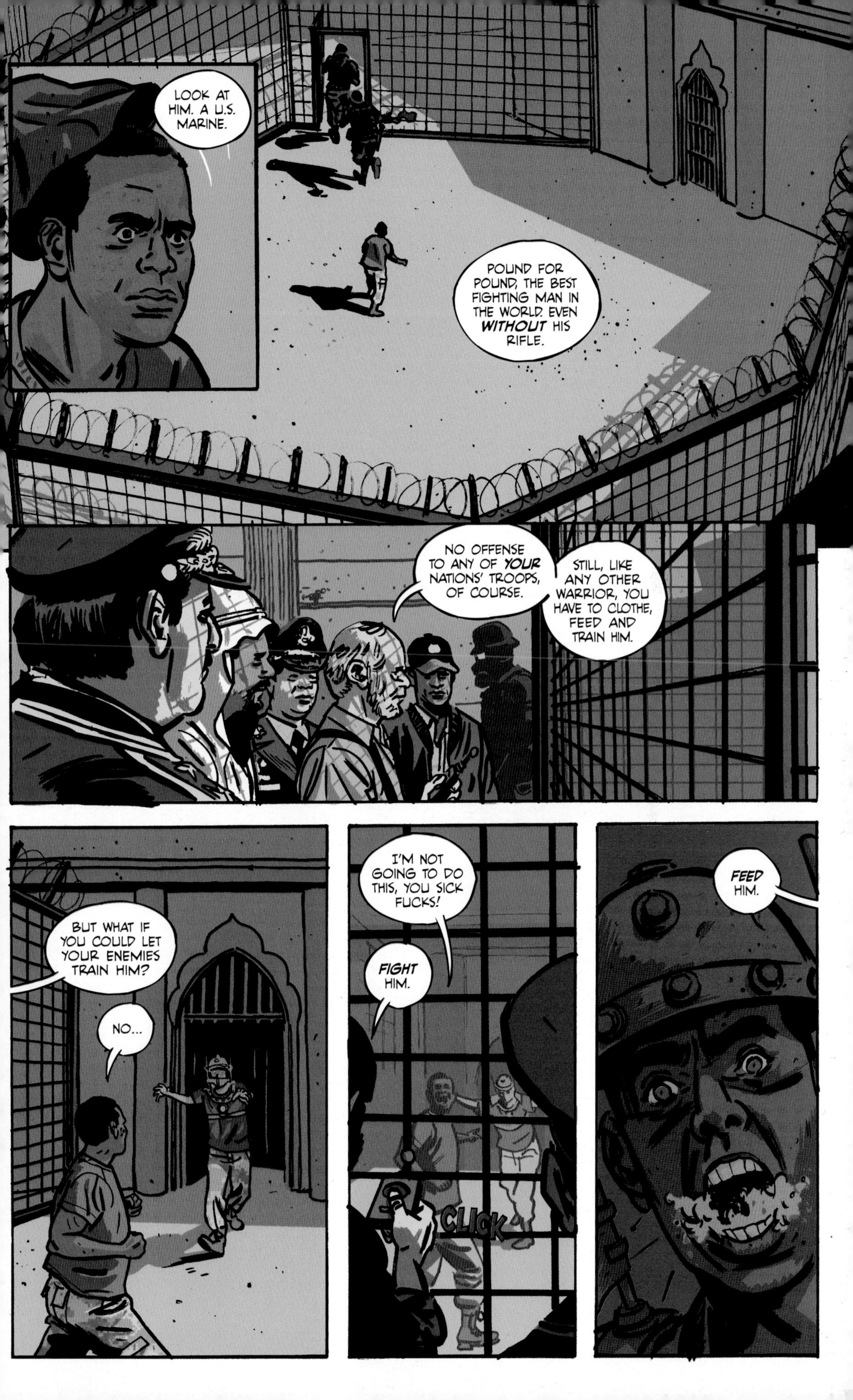
LOOK AT HIM. A U.S. MARINE.
POUND FOR POUND, THE BEST FIGHTING MAN IN THE WORLD. EVEN WITHOUT HIS RIFLE.
NO OFFENSE TO ANY OF YOUR NATIONS' TROOPS, OF COURSE.
STILL, LIKE ANY OTHER WARRIOR, YOU HAVE TO CLOTHE, FEED AND TRAIN HIM.
BUT WHAT IF YOU COULD LET YOUR ENEMIES TRAIN HIM?
NO...
I'M NOT GOING TO DO THIS, YOU SICK FUCKS!
FIGHT HIM.
CLICK
FEED HIM.

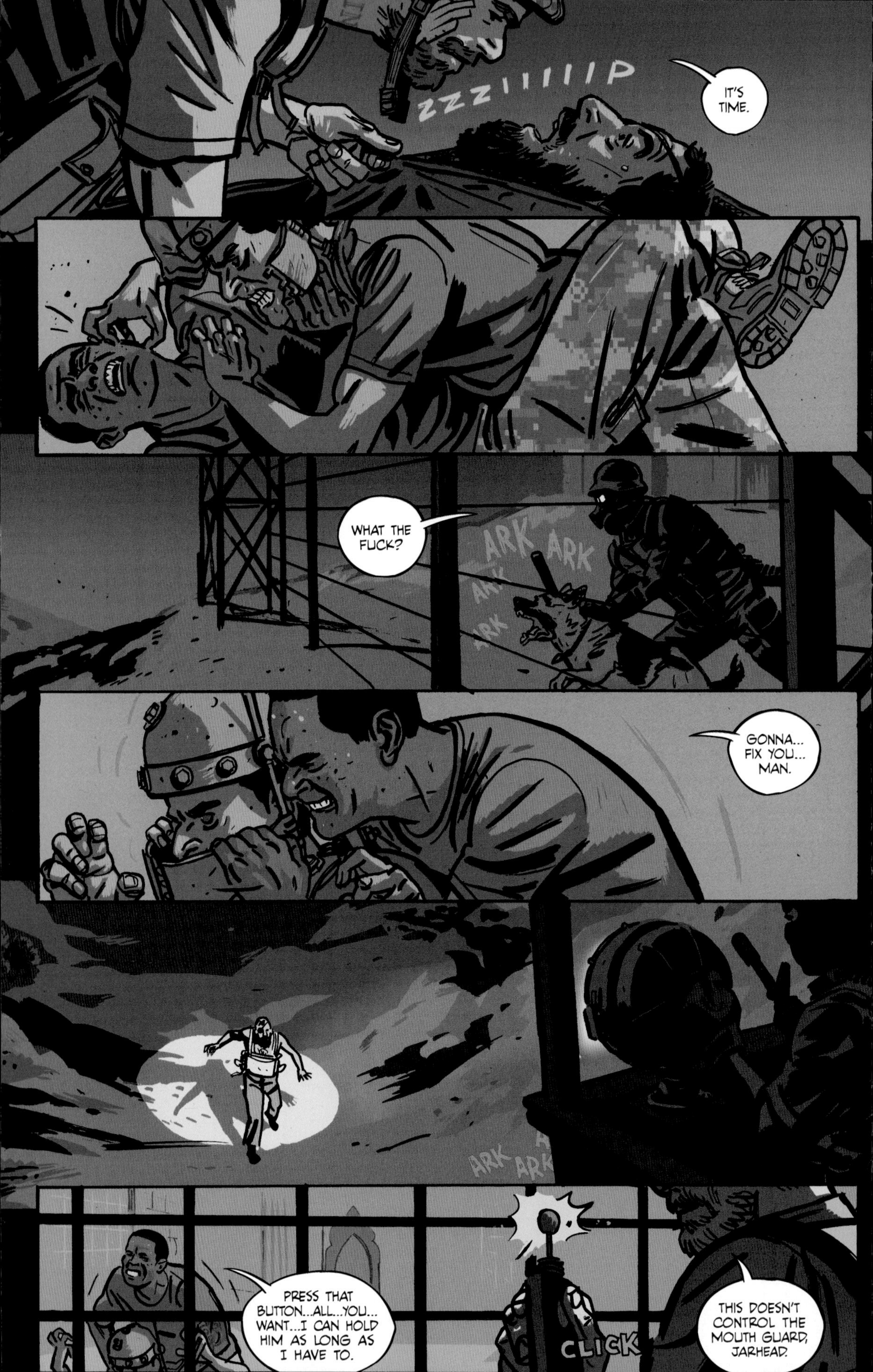
ZZZIIIIIP
IT'S TIME.
WHAT THE FUCK?
ARK ARK ARK ARK
GONNA... FIX YOU... MAN.
ARK ARK
PRESS THAT BUTTON...ALL...YOU... WANT...I CAN HOLD HIM AS LONG AS I HAVE TO.
CLICK
THIS DOESN'T CONTROL THE MOUTH GUARD, JARHEAD.

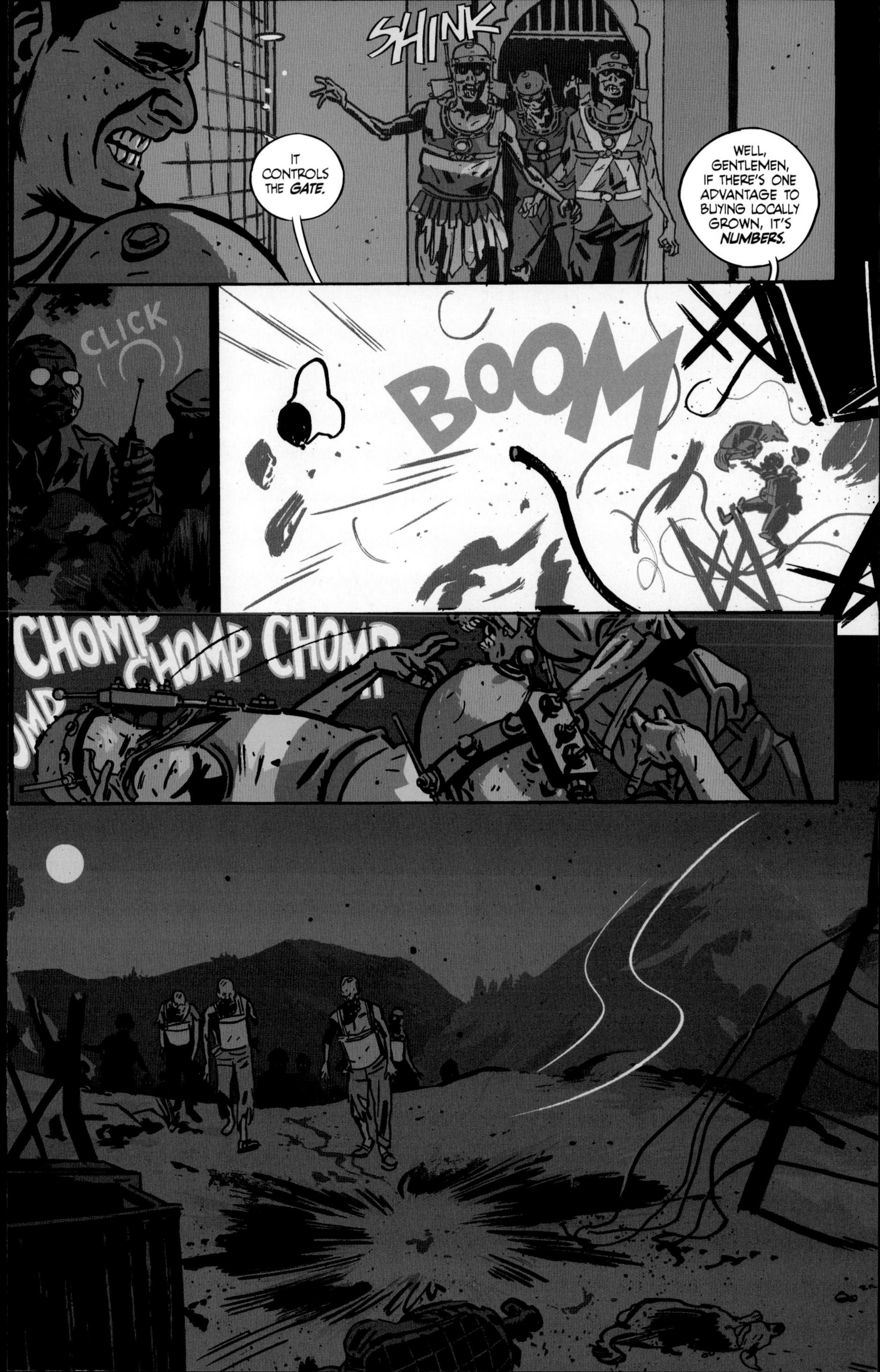
SHINK
IT CONTROLS THE GATE.
WELL, GENTLEMEN, IF THERE'S ONE ADVANTAGE TO BUYING LOCALLY GROWN, IT'S NUMBERS.
CLICK
BOOM
CHOMP CHOMP CHOMP

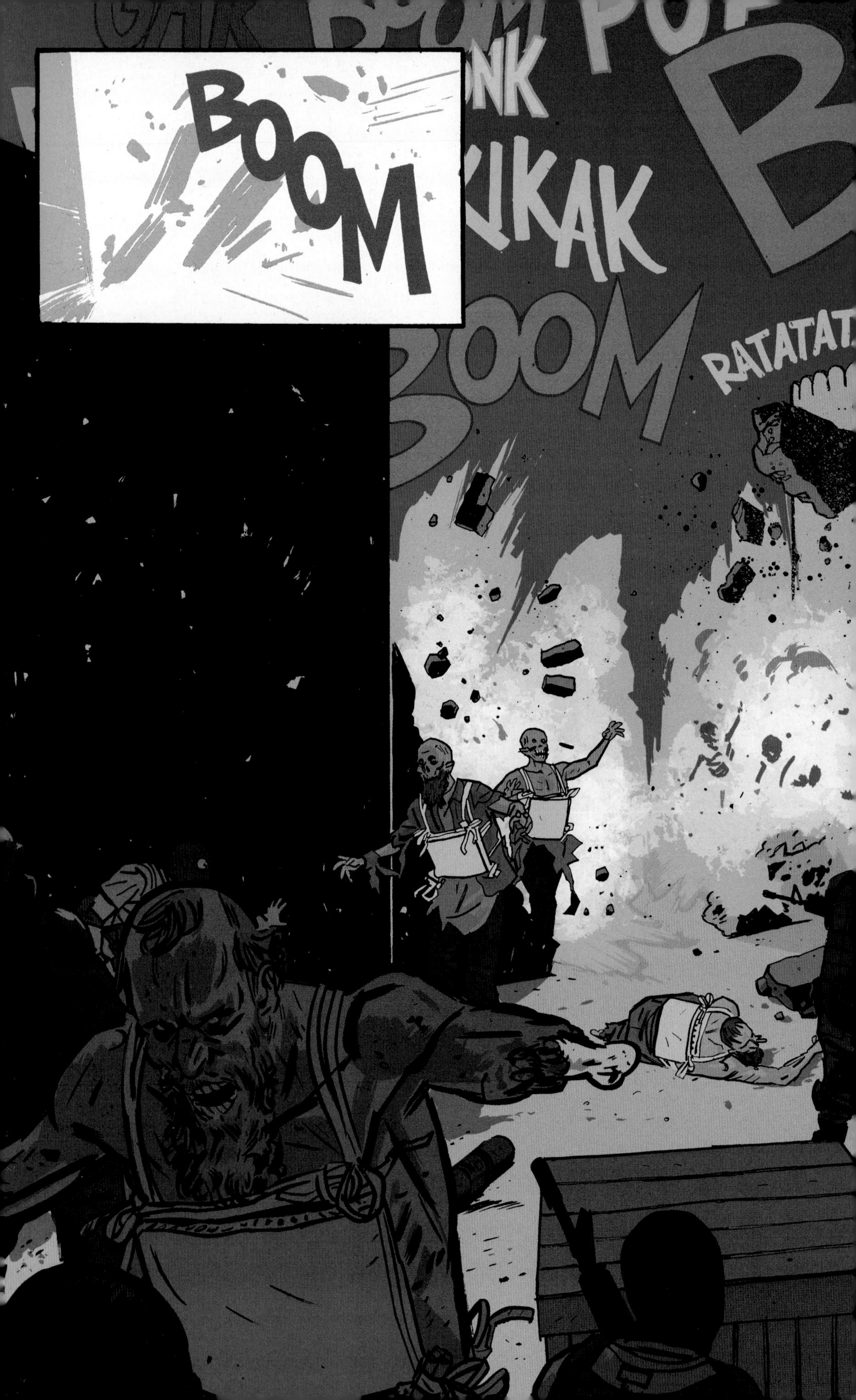
BOOM
RATATAT

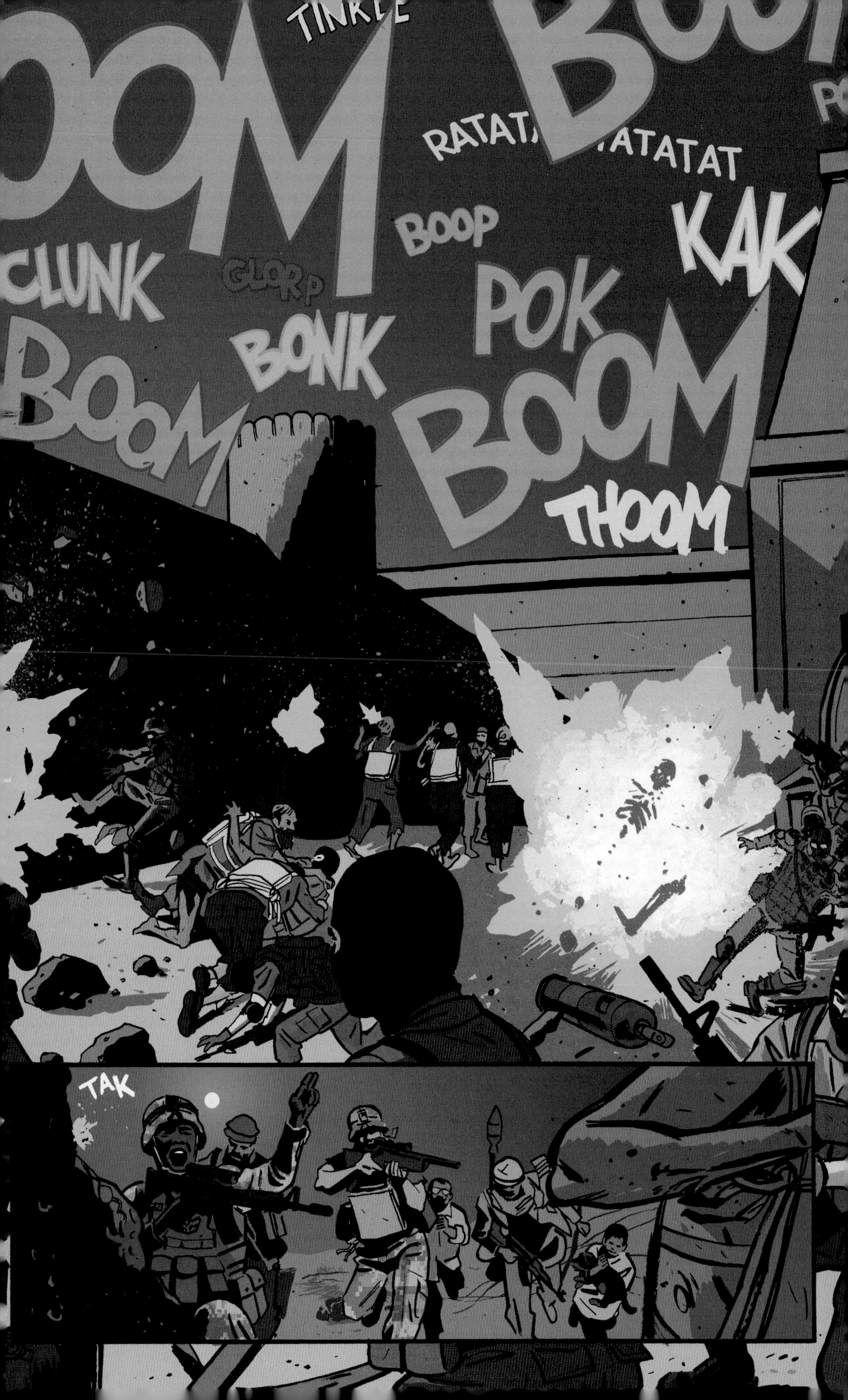
TINKLE
BOOM
BOOM
PO
RATATAT RATATAT
BOOP
KAK
CLUNK
GLORP
POK
BONK
BOOM
BOOM
THOOM
TAK

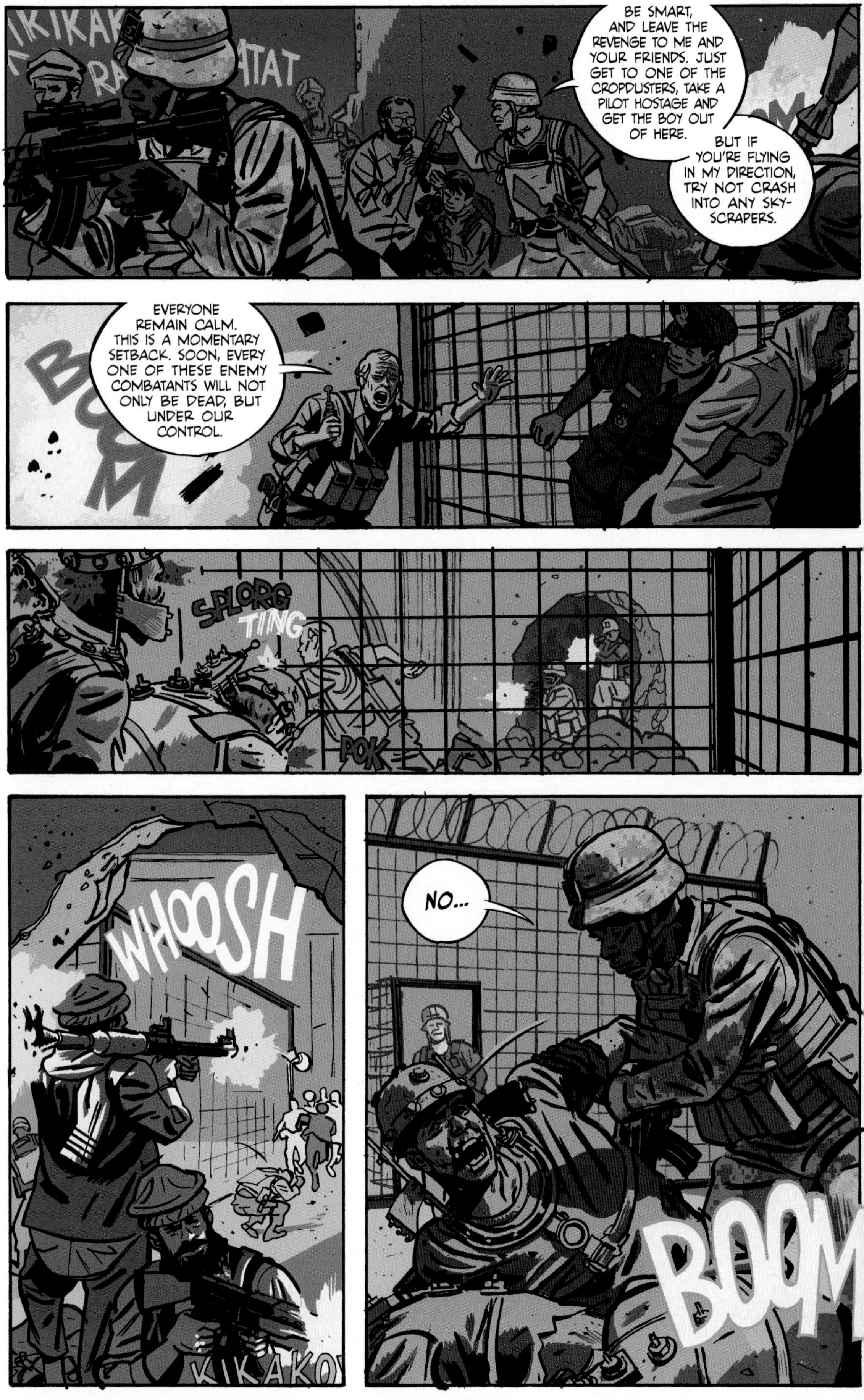
BE SMART, AND LEAVE THE REVENGE TO ME AND YOUR FRIENDS. JUST GET TO ONE OF THE CROPDUSTERS, TAKE A PILOT HOSTAGE AND GET THE BOY OUT OF HERE.
BUT IF YOU'RE FLYING IN MY DIRECTION, TRY NOT CRASH INTO ANY SKY-SCRAPERS.
EVERYONE REMAIN CALM. THIS IS A MOMENTARY SETBACK. SOON, EVERY ONE OF THESE ENEMY COMBATANTS WILL NOT ONLY BE DEAD, BUT UNDER OUR CONTROL.
SPLORG
TING
POK
WHOOSH
KIKAKO
NO...
BOOM

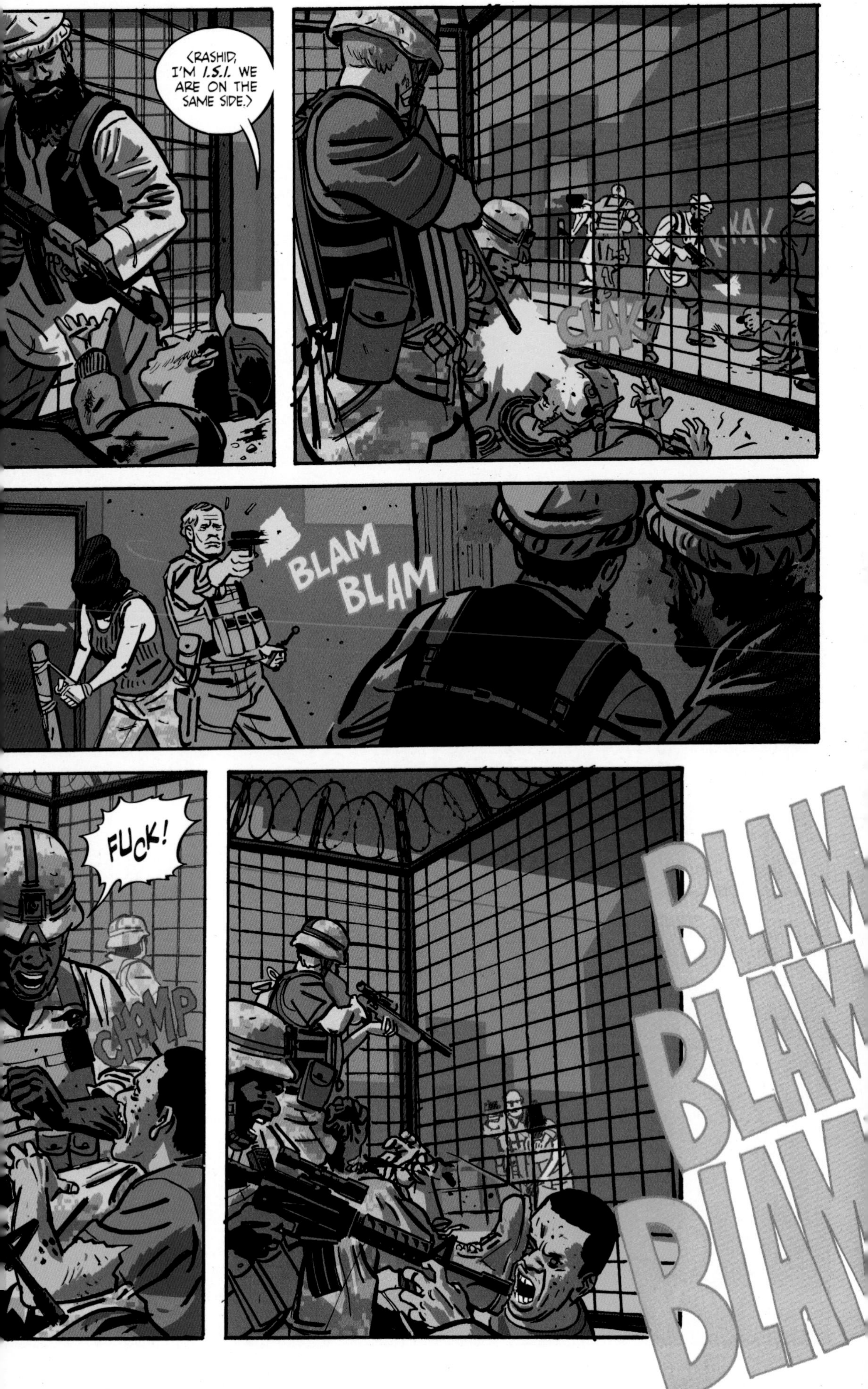
<RASHID, I'M I.S.I. WE ARE ON THE SAME SIDE.>
KKAK
CLAK
BLAM BLAM
FUCK!
CHAMP
BLAM BLAM BLAM

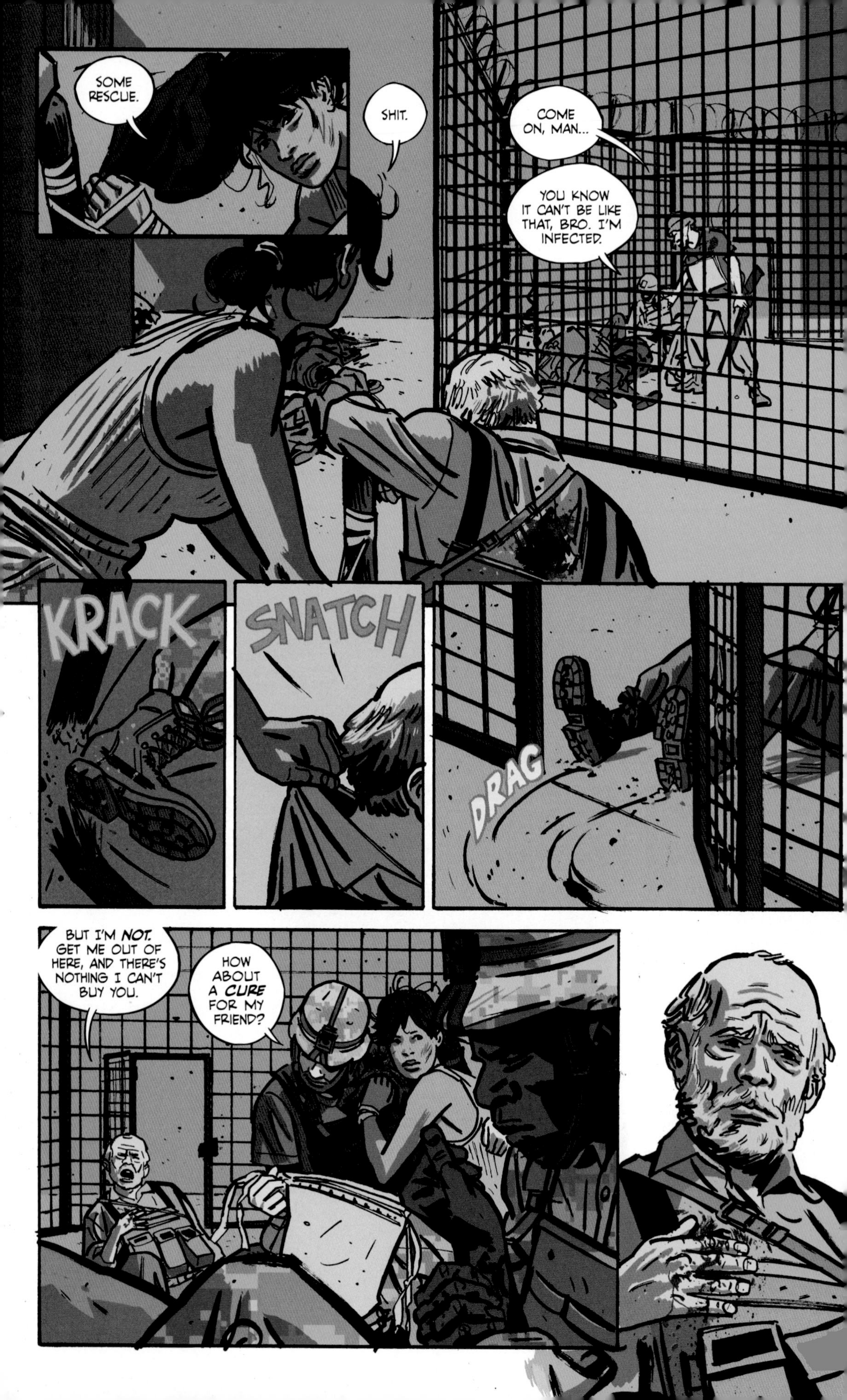
SOME RESCUE.
SHIT.
COME ON, MAN...
YOU KNOW IT CAN'T BE LIKE THAT, BRO. I'M INFECTED.
KRACK
SNATCH
DRAG
BUT I'M *NOT.* GET ME OUT OF HERE, AND THERE'S NOTHING I CAN'T BUY YOU.
HOW ABOUT A *CURE* FOR MY FRIEND?

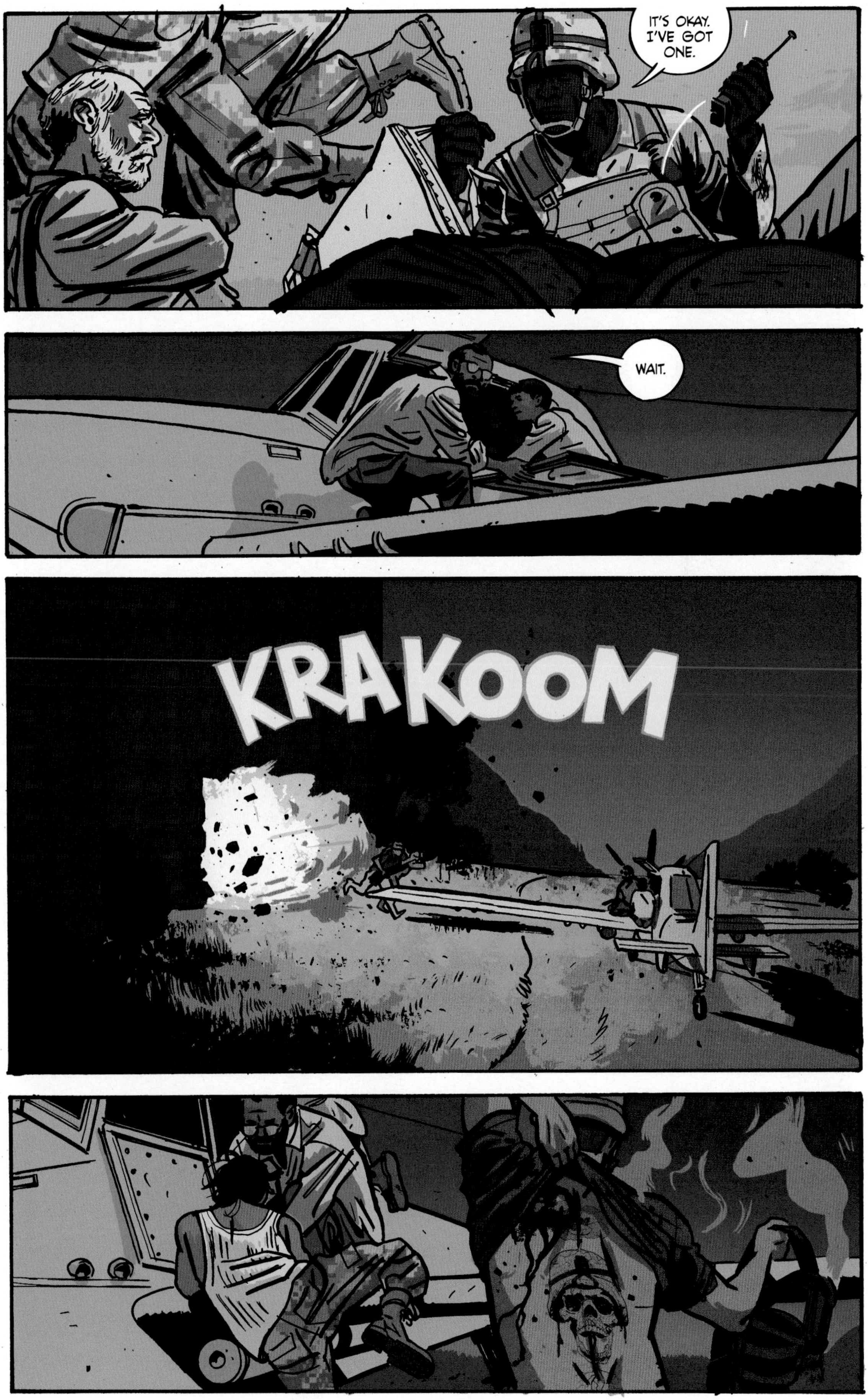
IT'S OKAY. I'VE GOT ONE.
WAIT.
KRAKOOM

END.

EPILOGUE

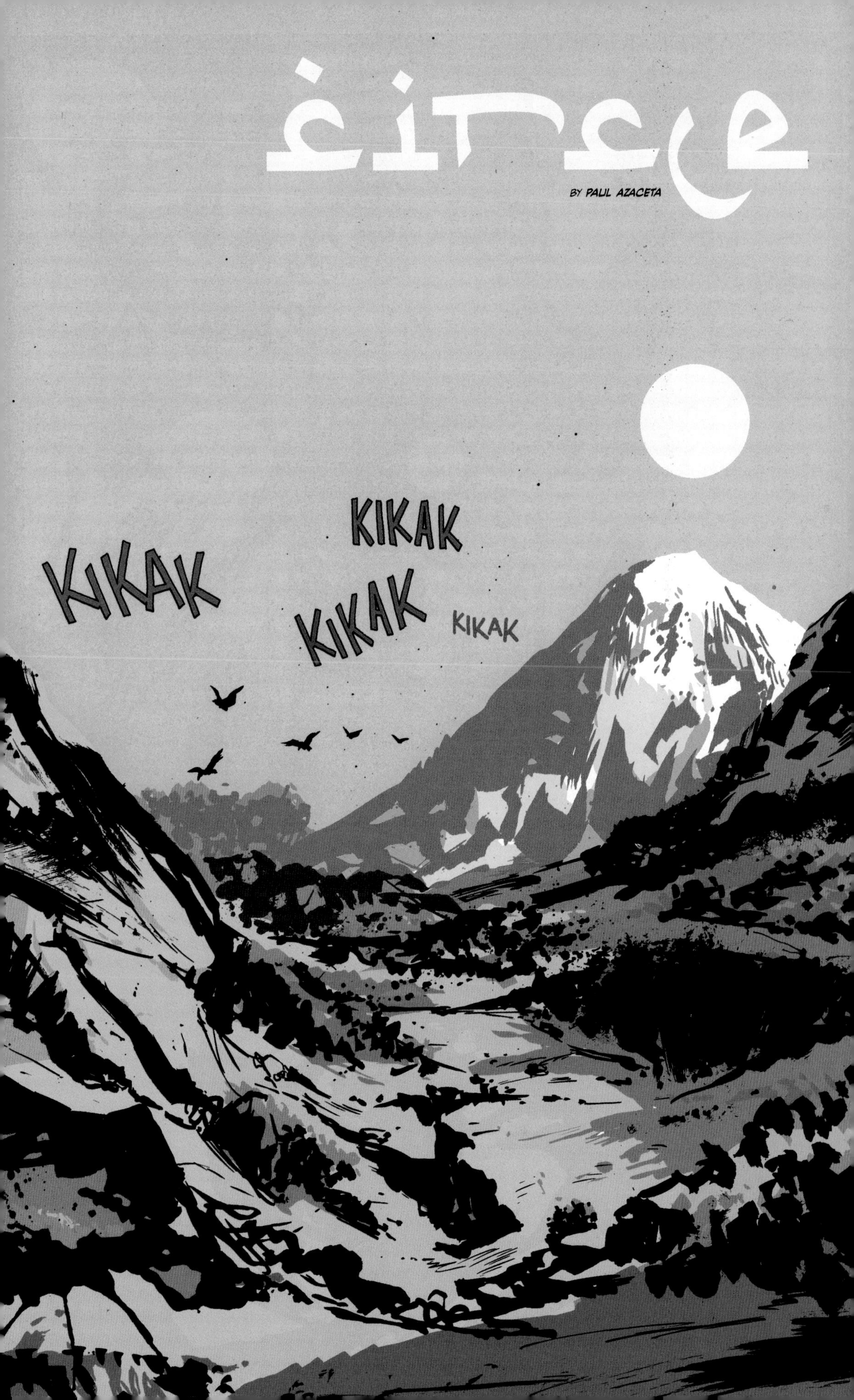
Circle
BY PAUL AZACETA
KIKAK
KIKAK
KIKAK
KIKAK

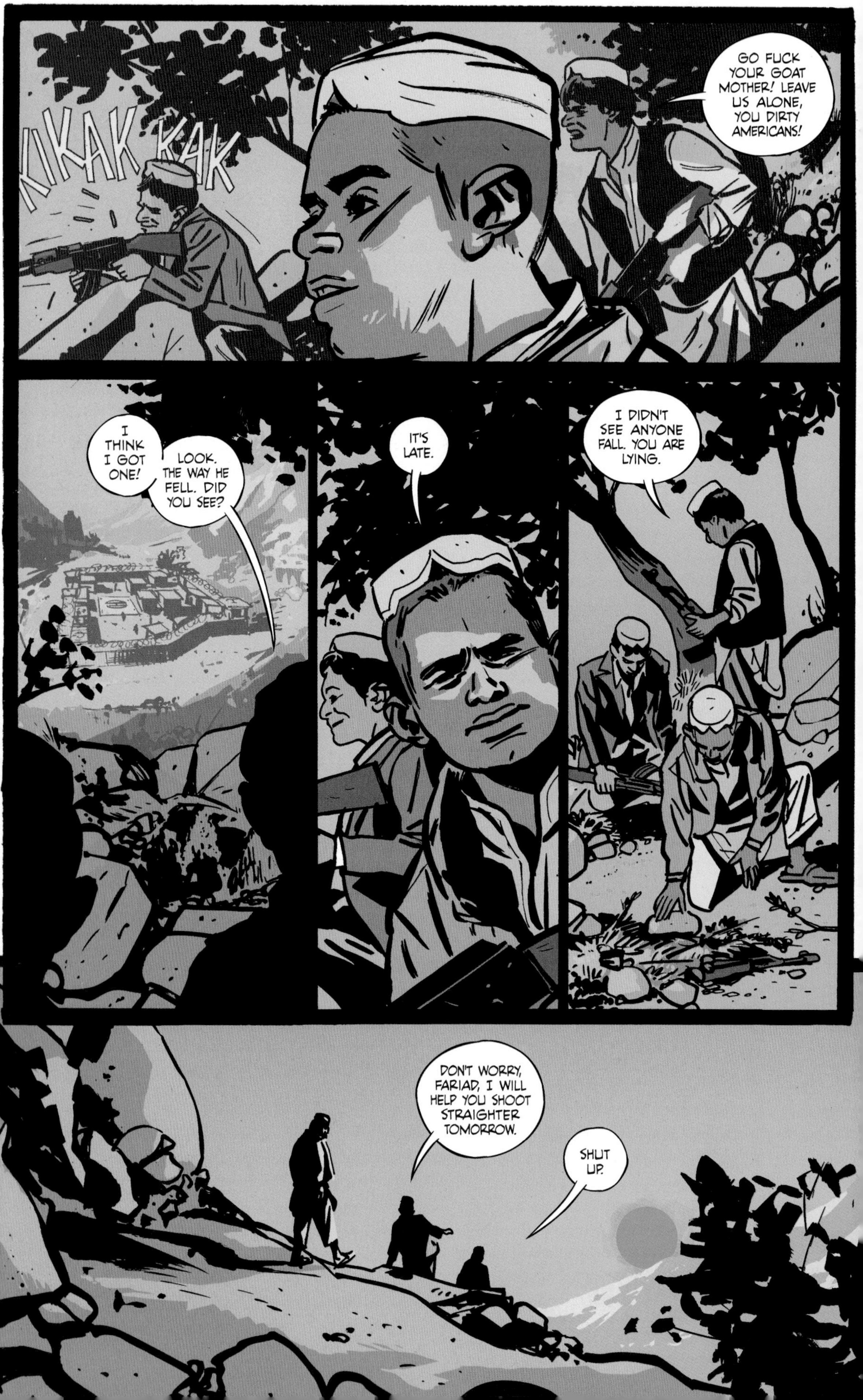
KIKAK KAK
GO FUCK YOUR GOAT MOTHER! LEAVE US ALONE, YOU DIRTY AMERICANS!
I THINK I GOT ONE!
LOOK. THE WAY HE FELL. DID YOU SEE?
IT'S LATE.
I DIDN'T SEE ANYONE FALL. YOU ARE LYING.
DON'T WORRY, FARIAD, I WILL HELP YOU SHOOT STRAIGHTER TOMORROW.
SHUT UP.

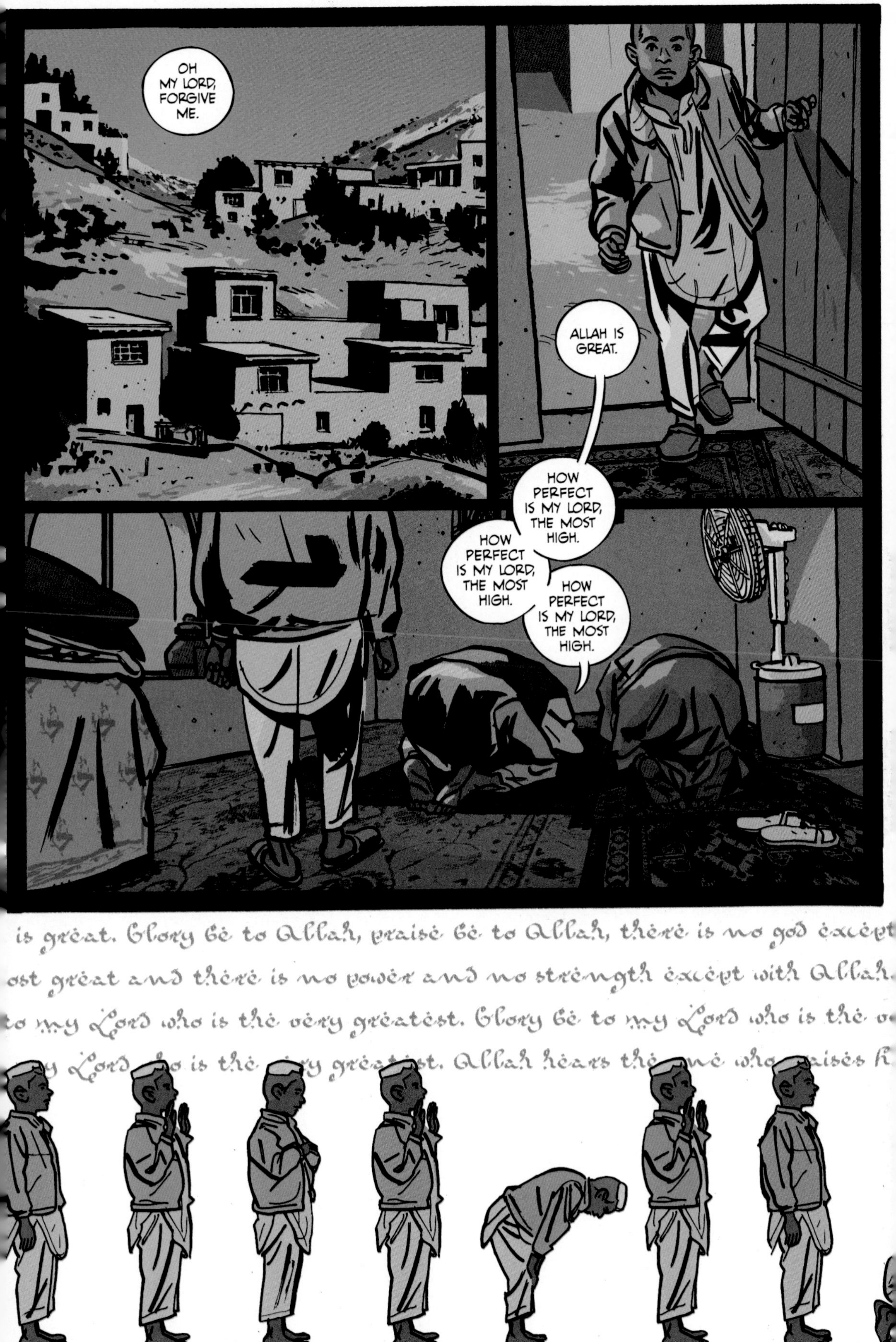

OH MY LORD, FORGIVE ME.
ALLAH IS GREAT.
HOW PERFECT IS MY LORD, THE MOST HIGH.
HOW PERFECT IS MY LORD, THE MOST HIGH.
HOW PERFECT IS MY LORD, THE MOST HIGH.
is great. Glory be to Allah, praise be to Allah, there is no god except
ost great and there is no power and no strength except with Allah.
to my Lord who is the very greatest. Glory be to my Lord who is the ve
Lord is the greatest. Allah hears the who

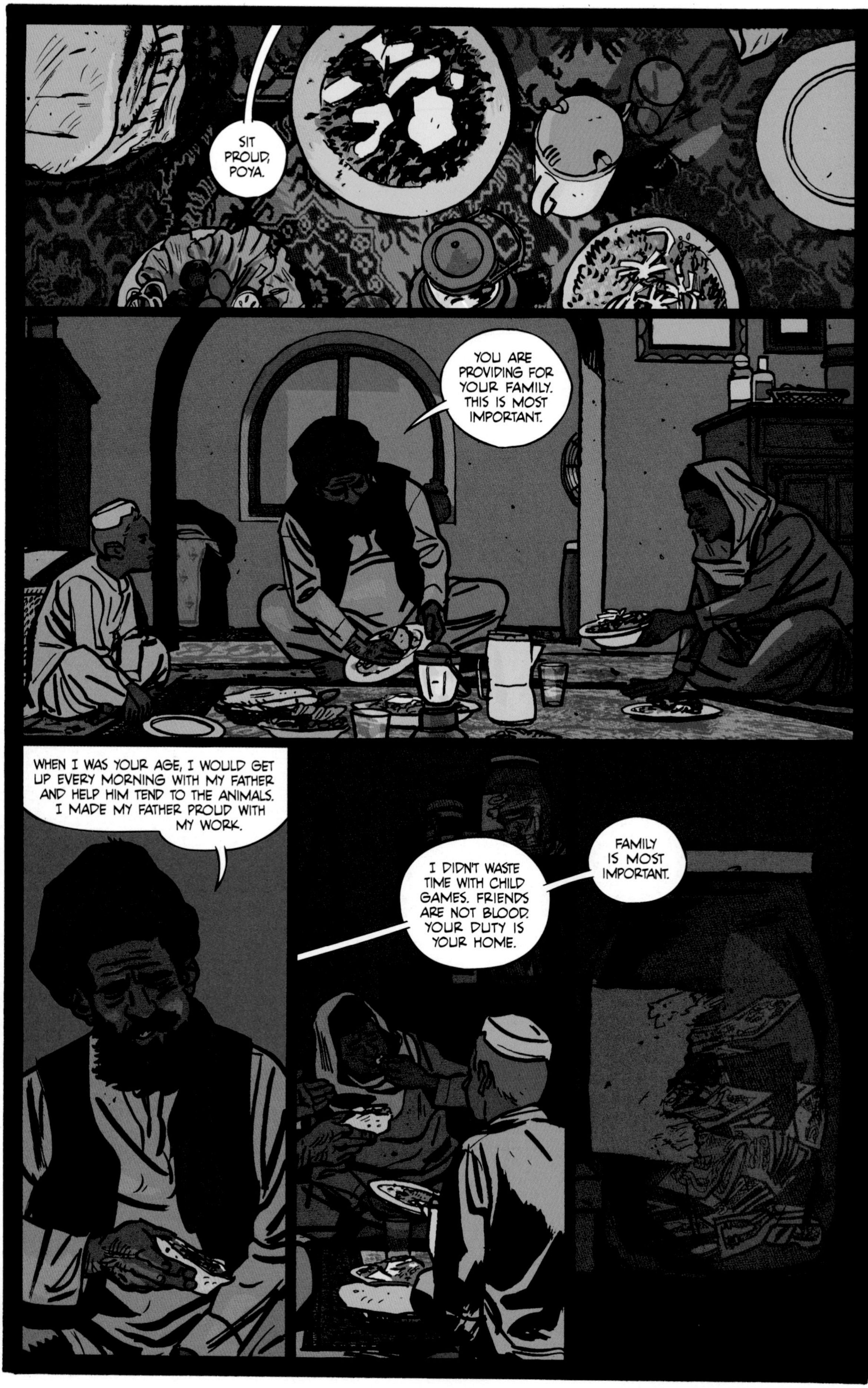
SIT PROUD, POYA.
YOU ARE PROVIDING FOR YOUR FAMILY. THIS IS MOST IMPORTANT.
WHEN I WAS YOUR AGE, I WOULD GET UP EVERY MORNING WITH MY FATHER AND HELP HIM TEND TO THE ANIMALS. I MADE MY FATHER PROUD WITH MY WORK.
I DIDN'T WASTE TIME WITH CHILD GAMES. FRIENDS ARE NOT BLOOD. YOUR DUTY IS YOUR HOME.
FAMILY IS MOST IMPORTANT.

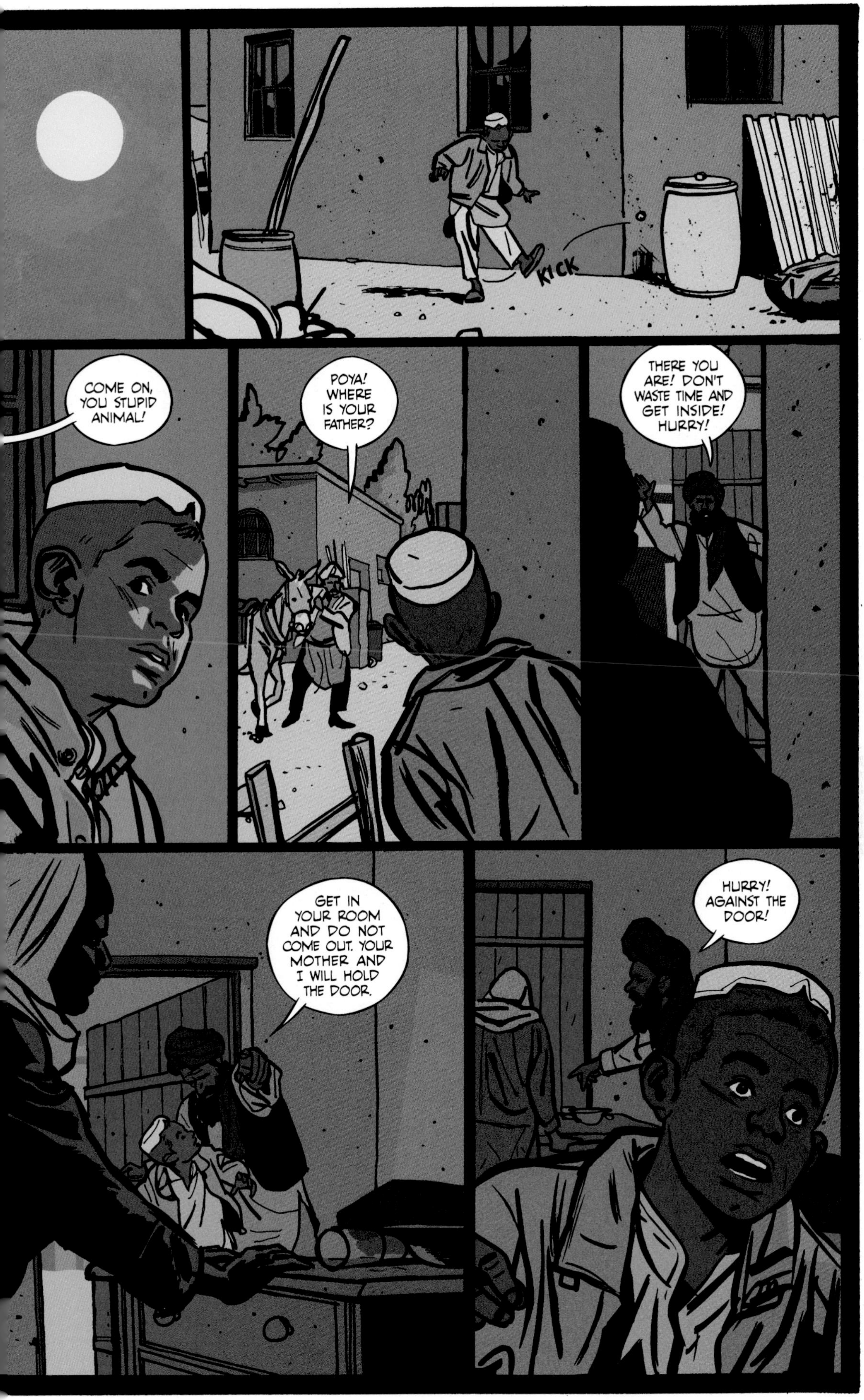
KICK
COME ON, YOU STUPID ANIMAL!
POYA! WHERE IS YOUR FATHER?
THERE YOU ARE! DON'T WASTE TIME AND GET INSIDE! HURRY!
GET IN YOUR ROOM AND DO NOT COME OUT. YOUR MOTHER AND I WILL HOLD THE DOOR.
HURRY! AGAINST THE DOOR!

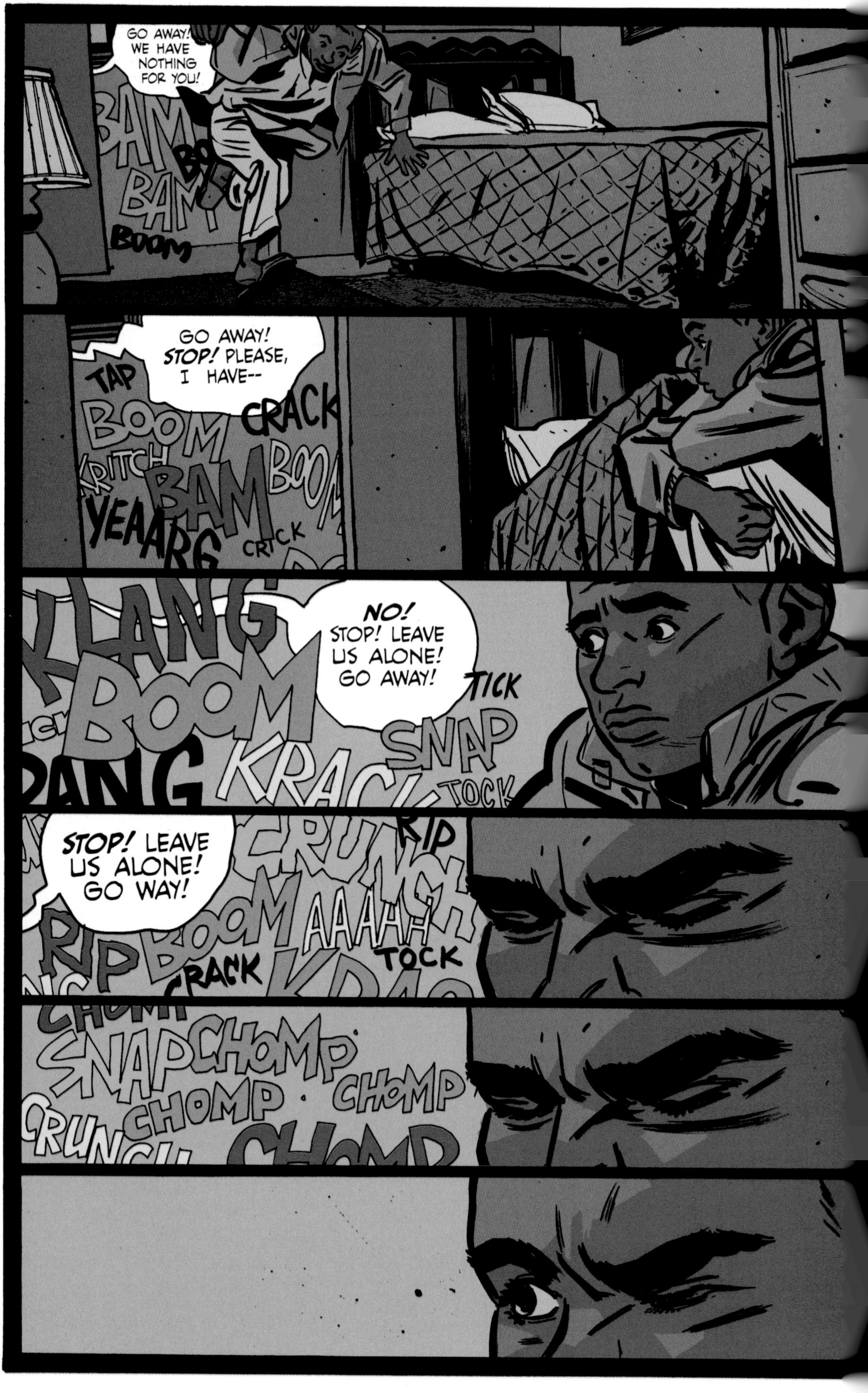
GO AWAY! WE HAVE NOTHING FOR YOU!
BAM
BAM
BOOM
GO AWAY! STOP! PLEASE, I HAVE--
TAP
BOOM
CRACK
KRITCH
BAM
BOOM
YEAARG
CRICK
NO! STOP! LEAVE US ALONE! GO AWAY!
KLANG
BOOM
TICK
SNAP
KRACK
TOCK
STOP! LEAVE US ALONE! GO WAY!
CRUNCH
RIP
RIP
BOOM
AAAAH
TOCK
CRACK
SNAP
CHOMP
CHOMP
CHOMP
CHOMP

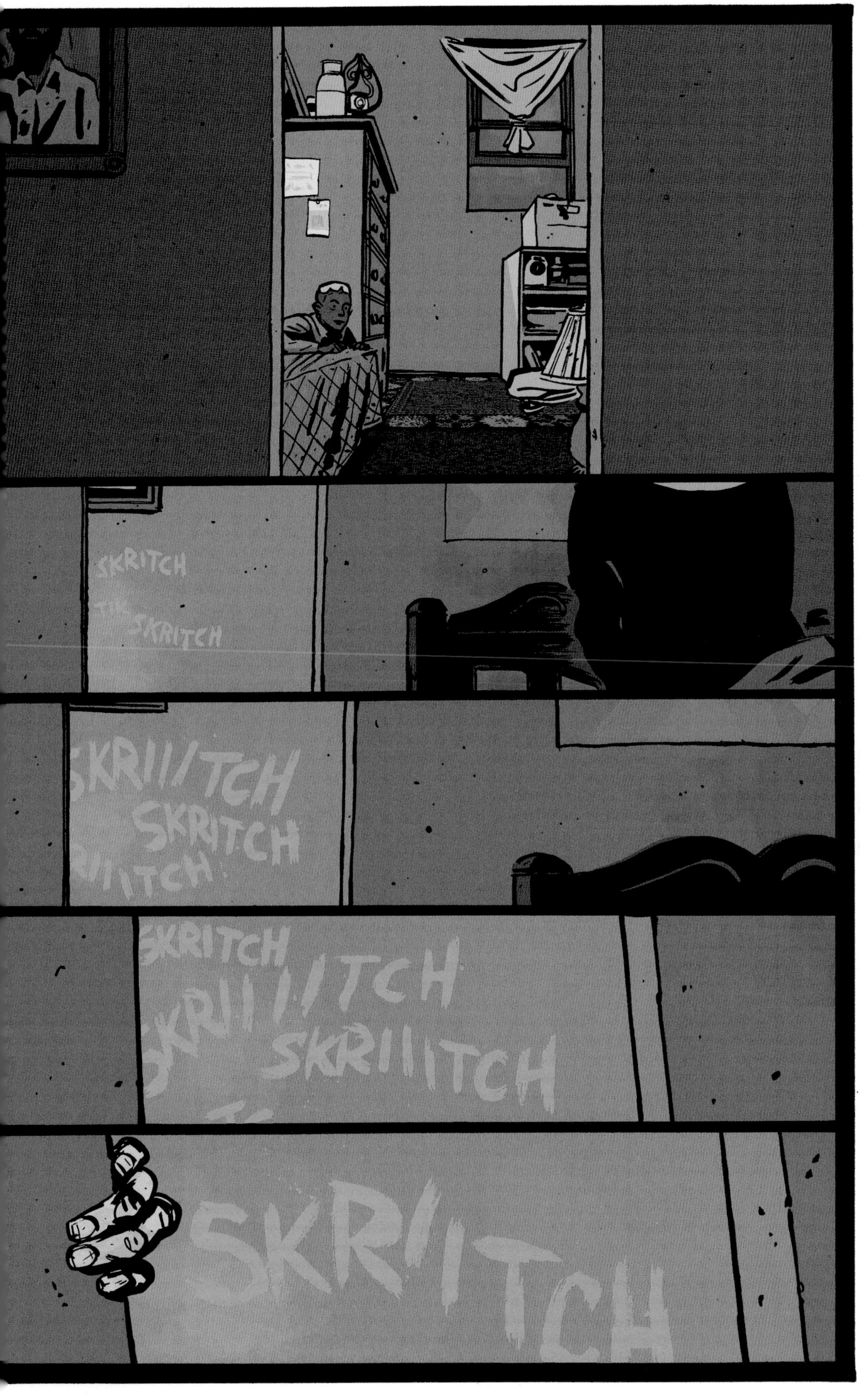
SKRITCH
TIK
SKRITCH
SKRIITCH
SKRITCH
SKRITCH
SKRIIIITCH
SKRIIITCH
SKRIITCH

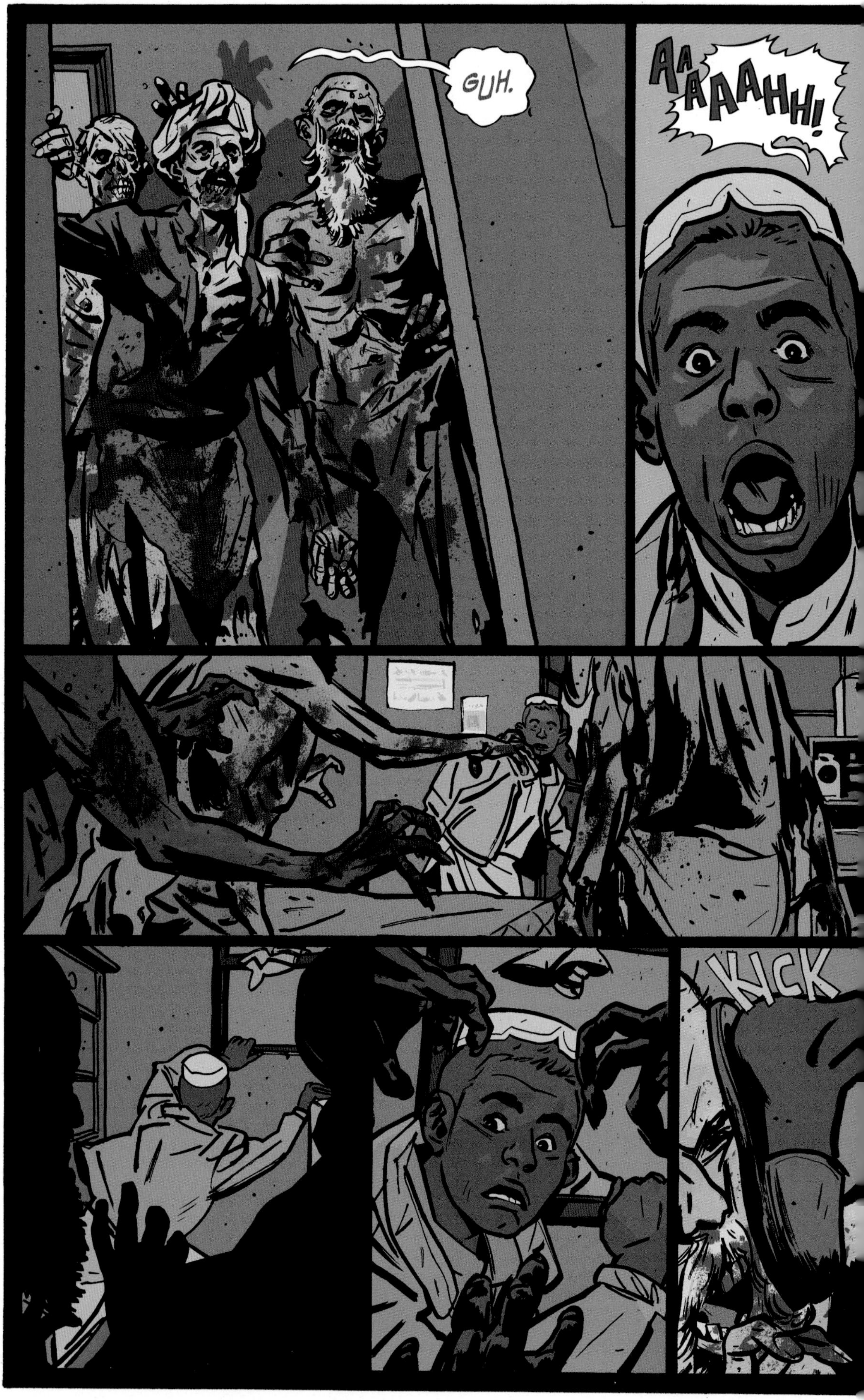
GUH.
AAAAAHH!
KICK

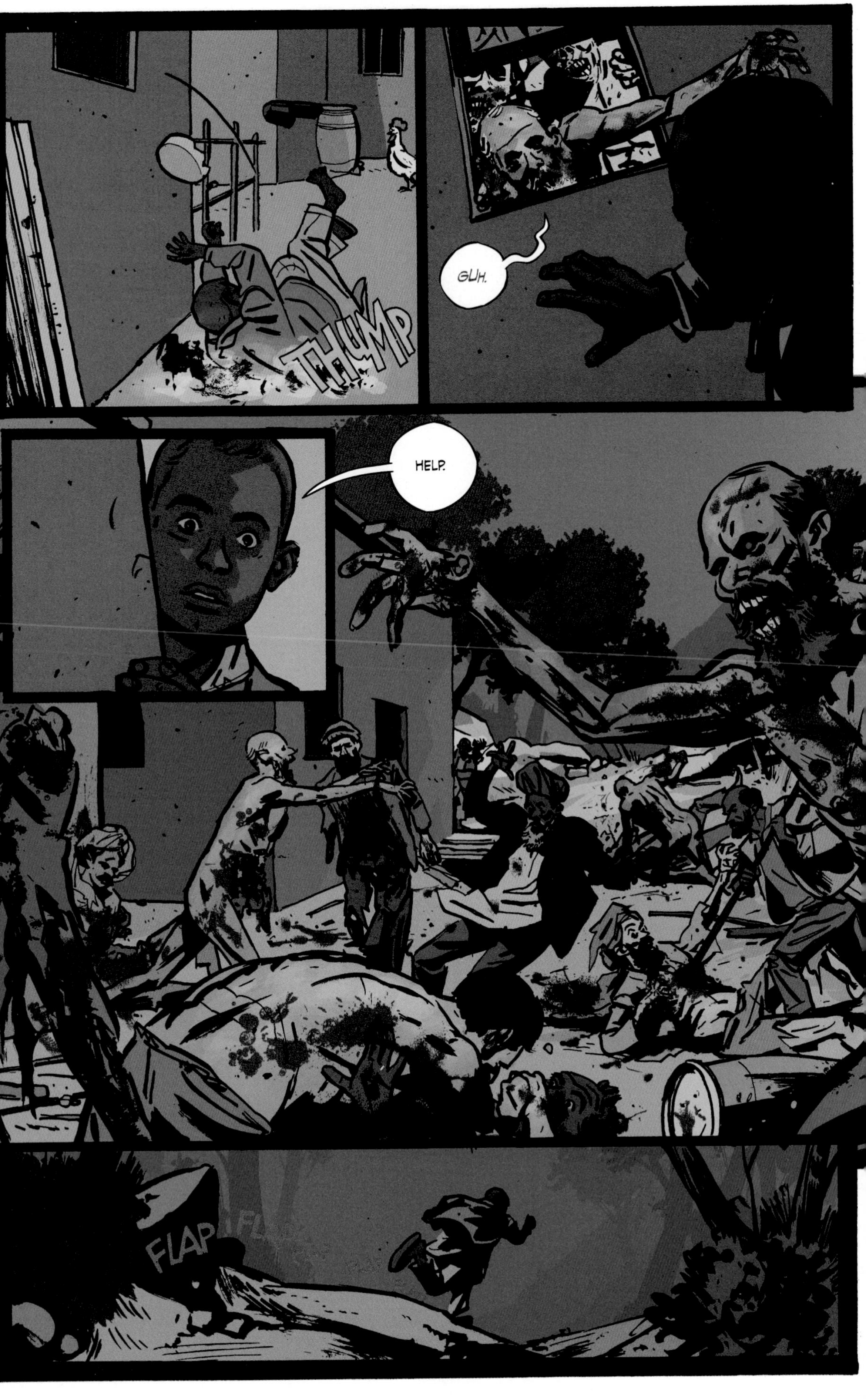
THUMP
GUH.
HELP.
FLAP

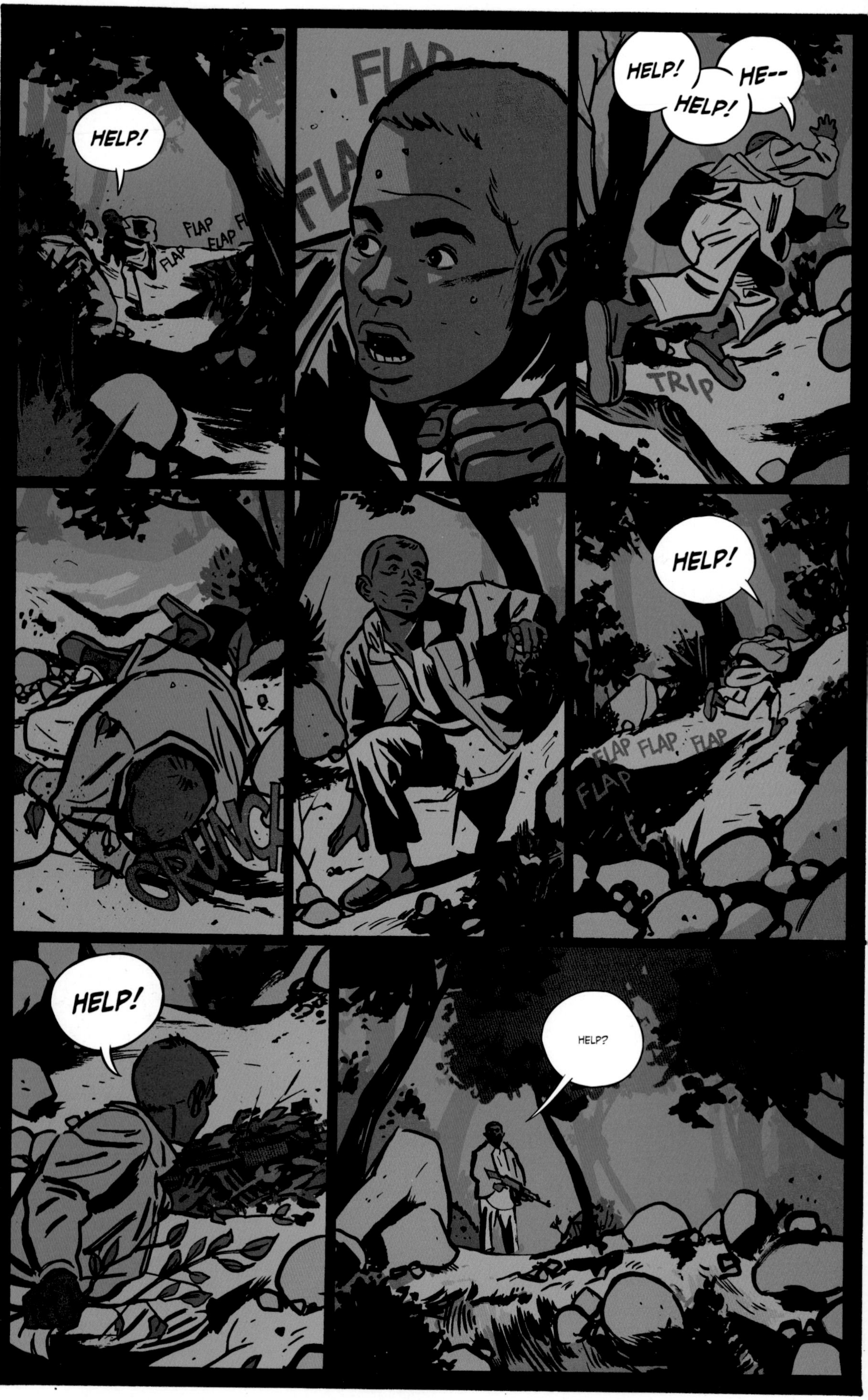
HELP!
FLAP
FLAP
FLAP
FLAP
FLAP
FLAP
HELP!
HELP!
HE--
TRIP
CRUNCH
HELP!
FLAP
FLAP
FLAP
FLAP
HELP!
HELP?

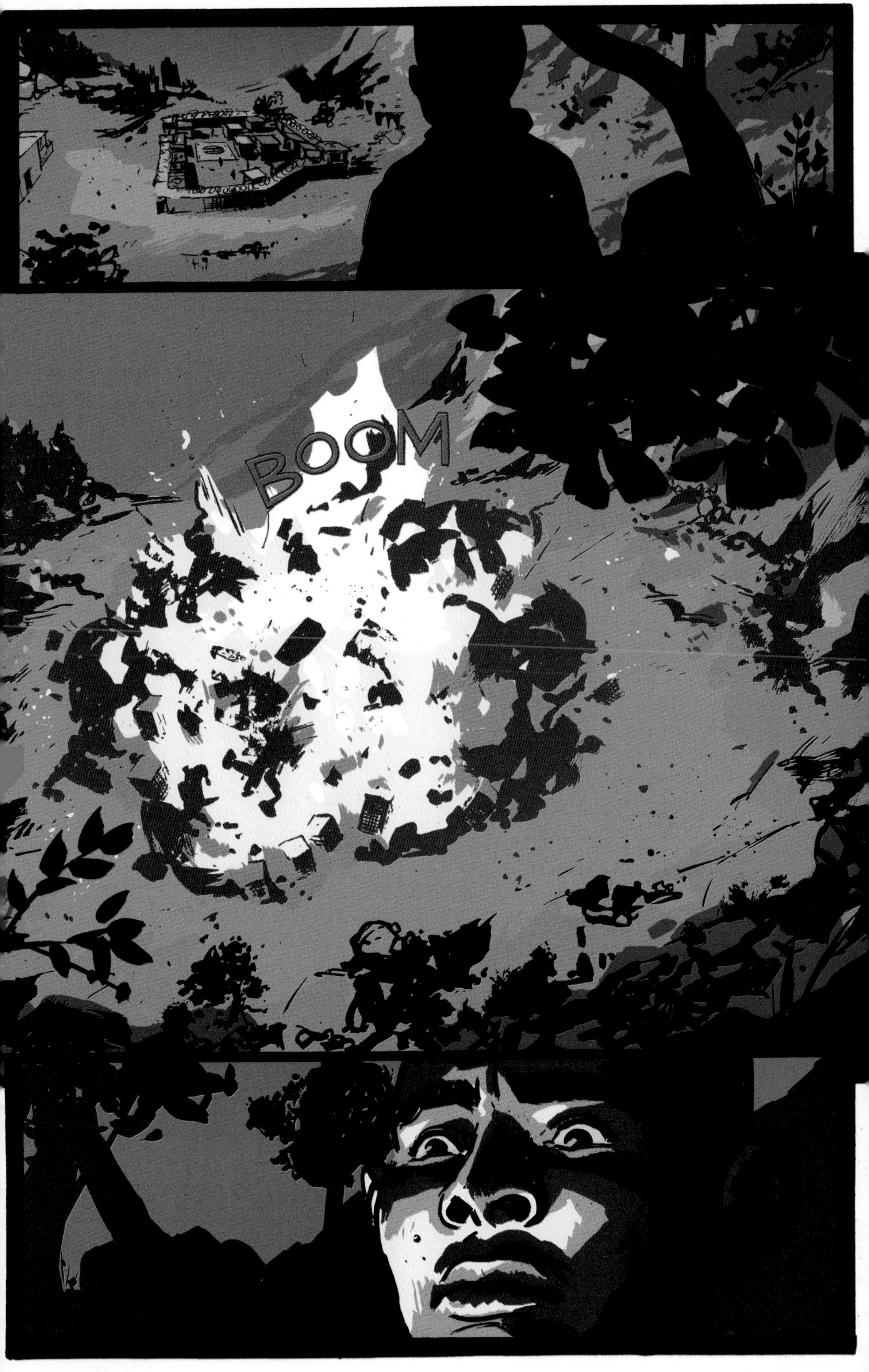
BOOM

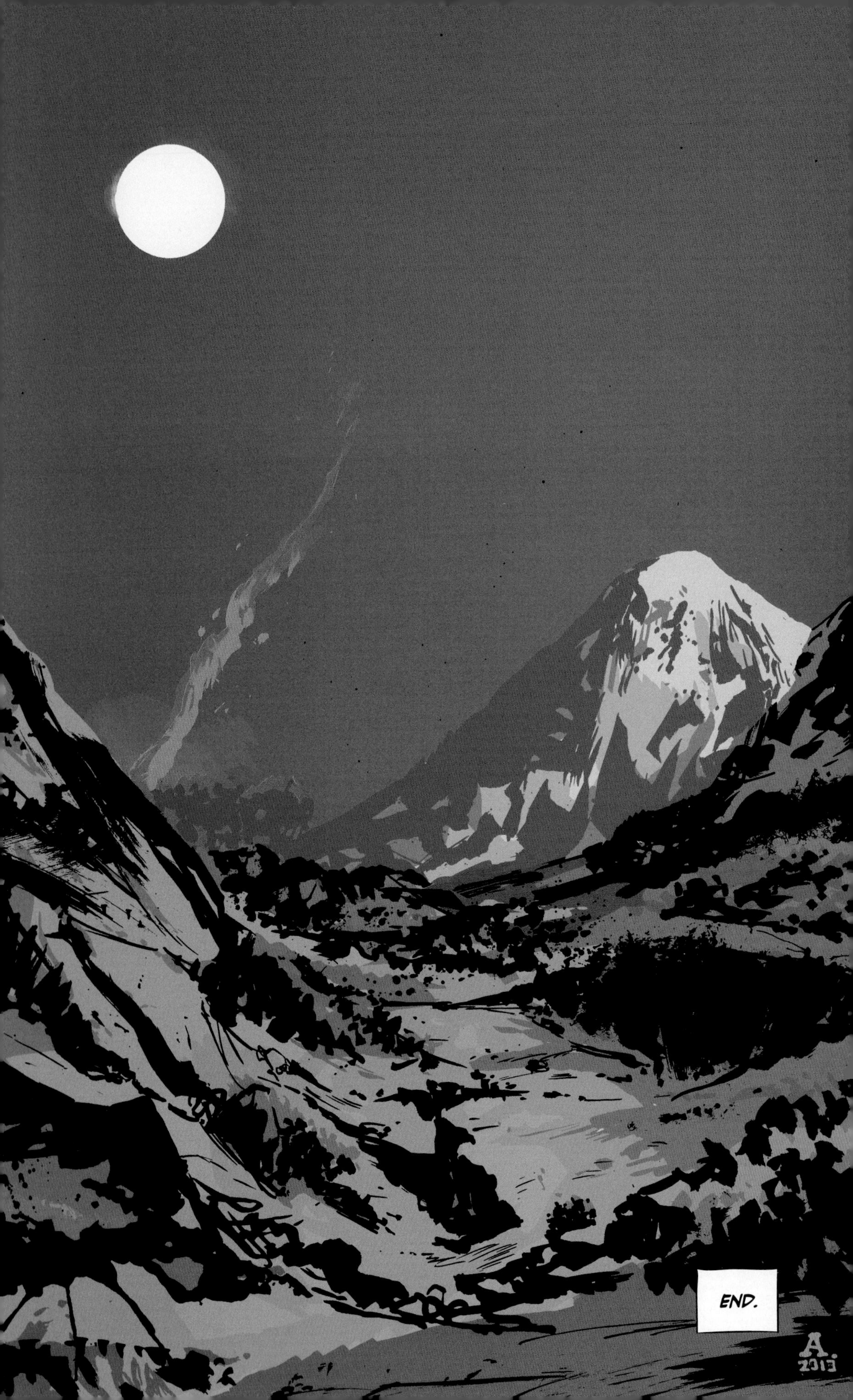
END.
A.
2013

EXTRAS

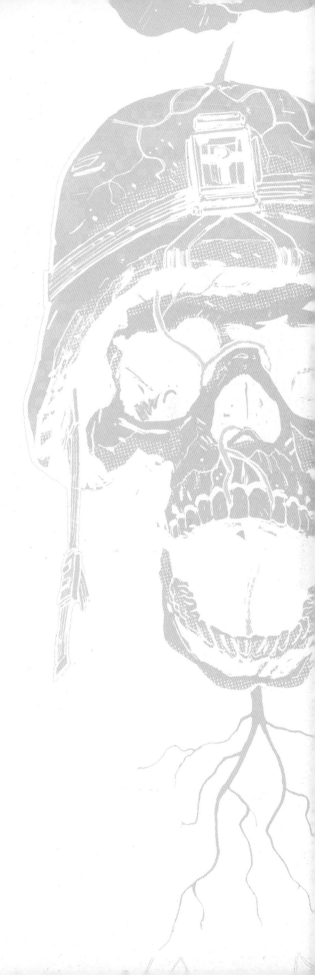

From Concept to Cover.

We quickly agreed on the iconic image of a poppy growing out of a skull for our first cover. Paul sketched out a few ideas before deciding on the final design.

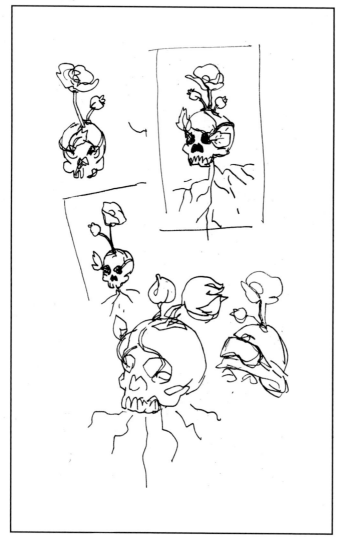

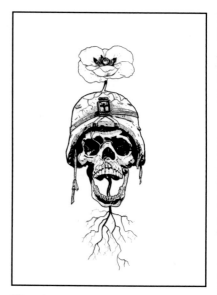

Here's the fully inked cover...

...with final colors applied.

An equally important part of designing the voice of the book was the logo, and shown here are the first steps toward the final result on the cover.

GRAVEYARD OF EMPIRES

GRAVEYARD OF EMPIRES

Combat Outpost, Afghanistan.

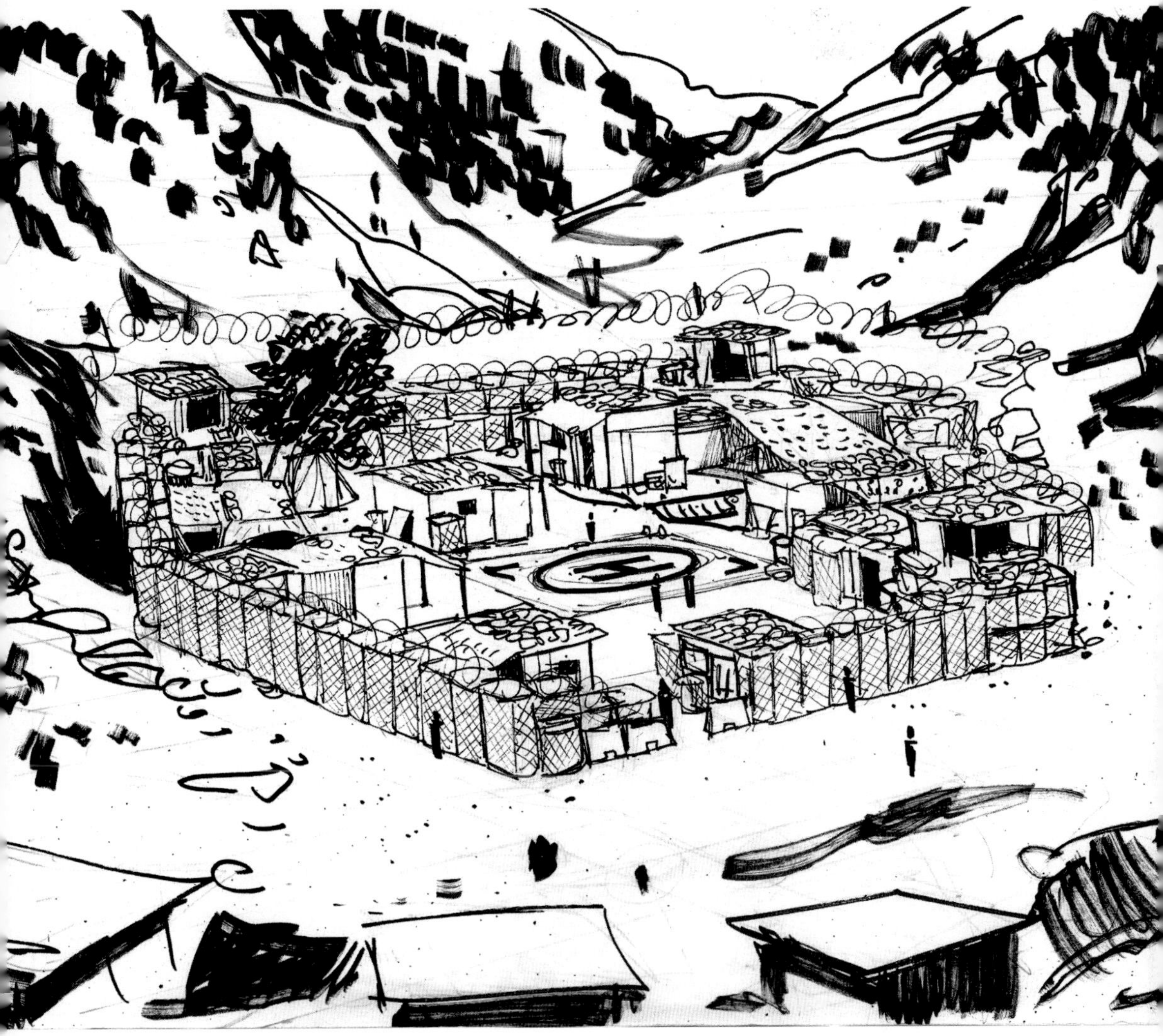

We wanted to give the base the worst tactical placement ever. It's in a valley that's practically unreachable by land vehicles. It's WAY too close to the village, which makes avoiding civilian casualties a virtual impossibilty. And it's located downhill—ceding the high ground to the Taliban so they can shell the base and harass choppers coming to resupply and evacuate casualties. If all these sound unbelievable—combat outposts have been placed in these precarious situations before (although maybe not all at once).

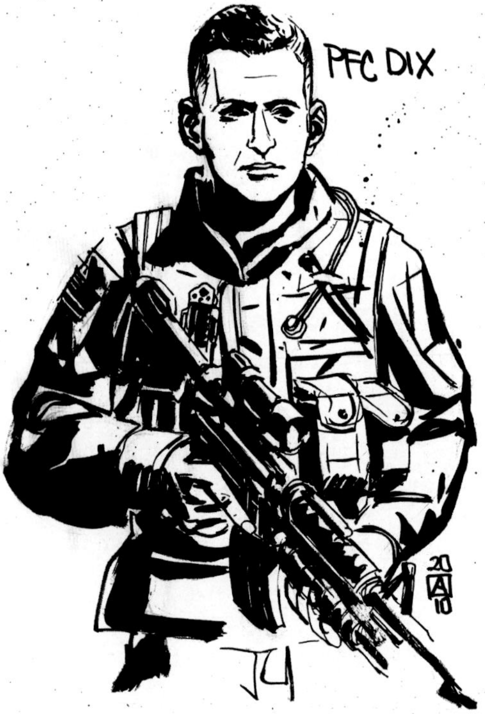
PFC DIX

DIX, who later became Wilson, was one of the first characters we conceived of—along with the other characters you see here. The first scene of the first issue—between Wilson, Reddick and the suicide bomber—was literally the first scene I imagined. Why the name change? Almost all the Marines' names are a combination of Howard Stern show staffers (where I used to work) and Duke Basketball players (of which I remain a lifelong fan).

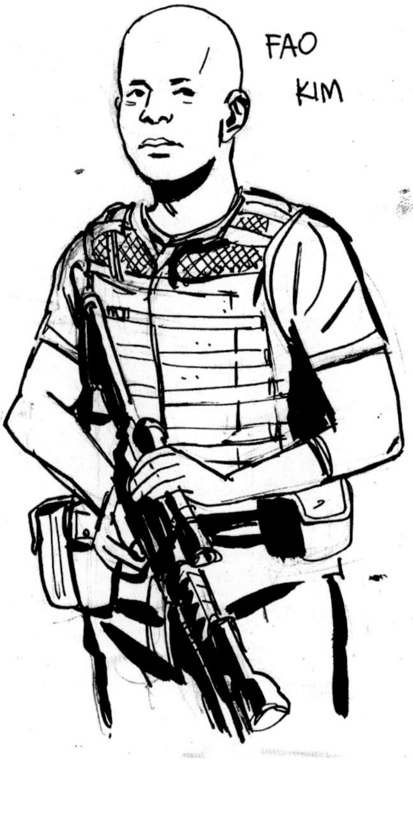
FAO
KIM

One of the things Paul and colorist Matt Wilson deserves the most credit for was making the characters visually distinguishable. This was an especially difficult challenge because almost everyone is wearing the same Marine uniform or is in Taliban dress. Racial diversity was one way to do this. That wasn't just a politically correct choice—it reflects the diversity you'll see on the battlefield. Paul did this with the Taliban as well. Afghanistan is filled with many different ethnicities and even more tribes (some would argue it shouldn't even be a single country).

MEDIC

Once we decided they were Marines, the medic would become a Navy Corpsman, as they serve the role of medic in the Marines. Story-wise, we also knew he'd have to be one of the first to get wounded, forcing the Marines to turn to a twisted Taliban doctor and putting them in even more jeopardy. F.A.C. Kim would also have to take a hit along with his radio, so the Marines would be cut off from outside communication and unable to call in airstrikes against the zombies. Assuming there even was an outside world left...

LIEUTENANT

LT. VASQUEZ is someone we wanted to set up as the guy you think is the antagonist. His decisions to both be more pro-active in the field, hunting Taliban rather than cowering behind the wire as well as trying to win the hearts and minds of the local villagers, are based on his experiences with the surge in Iraq's Anbar province. But as he starts getting Marines killed, it seems like he's an obstacle that our protagonist—Reddick—needs to overcome in order to keep himself alive. He's really a supporting character, however, meant to change Reddick from a loner who cares only for himself to someone who literally dons a suicide vest in order to save his surviving comrades in the end.

PINEAPPLE

Before we came up with names for the Marines, I did a kind of G.I. JOE thing where I started referring to them by the weapons they favored. In this case, "Pineapple" earned his name because his weapon of choice was a grenade launcher. No, the grenades he's launching aren't pineapple-shaped...but I thought making his face pockmarked like a pineapple would help make him stand out from his fellow Marines.

SNIPER

REDDICK. Very early on I knew the most valuable Marine to have in a zombie apocalypse would be a scout sniper. That also presented the chance to create a character who was a loner who would need to learn to work with others. Yes—I know scout snipers work in pairs, but for the stake of story simplicity and smoother dialogue it made more sense to have him say he was trained to work alone. It's never stated, but one of he Marines killed in the firefight in issue one was his spotter. That's part of why Reddick takes his death so hard...and why he tortures the doctor.

At some point in the writing of the first issue, Paul said we should have more Marines...and this was one of them. For one thing, we'd need more cannon fodder for the Taliban and food for the zombies. For another, even with the number of Marines we wound up with, this is still a severely undermanned combat outpost.

The problem? We were already pushing, I think, 30 pages. If we were going to create new characters, we'd have to find a way to make you care about them. I think Paul and I arrived at an elegant solution in the double-page spread in the 1st issue. In 18 panels—which can be read vertically or horizontally—we establish downtime at the combat outpost and give you little bits of insight into characters that might only appear on a few pages. It's one of the sequences in comics I'm most proud of writing, and one of my favorite things Paul has ever drawn.

VANCE. Ultimately, our real antagonist. A CIA man in the "ghost wars" of the 80s, he returns to the Afghanistan/Pakistan border to test out and create an undead army. I love how Paul found a way to age him while still making it clear that he is the same guy. Thematically, it's also fitting that he's handing out Stinger missiles in the Cold War to the very people who are shooting them at Marines today.

VANCE

Maybe sunglasses

YOUNG 1980s

some grey

OLDER 2011

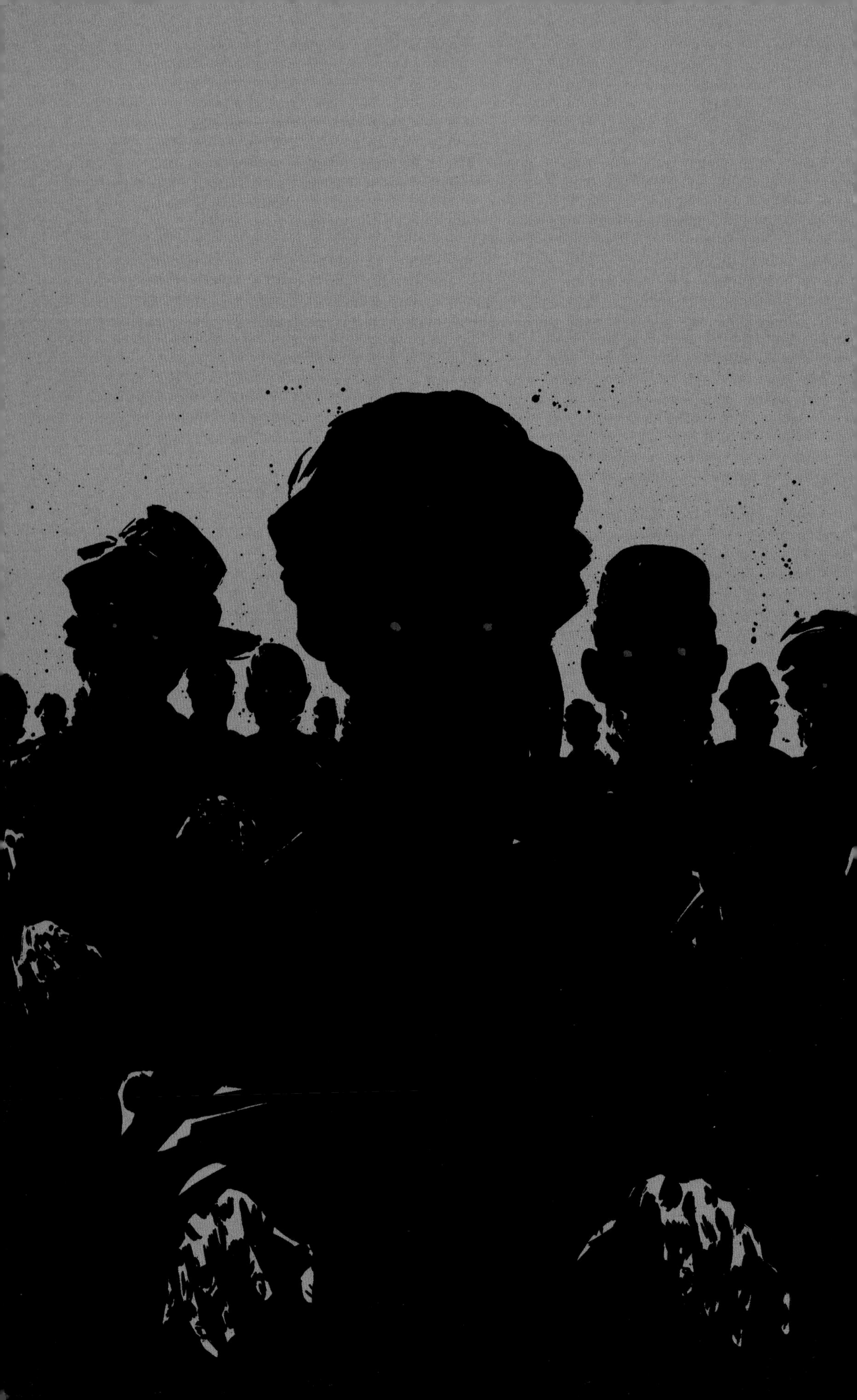

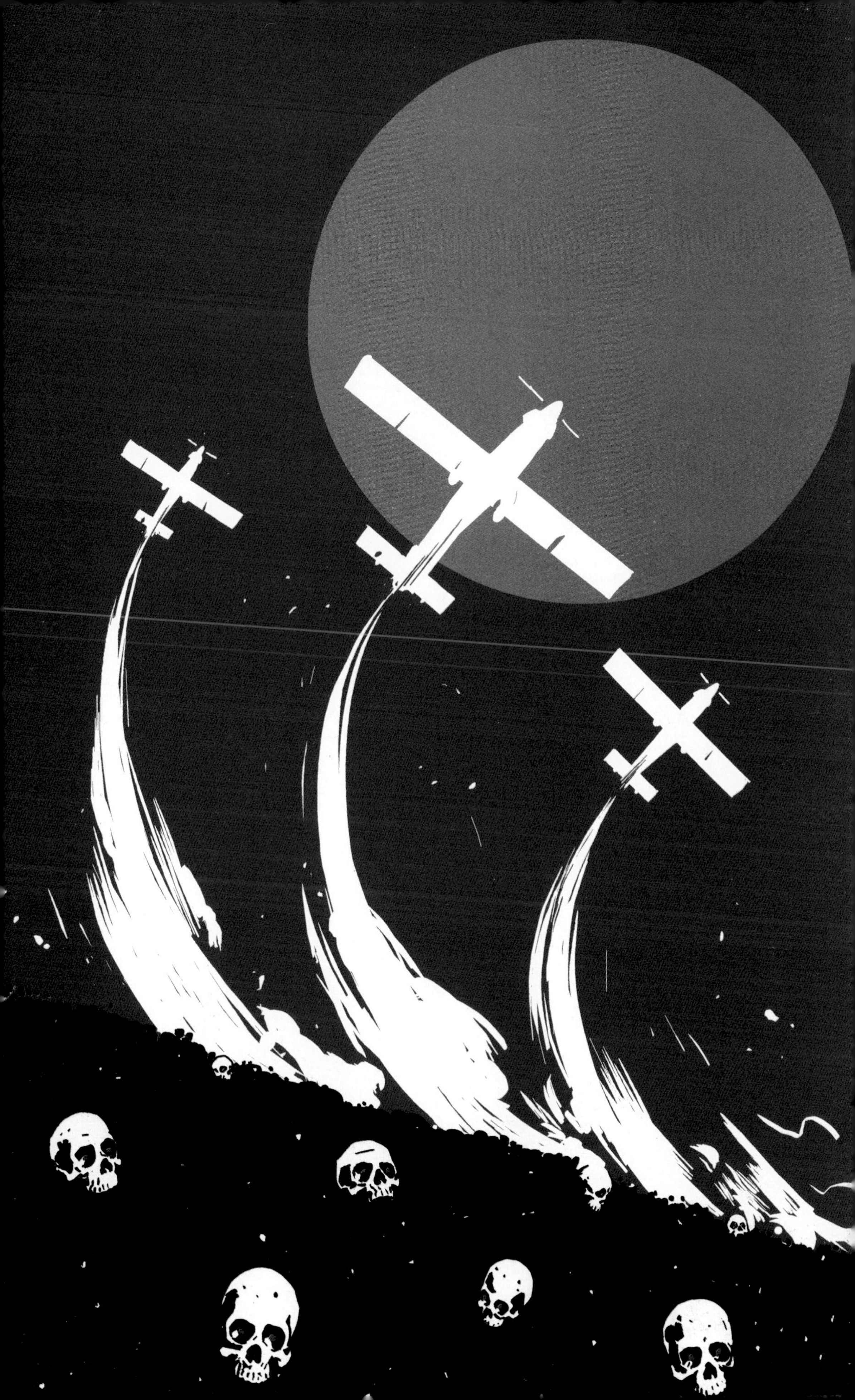

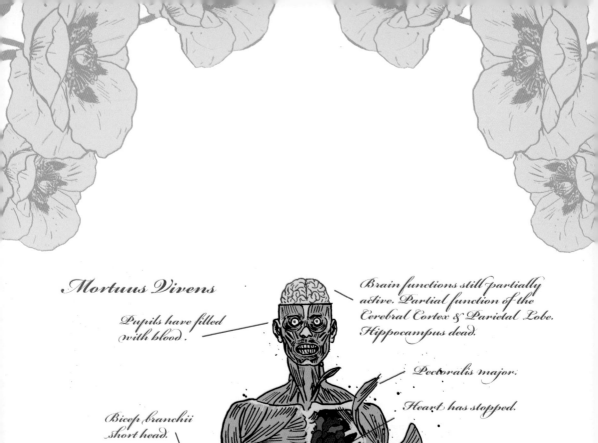

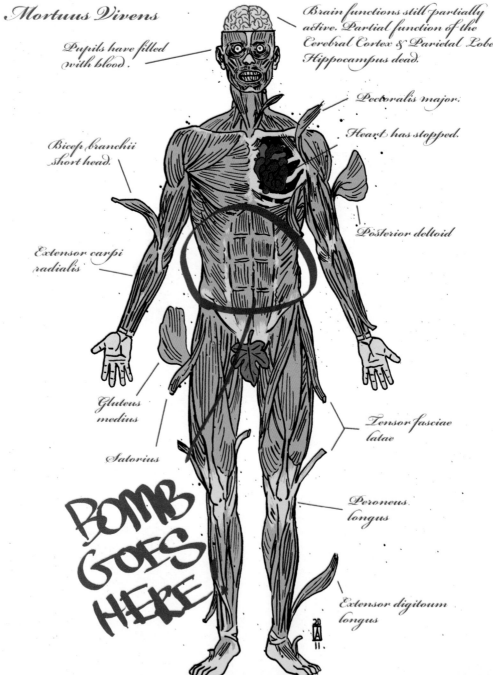

Mortuus Vivens

Pupils have filled with blood.

Brain functions still partially active. Partial function of the Cerebral Cortex & Parietal Lobe. Hippocampus dead.

Bicep branchii short head.

Pectoralis major.

Heart has stopped.

Extensor carpi radialis

Posterior deltoid

Gluteus medius

Tensor fasciae latae

Satorius

Peroneus longus

Extensor digitoum longus

BOMB GOES HERE

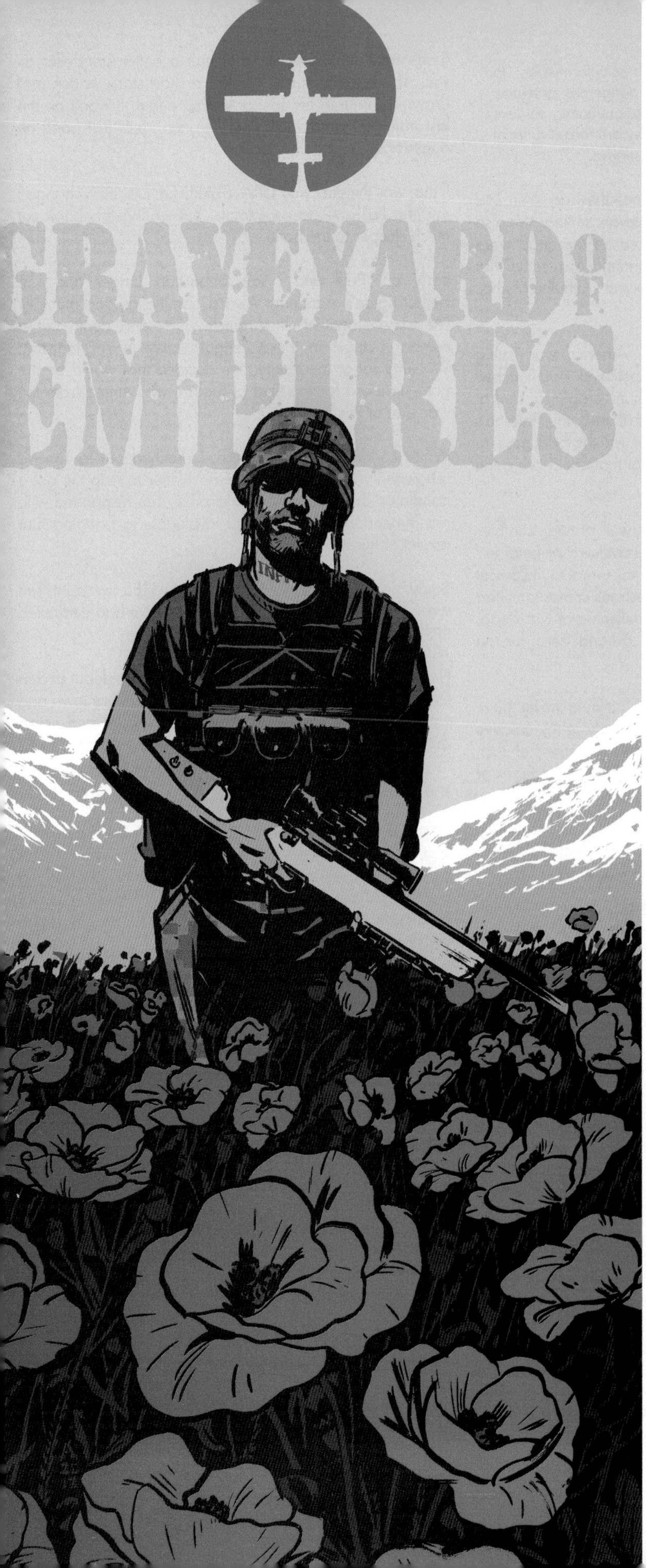
GRAVEYARD OF
EMPIRES

AFTERWORD BY MARK SABLE

What you hold in your hands is the second book I've done with Paul Azaceta, and writing each of them has been a life-changing experience.

GROUNDED was life-changing because it was my comics debut. I'd written many things before, but GROUNDED marked my publishing debut. The day before it came out, I was a law student who liked to tell people he was a writer. The day it hit the stands, I had permanent, physical proof that I *was* a writer.

More importantly, I learned that the words I put down on paper could be transformed into something even better than I had imagined.

The fact that GROUNDED sold out its first printing—and gave me a career that has had me writing comic books for nearly every major publisher ever since—was gravy.

GRAVEYARD OF EMPIRES also sold out its first print run, but that's not why it changed my life.

When I wrote GROUNDED—which I adapted from a screenplay—I basically handed Paul the script and hoped for the best. When I approached Paul with the idea for GRAVEYARD (more on that soon), he insisted on a more collaborative approach.

If you're wondering why GRAVEYARD took so long to get into your hands, a good part of that was the back and forth between Paul and I, which started with the idea itself. It had been over five years since we'd worked together, and I think I'd pitched him every story fragment I'd had in the hopes of working together again on a creator-owned project.

Here's the idea I sent Paul in 2009, originally entitled (I know) "THE MARCHING DEAD:"

> *"A group of fuck-up Marines screw up guarding the Iraqi Museum of Heretical Antiquity during the looting that followed the War in Iraq. When the army brass finds out it was the infamous Necronomicon that*

was stolen, they are assigned on a suicide mission: To recover the book from Iraq's most dangerous province. There, they learn that someone is re-animating soldiers and insurgents alike as zombies. They are forced to team up with the remaining insurgents to survive."

Together, Paul and I decided that since the Iraq War was winding down, we needed a more relevant setting. We also knew we needed a more original reason the dead were coming back to life than the Necronomicon, a tome that had been passed down from HP Lovecraft's Cthulhu Mythos to Sam Raimi's Evil Dead trilogy.

Afghanistan met both those needs. America was trying to replicate the surge that many believed had worked in Iraq. The elimination of the opium crop—so central to Afghanistan's economy in general and the Taliban's fortunes in particular—gave a cover for the bad guys to spray the kind of mysterious chemical that could bring the dead to life.

And what better place to throw our well armed, zombie-fighting protagonists into than the *Graveyard of Empires?* Not only had armies from Alexander the Great to the Soviet Red Army failed to tame it, their disastrous campaigns had led to the fall of their empires. With millennia of war-dead, Afghanistan would be the perfect ground zero for an unending zombie uprising.

When I first started writing comics, I would never have shown an artist a pitch paragraph so early in my creative process, nevermind seriously entertain suggestions of such drastic changes. This was a new frontier for me in terms of artistic collaboration. But it didn't stop there.

Paul was insistent from the beginning that we needed to ground the military aspects of our story in realism in order to make the reader accept the fantastical element of zombies. We killed ourselves doing research, not only reading books, watching films and all-too-easily-available war footage, but speaking to journalists and members of the military and intelligence communities.

If Paul felt something wasn't real, I had to prove to him that it at least *could* be, or I had to cut it. The example I've cited most is the suicide bomber with explosives implanted in his chest. Paul didn't believe it could be done—it felt too much like something Heath Ledger's Joker in "The Dark Knight" would do, not Al Qaeda. I remember feeling a mixture of pride and revulsion when I showed Paul some rather gruesome evidence that surgically implanting explosives were not only possible but also a growing fear among terrorism experts.

This back and forth between Paul and me—as well as colorist Matt Wilson and letterer Thomas Mauer —continued with every issue. We asked a lot from each other, and we went from what was supposed to be three 22-page issues to the four over-sized issues with 124 pages of total story. (That's the equivalent of six issues in a world where the Big Two put out 20 page, decompressed issues). I think GRAVEYARD OF EMPIRES was better for it, and I know I'm a better writer from working with this dream team of talent.

(I suspect Paul would say that he's a better storyteller as well. This book features "Circle," a short story written *and* drawn by Paul in his comics writing debut. It won't be the last time you read work Paul's written…let's just hope he doesn't put me out of a job.)

If that was the only way GRAVEYARD OF EMPIRES changed my life, I'd have no complaints. But writing this book cut much deeper to the bone.

Early on, Paul and I saw Sebastian Junger and Tim Hetherington's Academy Award nominated documentary "Restrepo" together. It chronicles life—and death—at a combat outpost in the Korengal Valley in Afghanistan. Walking out of the theater, we decided that would be the gold standard for the kind of realism we wanted from the war side of this book.

While conducting my research, I reached out to Tim—a renowned war photographer—on Twitter to help me get a handle on the Taliban. To my surprise, Tim responded with recommendations that proved invaluable to bringing that aspect of the story to life.

Sadly, right before GRAVEYARD OF EMPIRES saw print, Tim was killed covering the conflict in Libya. We had dedicated the book to him, and I was devastated.

Flash forward a few months to GRAVEYARD's debut at San Diego Comic-Con, 2011. San Diego is a military town and we were approached by a number of veterans and active duty military personnel. Not only had many of them served in Iraq and Afghanistan—some were due back for their second and third tours.

I braced myself for their response. I thought they might lecture us on how we got the camo scheme wrong or be angry that we were exploiting the conflict they'd fought and bled for. At the very least, I thought they'd want to avoid reading a war comic the way I hate watching courtroom dramas.

Instead, they were appreciative that we shone a light on what's going on over there. Walking around the U.S. in the past decade, you could forget there's a war or two (or more) being fought on the other side of the world. They were happy that we got more right than we got wrong (to be fair, we haven't heard from the zombies, so the jury is still out on our accuracy as far as the living dead are concerned).

But most of all, they wanted to share their stories. One Marine—after showing us his shrapnel wounds—wanted something more. He asked us if he could use Paul's iconic cover image—a helmeted skull with a poppy growing through it—as a tattoo. He wanted to ink the names of his fallen comrades in the roots, forever entwined with his.

I've never had that kind of reaction from a reader before, and writing about it still gives me the chills. Yes, GRAVEYARD OF EMPIRES was a comic book about zombies. But it was—and always will be —a reminder to me of all those that have made a sacrifice to fight, and to bring those stories of their fight home. If you've heard just one of those stories and your life isn't changed…you haven't been listening hard enough.